afloat again, adrift

Andrew Keith

In memory of my mother
and
for dad

afloat again, adrift

three voyages on the waters of North America

by Andrew Keith

Maps by Salvador Yrízar

ALIFORM PUBLISHING
MINNEAPOLIS, OAXACA

ALIFORM PUBLISHING
is part of The Aliform Group
117 Warwick Street SE/Minneapolis, MN USA 55414
information@aliformgroup.com   www.aliformgroup.com

First published in the United States of America by
Aliform Publishing, 2006

Library of Congress Control Number
2006927406

ISBN 0-9707652-8-2

Set in Times New Roman

Cover design by C. Fox Design

Table of Contents

HUDSON
BAY

Nelson
River

York
Factory

GULF
OF ST.
LAWRENCE

Quebec

GREAT
LAKES

NORTH
AMERICA

MISSISSIPPI
RIVER

New
Orleans

GULF
OF
MEXICO

SYD

Introduction: WHERE THE WATER FLOWS

I heard my dream
went back downstream...
And I followed you, Big River,
when you called.
Johnny Cash, "Big River"

It might have been the canoe my parents bought when I was a kid, 17 heavy feet of shiny new aluminum. My brothers and I took turns portaging it to the nearest pond, Lake Cornelia. Once we got to the middle, we'd leap into the water and crawl back in the canoe, often tipping it over while exploring our limits. Years later on graduation day from high school, my friend Mike and I paddled it along Minnehaha Creek all the way to the Mississippi, my first time following a river downstream.

Perhaps it was even earlier, learning how to swim as a boy, feeling brave enough in the water. Or the first time seeing the ocean? It's hard to say when the adventure truly began, but one letter changed everything.

When I was 19, I received an invitation by mail from my friend Pat to meet at the start of the Mississippi River and then paddle back to his home near Davenport, Iowa. He included his parents' telephone number and I was to call if interested.

Not long before that I had quit college—there was a world to be discovered and movement was required. Convinced that I had to get lost in order to find myself, I walked off campus one morning without looking back. And I did disappear for several months: hitch-hiking out west, spreading my wings, climbing mountains, walking Pacific beaches, meeting a cross-section of humanity and ultimately going broke. When I returned to Minnesota in the spring, I found employment as a tree-planter. The work was hard but the pay was good; at ten cents a tree I managed to plant 20,000 red pine seedlings in a month and earned $2,000. In July when Pat's letter arrived, I was free and liquid.

We had met in college and became friends sharing music, forest walk-abouts, intellectual rants and a similar sense of humor. Pat's intense curiosity, his vitality and his virtuoso guitar playing captivated a lot of people. We all missed him during the second year when instead of resuming school, he hopped on a west-bound freight train. Every now and again I'd get a postcard: Billings, Seattle, Denver. He returned to Iowa in the fall but didn't stay long. Borrowing the family canoe he paddled, alone, down the Cedar River to the Iowa River to the Mississippi River. By then it was getting cold so he continued south; a few more postcards trickled in: Quincy, Helena, New Orleans.

Now my friend wanted to explore the upper Mississippi—and with me. It didn't take me long to decide. When I called Pat answered and in one short conversation we formed our plan. My sister lived in Bemidji, a town near Lake Itasca, which is considered the river's source, and we could rendezvous at her house. He would bring the canoe and his personal supplies; I was to supply my tent, a paddle and any other camping equipment I could scrounge. We set the date for August 15, 1977. A letter and a phone call was all it took to send us down the Great River.

Not exactly sure where we were going, I went to the public library the next day to study an atlas, and while paging through North America I found a map that showed the continental divides and watersheds. With my finger I traced the river upstream to the height of land at Lake Itasca. In that moment I noticed something very peculiar about northern Minnesota: not one but three major watersheds begin there. Just a few miles from the birth of the Mississippi, on the other side of the divide, a separate watershed flows north to Hudson Bay. A little to the east and over another nearby divide is the origin of the Great Lakes, which drain off into the St. Lawrence Seaway and ultimately the Atlantic. From just about the same location we could paddle three different directions and arrive at three different seas: south to the subtropical Gulf of Mexico, north to the subarctic Hudson Bay or east to the Gulf of St. Lawrence. New Orleans, York Factory and the city of Québec were all downstream from my backyard.

Pat's overture to join him on the Mississippi was a spring that welled into something much broader. It would take plenty of patience and several years navigating my own personal watersheds, but over a couple decades I eventually paddled those three separate routes. Rivers, like memories, are a blending of currents; when streams merge they become inseparable, like these three woven travelogues.

AWAKENED GIANT
Lake Itasca to Lake Winnibigoshish

Down the Mississippi

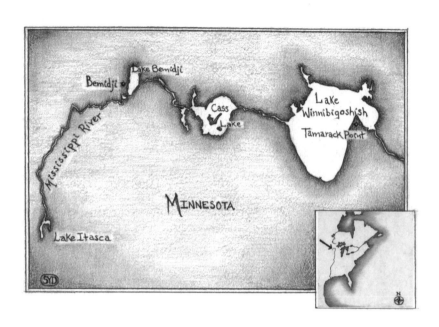

wo weeks after receiving Pat's letter I hitchhiked from Duluth to Bemidji. That same day Pat and his brothers drove north from Iowa in their family station wagon. When a traveling salesman dropped me off downtown at the lakefront, I noticed a car approaching with an upside-down canoe strapped to the roof. Thinking it might be the Iowan entourage, I waved and a hand dangling from the window shot straight up and waved back. We had arrived at the same moment, a good omen. After loading my worldly possessions into their car, we drove to my sister Polly's home. Our sojourn had begun.

We knew portages awaited us, along with several dams to walk around, so it was important to keep our supplies to a minimum. There were intermittent towns along the way for restocking, so we didn't need to buy much. The next day we packed and organized, and between us we had the essentials: canoe, tent, packs, sleeping bags, tarpaulins, food for several days, extra clothes, matches, two guitars and one Minnesota state highway map.

My brother-in-law Lee shuttled us to Lake Itasca in his truck. We loaded and debarked, heading for the lake's outlet. The day was ours, the only thing pressing was to find a place to camp before sundown. We paused for a ritual smoke and a blessing, offering tobacco into the water. A loon sang to claim its territory nearby, a great blue heron took flight leaving wingprints on the water's surface.

The word Itasca is derived from the Latin phrase *veritas caput* which means "True Head." When Henry Schoolcraft arrived here in 1830 after ending his search for the source of the Mississippi, he combined the last four letters of *veritas* and the first two letters of *caput*, inventing a new name. Every summer tourists come to this lake's outlet to wade across the birthplace of the longest river on the continent. They spit, splash and rock-hop all the way across the Mississippi River. At this point it is 1467 feet above sea level and over 2500 miles long. Parting through the tourists, we slipped the boat over the lip of water spilling from the lake and entered the infant river ready for discovery.

The tiny creek was low that summer, only a scant few inches flowing over the sandy bottom. At first we actually dragged the canoe more than we paddled. Fortunately it was a hot day because we spent most of it wet. Between the shallow stretches we meandered through marshes filled with cattails, bulrushes, flowering white lily pads, arrowroot and wild rice. Sometimes the aquatic vegetation grew so thick it became impossible to distinguish the river from the swamp. I'd stand up in our canoe and glance out over the reeds, searching for a route. Even from that angle it all blended into a sea of verdant stalks. When we parted the stems with our blades, we could peer down to the river bottom, the gentle current bending the submerged plants and pointing the way.

Late in the afternoon we finally came upon solid ground and made our first camp. I pitched the tent while Pat cooked up a skillet of river-rat fricassee. After dinner we pulled out the tobacco and chart, that is, the state highway map. We surmised Bemidji was just one day's paddle away. It began to rain, the fire hissing as it was doused. Safe in our tent, warm and dry, I thought about the youthfulness of those raindrops falling into the newborn creek, every drop continually refreshing the hydrological cycle. It felt good to sleep upon the ground. It felt good to know so much journey awaited.

The first of many lessons learned on the river was that plans are useless. After breaking camp, we hopped into our canoe and started paddling towards town. We entered another swampy area where the slow river snaked from one bank to the other in the most crooked possible fashion, one crazy loop after the next. Our map was definitely not suitable for navigational purposes we learned. It actually ended up taking four more days of slipping, shoving and sliding through the reedy waters before we finally arrived to Bemidji. The beauty was it didn't matter—we had no itinerary. We were not alone on the nascent Mississippi. During those first few days we met several other canoeists whose purpose was much different than ours; they had come to harvest wild rice. *Zizania aquatica*, or *mahnomen* as the indigenous people call it, is a very nutritional foodstuff packed with minerals, protein and carbohydrates. When the rice matures at summer's end, the locals come to gather their yearly supply. Each canoe has two "ricers" working in tandem. One stands in the rear with a long pole and slowly pushes the boat through the water. The other sits in the middle with a pair of short sticks; the first is used to bend the grass heads over the gunwale and the second to flail the tassels so the ripened seeds fall into the canoe. An experienced team can gather 200 pounds a day if they know where to go and when. Too much rain, or not enough, affects the grasses; in times past, if the season was poor it signaled hunger. That year it was plentiful and people feasted.

Curving through the stream we crossed delicate wakes with an Ojibwa couple. Their hushed voices blended with the swish-swish sound of their light thrashing. As we neared I could hear the grains falling into the canoe. Behind them to the east, the full "rice moon" was rising from the swamp. Behind us to the west, the sun was sinking into the forest. The air was filled with pine and fecund marsh. Suspended in time over the water, we enjoyed the human bounty with the couple in a millenia-long rite, sharing a smoke.

In the middle of a small field an old log cabin came into view, a noble shelter still holding together with its tight dovetail grip. Believing no one was around, we beached. At the same moment somebody in a nearby house spotted us and quickly fired up a tractor. Not sure whether to retreat or wait, we stalled. A smiling old farmer approached and waving amicably dismounted from his rusty John Deere. The cabin belonged to him, he explained, and he invited us to spread out our camp beneath its roof. His father had hewn and assembled the cedar logs back in the early 1900s, homesteading the land and raising a family. Our farmer had been born in this very shack one cold January night and other than a few wrenching war years in Europe, he had spent his entire life on the family forty. He intended to die there, too. We accepted his offer and slept peacefully like two chinked logs.

The next afternoon we pitched camp near someone's manicured green lawn. The air was permeated with that peculiar smell of freshly mown grass, an aroma that seemed out of place in the Great North Woods. When the homeowner noticed the smoke from our fire he stomped out his door and onto the front porch, shouting, "Don't you even think about crossing this property line. Stay the hell out, you damn rascals! This is private property!" What divergent mentalities: an old farmer who opened up his heart and home to share a world, and another old grouch who chose to shut it all out.

Bird life was prolific. Great blue herons that recalled pterodactyls became our constant companions, often playing hide-and-seek with us. As we neared they would clumsily take off and then, with a few wing-beats, arch gracefully around the bend and out of eyesight. As we rounded the curve and approached them once more, they'd repeat their escape. Sometimes the game would continue for a half hour before they finally flew up and over the forest canopy, returning to their solitude.

Red-winged blackbirds hid within the cattails. Whenever we got too close for their comfort, they would alight in one communal wave, the black cloud of chatter undulating with the gusts. A teal spanked the river surface feigning a broken wing, trying to lead us away from its nest. It flopped up to a clump of reeds and, miraculously healed, lifted out of the water and flew home, having thoroughly fooled us. Inside the clump a bittern stood perfectly still, sharp beak to the sky, blending in cleverly with the bulrushes.

From the deep blue loft a black feather came twirling down. When I scooped it up, a shining raven cried hoarsely into the air. These magnificent creatures have more distinct calls than any other songbird. Far off, another of its kind replied. Gliding through the scenario, only whispering from time to time, we lay back listening to their conversation, watching summer cumulus clouds roll on by in the boundless heights.

As we passed through the shadow of a pine grove, I noticed two Ojibwa lads sitting beneath the towering trees passing a pipe. They had come to have a river moment so we joined them. Thunder boomed from an approaching storm; our stomachs were growling from hunger; we had yet no place to sleep but didn't care. As the smoke rose from the shared pipe, each presented his own invocation. When it came my turn, I tied the feather onto the stem.

After five slow and winsome days we finally crept into Bemidji. It seemed strange abandoning our canoe and wandering into town. Walking was a relief, although the pavement felt foreign. Melodic notes from a Bob Wills tune spilled from a tavern, inviting us inside for draft beer and a hamburger. We picked up a few supplies and headed back to the boat.

Between the towns of Bemidji and Grand Rapids the river passes through several lakes, the first Lake Bemidji. In the afternoon when we began the traverse, the water was oily calm so we shot the three miles across. An hour later we reached the far side and scouted for the outlet. Again our map was useless; all we could do was weave through the cattails fringing the shore. As we passed through one patch, instantly a storm of red-winged blackbirds took flight, leaping in unison and blackening the reddened skies: one moment utter silence and the next a rowdy fluttering exhale. We finally located the outlet and set up camp beside the marsh, listening to the pulsing song of cricket and frog.

We began the next day portaging around the first of fourteen man-made dams between Bemidji and Minneapolis (to which you can add a few beaver dams). The portage was easy enough, but being late August during a dry year there was precious little water released downstream. We had to drag the aluminum tub over sharp rocks for an hour until we found deeper water.

Eventually the river did return and pulled us through more swamps filled with feasting flocks of mallards, blue-winged teal, goldeneyes and wood ducks. It also led us through a couple of smaller lakes, Andrusia and Wolf, dotted with fishermen trolling for walleye and northern pike. Along the way I noticed a rope swing hanging from a poplar tree so we took time off to dunk, bathe and refresh ourselves. It's always great to be a kid, at any age, and have nothing better to do than swing on a rope and do back flips into summer waters.

Late in the afternoon we entered Cass Lake. A steady tailwind pushed us across to Star Island whose shores were lined with cottages. There are no roads, only sidewalks and footpaths, but the residents make up for their lack of automobiles with their luxury powerboats, small fortunes docked in front of each cabin. At the far end in a small public park, we set up camp illegally.

Star Island's claim to fame is that it contains the largest lake within an island within a lake in the state of Minnesota, called Windigo. According to Ojibwa legend, a giant, or windigo medicine-man, resides at the bottom of the lake. This much feared spirit-being surfaces occasionally to haunt and devour people. Several drownings on nearby lakes have been attributed to him.

As the sun rose in our face, gray skies scattered into blue, and after portaging Knutson Dam at the outlet of Cass Lake we were back on the river again. The morning was exceptionally calm, and up ahead was the largest lake on the Mississippi River, Winnibigoshish. Where the river ended and it began was a small resort with a Hamm's Beer sign. Sipping frosty mugs, we asked the owner for his advice on crossing the lake. Could we go straight across to reach the outlet, or would it be better to paddle the long way around, following the shore for 35 miles? Going straight across implied an easy afternoon of paddling, especially in those halcyon conditions. Hugging the shore would take two days, at least.

He opined, "This lake is very shallow and when the wind picks up the waves can turn murderous in no time. If a thunderstorm happens to blow in, why you boys would be swamped ducks. Only a fool would make the crossing in a little boat like that. Take my word, follow the shore."

We returned to our craft. It was still early and very calm. Why not spend a few hours in the middle of a little sea? Do the math: 12 miles across or 35 around.

When you're sitting in a canoe looking out over a 12-mile fetch of water, the distant shoreline is barely discernible. Even on a clear day it's nothing but a thin line way over yonder. So Pat and I dug in towards the middle of the immense lake. After two hours of nonstop paddling that distant shoreline became as close as the one we had left behind. We were in the very heart of the lake, six miles from any soil, and paused to admire our position.

What we saw was disturbing. A nasty prairie storm front was breaking the western horizon with its wall of thunder-heads moving right for us, and we were two hours from safety. Our timing couldn't have been worse. The windigo was awakening and our paddle blades swung furiously. The storm consumed the sun, lightening was constant, booming thunder broadcast severe warnings. Only once before had I seen green clouds and that was shortly before a tornado touched down. Those fast-moving clouds were green and purple and black. For a while it remained eerily calm and we paddled on nervously; then the wind pelted us, well ahead of the rains. At that point we were still a couple miles from shore. The lake's surface erupted and choppy waves grew in size with each packed gust, the spindrift spraying us. Chop turned into breaking, five-foot waves. Fortunately the wind was to our back and we sailed and surfed the roil, shipping water. I grabbed our biggest pot and bailed when I could while we continued stroking as fast as possible.

When we neared shore some people noticed us and leapt into their motorboat to attempt rescue. As soon as they left dock they realized that is was too rough, and we watched them return to shore while keeping a watchful eye on us. Paddle on! The giant had surfaced for a snack. Paddle on! We literally surfed onto the sand beach at Tamarack Point with a quarter-filled canoe and thankful hearts. We tossed the gear, drained the canoe, pitched the tent and then jumped in. Gale-force winds began bending trees and buckets of cold rain puddled the land. Lightening grounded out all around. We could have easily been swamped and lost the canoe, perhaps even drowned, but we had made it, barely. High and relatively dry in our tent, we waited out the storm with that rare appreciation for life, full of charged ions.

LAURENTIA
Sawbill Lake to Crooked Lake

To Hudson Bay

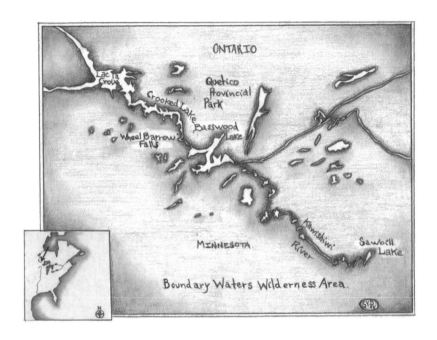

Herb and I met in the middle of the winter while working at a ski resort in northern Minnesota. The owner of the mountain compensated for our meager pay by giving everyone a free beer in the chalet at the end of the day. During those happy hours we shared life and travel stories and one thing became clear: we both enjoyed canoeing. The autumn before we met, he and a couple of his friends had wandered for two months through remote northern lakes. When I told him about my journey down the Mississippi River, he replied, "That's something I've always wanted to do." I bought us a pitcher of beer; here was a pump that needed priming.

I borrowed a pen from the bartender and scrawled out a map of the continent. After explaining the three different watersheds that flowed from Minnesota, I told him that a ride north to Hudson Bay was next. Backing away from the bar, Herb turned toward me and said convincingly, "I'll join you. Let's go this summer." We clanked our steins together, making the proposal official. We had never even been in a canoe together. Outside the snow was falling, a couple of feet already piled on the ground.

Five months later when those same snows began to melt off, already flowing toward faraway seas, we were organizing our packs. Where floating down the Mississippi had been easy and spontaneous, this voyage required careful planning. The route to Hudson Bay was complicated and involved navigating through various connected lakes and streams that traversed large tracts of wilderness. A state highway map would not suffice. Instead we invested several hundred dollars in detailed topographical maps purchased from the Canadian government. Herb and I would encounter a lot of rapids and an aluminum canoe would be inadequate. Indestructible plastic canoes had come onto the market and even though heavy were a safer bet. Finally, there would be very few towns along the way for restocking so we had to carry a month's worth of food and, with the assistance of our friend Sonja, we prepared two resupply packages to be mailed later.

In early May we drove away from my cabin fully provisioned: we had a new red canoe, over a hundred pounds of food, a dome tent, four packs, maps, water filters, a first aid kit and paddles—everything necessary for the summer-long adventure. Winding along the back country gravel road, we headed up to Sawbill Lake, our launching pad.

The borderland between northern Minnesota and southern Ontario contains thousands of pristine lakes, and over a million acres in this region have been set aside as wilderness areas. On the U.S. side is the Boundary Waters Canoe Area Wilderness; its 1978 creation was quite controversial. When the federal government proposed buying all of the private lands and forbidding the use of motors, the locals cried foul and fought to keep their cabins, resorts and outboards. Eventually a compromise of sorts was reached, removing some of the lakes near existing roads from the proposal and allowing the resorts within these corridors to continue operating. However, the majority of the previous landowners were bought out and their buildings demolished.

Across the border in Ontario a sister park was formed, Quetico Provincial Park, which is larger than the U.S. tract and even more remote. The designation of these two areas as wilderness has created one of the most idyllic places in the world for canoeing. You will likely encounter other parties when entering, but for those willing to endure a few hard portages much solitude awaits. One could paddle all summer there and never cross the same lake twice.

A few friends had gathered to send us off. While loading the canoe I kept glancing out over Sawbill Lake wondering what was around that first point. After the last kiss we embarked to find out and cheers from our fan club grew softer with each stroke. We turned to look back at them one more time, knowing we wouldn't see each other again for two months, maybe three. I tied a yellow bandana onto my paddle and waved it one last time. Herb and I then thrust our blades in the water and disappeared from their view. Suddenly we were alone and everything would be new: every bend, each island, every encounter, each body of water.

We soon came to the end of a small bay where we found our first portage, a footpath connecting Sawbill with Alton Lake. After unloading our heavy packs we paused to smoke a ceremonial pipe. I felt like a child again, reminded of that liberating sensation when school was out for summer. After all the winter's planning and preparation we were finally free to go. While savoring our newfound nomadic status, we hauled our cargo over the short portage, reloaded the canoe and then sailed with a tailwind across the length of Alton.

On the far side was another portage that went up and over the Laurentian Divide. This inconspicuous ridge parts the waters that flow either to the Gulf of St. Lawrence or to Hudson Bay. It was really our genuine starting place, and I dipped one of our water bottles into Alton and filled it halfway. Herb and I then left our boat and strolled the portage to Beth Lake on the opposite end. There I dipped the bottle in her waters, topping off the jug. We retraced our path to the highest point of land and held another ceremony, splashing the combination over each other. Officially baptized, we were ready to follow those waters all the way to Hudson Bay. The St. Lawrence would have to wait.

Now it was time to work. Trudging up and over the trail, we each shouldered a 70-pound food pack, then returned for the canoe and the other two packs. Once reloaded we set across Beth, the first in a network of interconnecting lakes that eventually flowed into Lake of the Woods. From there the waters continued ocean-bound via the Winnipeg River, Lake Winnipeg and ultimately the Nelson River. All the lakes were connected by streams but most were unnavigable, and so we had to portage from one puddle to the next. As we skirted the shore a pair of great blue herons greeted us. Just like meeting old friends, we played tag with them to the end of the lake.

All portages in the Boundary Waters are measured in rods, which come from the old English measurement system. One rod equals 16.5 feet, roughly the length of our canoe. The path connecting Beth and Grace was 280 rods long, which equals 4620 feet. With all the gear we had to lug, each portage required two carries. In other words, we walked through with a load, returned empty-handed, and then walked it again with the second load. Hence, a portage was really three trips. We shuffled over two and a half miles on that long haul, carrying 300 pounds of gear. The weather was unseasonably warm, in the 80s and quite humid for May, and by the end we were both tired and soaked in sweat. The lake ice had recently melted and water temperatures were cold, but we dove in just the same, a quick dunk to leap back out refreshed. We were out of shape and a little fazed to consider just how many more times we would have to repeat this weary exercise before reaching the sea. It felt great to get back into the canoe.

We camped early that day on Grace Lake. For our first few days we allowed ourselves the luxury of fresh food and that night we gorged on steaks, baked potatoes, and a salad. Food always tastes better outdoors, especially after a long day voyaging. After dinner we sipped whisky and watched our first sunset together; a three-quarter waxing moon reflected over the still waters. Beside the warm firelight, beneath the cold moonlight, we mused over the difficult trip ahead. With neither clock nor schedule, everything seemed possible. It wouldn't be easy, but we were where we wanted to be: sleeping under the stars, drifting away.

I arose first and sat by the lake watching the sunrise, a chorus of song-birds blending with the breezy pines. Several fish leapt from the water and, far off, a loon wailed. Despite all this company I felt strangely alone. It was a mixed emotion that surfaces whenever I enter the wilderness. Securities that had insulated me before, things like work, relationships and family, all belonged to the world I had left behind. I'm not even sure how to define wilderness, but waking up there, miles from the nearest town, road or power line, made me feel disoriented. There was some nostalgic hint that once long ago I was familiar with these surroundings, somehow connected to a distant, hazy animal origin. Not quite belonging to either world, I wanted both. The spell of loneliness was interrupted when Herb rolled over and popped out of his bag to join me. We shared a cup while cooking up bacon and eggs over a smoky fire before slipping back onto the water.

We intentionally began our journey in early May to get a jump on the fishermen and mosquitoes, both known to arrive in hordes. The "opener" was still a week away so during those first days we never saw another human. Since the snows had just melted, there were no pesky bugs either. We had both lived in the north woods long enough to know how a cloud of mosquitoes can affect one's mood and we were grateful for this fair start. Absorbed in our blissful solitude we paddled in silence. Winds sighed through the trees, wavelets splashed against the boat, patterns of light splayed over the surface of the water. It all mesmerized me as we crossed Thomas Lake. Deep and spring-fed, Thomas was more transparent and even colder than the previous lakes. A smooth black outcrop alongside the shore had been warming all day from the sun. We dove into the chilly waters and then scrambled out, hugging the hot bedrock like two amphibians soaking in the solar energy, diving and warming up again and again.

To traverse this region's myriad waters the indigenous inhabitants created the birch bark canoe. It was the perfect craft: fast, silent and easy to portage. Birch bark is an amazing material—waterproof and quite tough. Sharp rocks will puncture it to be sure, but the material is plentiful so patching a boat was doable. These original inhabitants also used birch bark to cover their wigwams and make containers to carry and store their supplies. Before the Europeans came with iron cookware, they would heat up rocks in a fire and then submerse them into birch bark containers filled with water. With this slow but sure method foodstuffs were boiled. Thus the multi-functional skin of the birch tree provided transportation, shelter, storage and cookware, not to mention fuel for fires.

And who were these indigenous peoples? Several different groups have occupied these waters since the last glacial retreat and archeologists have discovered the remains of encampments that date back several thousand years. We will never know the name of those first natives, but when the Europeans arrived the area was settled by a combination of Lakota, Ojibwa and Cree, tribes whose people are still here. Their ancestors left ample relics—stone implements such as axes, spears, mallets, and arrowheads; tooled copper and pipestone; bone fragments. And they left rock art, or pictographs. A combination of iron oxide and oil from sturgeon fish created a very durable blood-red pigment. Using this paint they adorned weather-protected rock faces with animals, canoes, hunters and a variety of enigmatic symbols, along with handprints.

A few days into the journey, Herb and I noticed on the map a pictograph site along our route through the Kawishiwi River. Next to it was a designated campsite. Barely missing several thunderstorms, we paddled hard all day to reach it and happily found it unoccupied. We pitched our tents and ate a deserved hearty meal. After dinner we got into our canoe and headed over to the "museum"; witnessing those ancient creative expressions felt like a privilege. As I placed my hand over one red hand, not touching it but hovering just above its surface, I was filled with a sense of timelessness. I couldn't help but wonder who had painted this rock, who had left their signature, who had traveled this very route once, perhaps dodging summer rains as we had. I reverently sprinkled tobacco into the water and lit my pipe, blowing smoke into the atmosphere of eternity.

After we returned to camp, Herb lit a fire while I sat on a rock cantilevered over the river playing the harmonica. Immediately I noticed that my music, my blown notes, reverberated off the painted rock wall across the river, producing an echo. Herb looked up from the fire and smiled, appreciating the good acoustics. Far down the narrow canyon came the sudden cry of a solitary loon and to our great surprise it quickly advanced towards us, wailing louder and louder. The closer it got the cleaner became our duet within those canyon walls. When it was right before us, between the pictographs and the fire, our music harmonized. It seemed our notes were one in the same. Indistinguishable. As it flew by I could both feel and hear its wing beats and dropping my harmonica to the ground, I listened to its haunting song fade into the distance. Within that reverie I believed that my notes flying down the canyon somehow, mysteriously, converted into a loon which then carried the notes back to us to deliver a message: the sacred is very much alive. I imagined some early inhabitant sitting in the very same place after painting his handprint onto that enduring wall. He would have played his flute, offering his own musical notes up to the Great Creator, and he, too, would have been granted a glimpse into the real magic that surrounds us every day: we are capable of singing the birds into existence.

The first Europeans to enter these waters were the French in the early 1700s, who came to trade with the natives for pelts. The fashion in Europe at that time was to don outrageous felt hats and it was discovered that beaver hair made the best processed wool. These French traders were divided into two distinct groups. The first were called the *mangeurs de lard*, or "pork eaters," a derogatory term referring to the fact that they never drifted too far from civilization. They paddled in birch bark cargo canoes from Montréal, traveling up the Ottawa River and through the Great Lakes of Huron and Superior to Grand Portage in Minnesota. Their exclusive role was to outfit the second group with all the necessary supplies and trade goods required to sustain them for a year in the interior. This later group was referred to as the *hivernants*, or "winterers." Once a year these two groups would rendezvous at Grand Portage, roughly halfway between Montréal and the hinterlands, to exchange their goods: blankets, traps, brandy, wampum, tobacco and gun powder going to the one party and the coveted furs to the other. It was a legendary celebration with plenty of spirits to go around. After the party dust settled, everything quickly returned to business. Freshly resupplied, the *hivernants* would paddle to the furthest reaches of North America in their small canoes to trade with the natives for yet more furs. The *mangeurs de lard* returned to Montréal with their goods for the European market.

The main voyageur route for penetrating the interior was precisely along what is now the U.S.-Canadian border, a series of lakes that link Lake Superior to Lake of the Woods. From there most *hivernants* headed to Lake Winnipeg and then branched off into various directions, some north towards Hudson Bay and others west to Great Slave Lake and the Rockies. The long ago established route to Hudson Bay was the same one Herb and I were pursuing. Our intentions were quite different but the waters we shared have changed little. Synchronizing history with our own paddle strokes, we honed in on that ancient byway.

Our entrance into the international boundary route was Basswood Lake, where an encounter awaited. We entered from the southeast at Bayly Bay and right away I noticed a strange object bobbing in the middle of the waters, so we set our bearings for it. As we neared, its shape began to take form. What originally seemed like a deadhead became a mother moose and her calf. I knew moose could swim but I had no idea so far and at such a young age. The calf was certainly born that very spring and could not have been more than a few months old, yet there it was at least a quarter-mile from shore swimming confidently. As we neared the mother went into an instinctual protective mode, frantically circling her baby. Huge mammals, moose in the forest can be daunting. When threatened they often charge and your best hope is to scale a tree, quickly, providing one is handy. But in the water moose are vulnerable. You could probably even straddle their shoulders and take a ride, but we backed off. With binoculars in hand we drifted along and watched them swim towards shore. Once on firm footing they turned toward us one more time, vigorously shook off the lake water and disappeared into the forest.

Before departing on the journey we had outfitted our canoe with a spray skirt to cover and protect our cargo during the rains. It was essentially a three-piece, hand-sewn nylon tarp that snapped onto the gunwales, sealing the inside of the canoe from the elements. One part covered the bow, another the midsection and the last the stern. When our first big thunderstorm rolled in, we fastened all of the sections into place and put on our rain coats. During the cold showers we remained warm and dry. As the thunder rumbled and the rain drops pocked the lake surface, we paddled along singing like sailors, skipping over the rippled waters, satisfied with our designs. The storm passed, the sun returned and soon we were paddling in shorts.

That night we camped among a large stand of white pines on Washington Island. It was pleasant having new ground to dream upon every night, a new earthly jewel, and I sat beside the fire and reflected on the day's gifts. Besides the moose, we had seen two bald eagles, a beaver, a pair of loons and several great blue herons. We heard songs from the first returning white-throated sparrows, a percussive partridge drumming and boreal owls hooting their territories. As the fire dwindled a stillness descended upon our world; the sun set and a full moon rose out of the mirror of Basswood Lake. Before the stars fully emerged, we were sound asleep.

It's really quite easy to get lost in the Boundary Waters. Navigating through the complexity of islands and bays is a challenge even with the best topographical maps and one has to constantly read the terrain and the chart simultaneously. We had gone to bed thinking we knew exactly where we were. In the morning we set out across a small bay, certain it would lead us to the main body of Basswood Lake, but as soon as we rounded a large island we knew we were lost because nothing matched the chart. I thought we should go forward. Herb disagreed, thinking we had made a wrong turn the previous day, and the solution was to retrace our path back to the campsite and head in the opposite direction. We paused next to an island, studied our choices and finally agreed to go with Herb's hunch. Within an hour we were back on track heading north with a strong tail wind, surfing three-foot waves right up to what is called United States Point.

More rain threatened as we cruised the remainder of Basswood searching for a campsite high and dry, but all those we passed were in low spongy areas. At the end of the lake was a 320-rod portage that skirted Basswood Falls. While we unloaded the canoe it began to drizzle upon our slippery, rough walk.

Halfway through the portage we met two older bucks also traveling in our direction and we paused together under the shelter of an old white spruce and had a snack. They were the first people we had encountered in a week and as much as I enjoyed Herb's company, it was nice to converse with someone else. They too were looking for the perfect campsite, a home base for the fishing opener. We paddled with them through a couple of smaller lakes and then shared another portage. Along the way we passed more campsites, all unappealing, and continued until reaching a section of whitewater called Wheelbarrow Falls.

Herb and I boulder-hopped along the fast river and studied the rapids, debating whether or not to run them in the canoe. Meanwhile, our companions unloaded their gear and prepared for the carry. The rapids didn't seem that vicious so we agreed to skip the portage and instead paddle through. Perhaps our decision was influenced by the fact we had started our day lost. Maybe there was a chance we had wanted to get a competitive lead on our companions for the next available decent campsite. Certainly we were tired from the heavy day of paddling and the long, difficult portage we had done earlier. Whatever the reason, we got into the boat and headed for the funnel created by the surging water that squeezed between two boulders.

What a thrill to enter into that point of no return. With heightened adrenalin we paddled hard and tried to coordinate our moves, slipping downstream fast and veering from bank to bank. The canoe plowed through a standing wave and I noticed how few precious inches there were between the crest and our gunwales. Suddenly I was scared. All that water colliding with rock made a thunderous noise. As we approached another standing wave, I heard a garbled scream: "Get out, jump!" There was nowhere to leap to but I felt the boat lighten as Herb hopped to shore. I bulldozed into the wave alone and the canoe immediately filled with water, becoming utterly impossible to maneuver.

Gear was floating in the boat and gear was now floating outside it, going downstream on its own. The canoe swept through another wave, glanced off a boulder, and then slowly began to list starboard. I clung to the gunwales as it smashed violently into yet another large rock and then the boat rolled over completely. I was trapped underwater and beneath the canoe, upside down and holding my breath. I heard the sound of rocks rolling on the bottom and thought, "This must be what it sounds like when bone grinds against stone." There was a sharp pain in my right leg, and then the noise subsided.

Surfacing in the still pool at the bottom of the rapids I noticed several things at once: the ache in my leg, the bobbing packs, the upturned canoe and Herb hollering, "Andy, are you all right?"

I simply reacted, swimming frantically after the floating packs and paddles, trying to herd them together before they sank. Herb dove into the pool, grabbed the canoe and pulled it back to shore. With Herculean force he turned it over and emptied it, then leapt back inside and floated over towards me, plucking our soggy packs from the river one by one. Swimming back to the bank, I saw our companions on the opposite shore shaking their heads as they loaded their dry packs into their dry canoe. They left us wet river rats behind and we never saw them again.

We paddled the boatload of saturated packs downstream to the nearest campsite, fortunately unoccupied. Our companions must have left it for us, knowing how much we needed it. Once on solid ground we both began shaking from retro-fear. With few words we expressed enormous relief and a new found respect for the power of water: "Damn. Shit. We are lucky idiots."

Then with great fortune the sun came out and we spread everything on the bedrock to dry, surveying the damage. A few food items had gotten wet along with most of our clothes. I had a gashed leg and a big fat lip. The only valuable item lost was my rain coat, which lay somewhere on the bottom of the river. There were indeed some lessons in this: we were too far into the wilderness to take unnecessary risks and had severely misjudged our capabilities. Water can be so powerful, even small rivers. Paddling a fully loaded canoe down rapids was not for us. Maybe if we had put on our spray skirts to keep out the standing waves we could have made it, but why wager on that? A portage path is there for a reason. We had survived and had learned. It was a rough job: the risks high and the hours long, and we weren't about to trade it for anything.

There are seven bays on Crooked Lake, each named after a day of the week. On the point between Wednesday and Thursday Bays was an enticing campsite. The view down the lake was beauteous; shear cliffs covered in orange, green and black lichen sliced out of the water and century-old white pines crowned the tops, the morning sun illuminating the wall and its vegetable tones. Even though it was early, we both felt like a day off. After our rapids fiasco my leg was stiff and sitting in a canoe all day would only aggravate it. Besides, we'd paddled every day since departure and needed rest and a cleansing.

At high noon I prepared a fire. While feeding the flames I gathered a dozen fist-sized stones and placed them on the embers. Within a few hours those cold, solid minerals became so hot they began to glow red, resembling their prior igneous state. Next to the fire was a large slab of glacially polished bedrock and carved in the ancient crust was a small cauldron, or scour hole, left over from the action of some long ago river. Using two long sticks I carefully rolled half of the cooked rocks into the hole, then crouched above it with a plastic tarp draped over me, sealing myself inside the improvised sweat lodge. The temperature inside soared immediately; my ritual purging had begun. I placed a bowl of water next to me and dipped a cedar bough into the liquid, splashing it over the ruby gems. Each droplet hissed into steam and the temperature rose higher until it was almost suffocating. Sweating intensely, I continued to sprinkle water over the cobbles and whip myself with the moist twigs. When I could no longer stand it, I flung off the plastic shell and dove into the frigid lake. With one long held breath I swam under the surface. Coming up for air, I took in a lungful of oxygen and returned to shore, cooling down quickly. Without haste I rolled the remainder of the nuggets into the pit and sealed myself off once more, repeating the rite. The lake's chill melted away into salty sweat. I offered up some herbs to the Vulcan altar, filling the womb-like space with sweet incense. Diving into icy Crooked Lake once more, I felt rejuvenated. It had been a solemn bath and I was totally relaxed. Crawling into the tent, I dozed off peacefully, dreaming of pictographs and birch bark canoes sliding over the water.

Waking from my siesta, I had a sudden urge to slip out alone over the transparent water. I headed into the middle of the lake and let the canoe glide to a slow stop, the ripples continuing forward. Eventually the lake surface calmed back down and became absolutely smooth. The reflection of the trees on the edge was as perfect as the actual forest. A steep cliff simultaneously rose and plunged; shoreline boulders doubled into gargantuan clams. The boat, myself, the clouds, a passing pair of mergansers all had their twin. I felt suspended over some scant immeasurable threshold and the two worlds I saw were both authentic, the tangible world easily confused for another assumed and reflected world, becoming indistinguishable. When I moved my head slightly, the other also moved his head. Witnessing this perfect duality had a dizzying effect. Then a fish surfaced from the underworld, disturbing the mirror. I cast my rod toward the center of the expanding circles; something nibbled and with a light tug I set the hook, reeling in a small walleye to add to our evening meal.

NANABOOZHOO
Paradise Beach to Horseshoe Bay

To the St. Lawrence Seaway

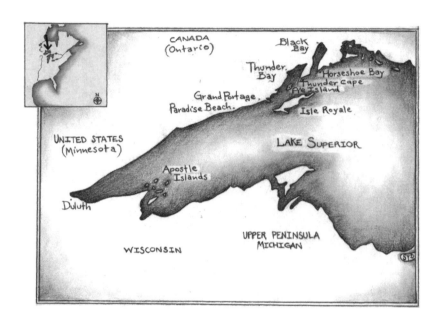

The Mississippi is a classic river, a thread that grows continually wider and deeper as it serpentines south to the Gulf. The passage to Hudson Bay is more discrete: a series of lakes cobbled together by streams that hopscotch north. The natural route east is through the five Great Lakes, the largest system of freshwater lakes in the world.

A letter initiated the trip down the Mississippi and a pitcher of beer led to Hudson Bay. The journey east, to the Gulf of St. Lawrence, began with a blind date.

Paula and I went out for dinner. After desert we walked around Lake Calhoun and that's when I discovered she was an avid whitewater kayaker. A week later she invited me to float down part of the Kettle River.

I'd played in rapids before but only in a canoe. The difference with a kayak was remarkable. Although slower, they turn on a dime, giving you much more directional control. Paula was a joy to watch as she danced effortlessly through the waves. If she tipped over, she simply popped right back up using the Eskimo roll technique. It took me a long time, but eventually I caught on.

We continued to date and a year later, in the spring, I bought us each a sea kayak. Where the whitewater kayak is designed for maneuvering through rapids, the sea kayak is meant for long distance travel over flat water like the ocean, or Lake Superior. When we took our first test run down the Mississippi River from Minneapolis to St. Paul, I was hooked.

The canoe had served me well enough in the past. It is much easier to portage so it was a good choice for the Mississippi River and Hudson

Bay trips. I learned, however, that without too many portages the kayak is the better boat: faster, safer and more comfortable. In a canoe you sit elevated on a flat seat and constantly shift your legs underneath trying to get comfortable. The kayak's bucket seat is down on the floor. Your legs rest against foot and knee pads and you lean into a backrest. The ergo-dynamics are more efficient as you essentially utilize your whole body to paddle instead of just the upper torso. Canoes are propelled with a single blade, but the kayak uses a double-bladed paddle, another advantage. One more notable difference is that a canoe is an open boat, while the kayak is completely covered. Once seated inside, you place a spray skirt around your waist which is attached around the cockpit and seals the inside of the boat from the weather. Herb and I had fashioned a nylon spray skirt for our canoe, but it leaked. The kayak's neoprene skirt was hermetic; breaking waves and snotty rains all washed away.

That fall Paula and I took our first serious float together, exploring the Apostle Islands on Lake Superior's south shore. Both of us were impressed with how quick and stable our new crafts were. Even though it was chilly outside we stayed warm. Beside the campfire one evening I proposed we take a longer trip the next summer and just keep going all the way to the Atlantic Ocean. Paula wasn't surprised, having already heard about the other excursions. And her school work would be finished by then.

Our plan was to follow the old "pork eater" route from Grand Portage to Montréal, first around the north sides of Lakes Superior and Huron, and then into the Ottawa River which leads to the St. Lawrence Seaway. Our destination was the city of Québec and sea level. By mid-June we were ready.

We chose Paradise Beach, just past Grand Marais on the north shore of Lake Superior, as our starting point. The long undeveloped littoral was close to my cabin and made an easy launch. We tried stowing all of our belongings inside the boats, but it was impossible. A few books were tossed, then a pot and a pan, clothes we thought we could do without, even some food. After the second attempt we succeeded. Paula and I entered the frisky waves and bobbed around the first telling point, leaving gathered friends behind.

Even though this was my third long paddling trip, the wonder of depar-ture was not lost. I felt like I had leapt across a threshold again and suddenly everything was new. We had shed the skins of our past, molted the jobs, the chores and the bills. The filters of everyday life, the known and predictable, all dissolved in a moment. It was the beginning of a lifestyle familiar to me but certainly new to Paula. Home now was on the move, entering a wild place of unforgiving cold water and immense boreal forest. We skimmed along the surface as if in a dream past small river mouths that streamed down from ancient hills.

That afternoon we found a smooth outcrop for our camp. I pitched the tent and collected firewood while Paula cooked pasta and toasted garlic bread. After our first dinner we sat on the shore and enjoyed the panoramic east-west view of Lake Superior, sipping tea. Our muscles were sore and sleep came quickly.

During the night the wind switched to the east. When we crawled out of the tent in the morning, we discovered three-foot waves colliding against the rocks. It had been so easy to pull off onto that knob the day before, but now it was going to be difficult to return to the lake without getting drenched. We had to delicately portage our gear over loose boulders, deadfalls and wide fissures to the far side of a point where the seas were calmer. Two important lessons were learned: first, never camp in a place you cannot exit from if the weather should change; second, the weather will change.

The same day we launched from Paradise Beach my friend Tom Hart had embarked on a different odyssey. He and his 12-year-old son Abe sailed from the south shore of Lake Superior to Grand Portage, bravely crossing 80 miles of cold open water in their 20-foot dory, the *Sanderling*. We had coordinated our separate departures so we could rendezvous and travel together for a couple days.

When Paula and I entered the marina at Grand Portage, they were on the dock waiting for us, and then we all headed out to an island in the middle of the bay to camp. Since they were sailing a goodly wind, they landed first. The fire was going and the coffee ready when we finally squeezed out of our kayaks. Earlier that day Abe had caught a lake trout and there was plenty enough for seconds. Licking our lips and sipping brandy, Paula and I listened to Tom describe their 30-hour crossing of the frigid lake. An excellent story-teller, by the end he had us all shivering.

At sunrise we left the island. They went fishing while we bee-lined towards Pigeon Point. Heavy gray clouds threatened to unload throughout the morning as Paula and I passed through wisps of fog shrouding the Susie Islands. Hermit thrushes sang their plaintive whistle, tiny wavelets splashed against the volcanic rock, fish leapt from the deep, a passenger ferry blasted its horn for the last call to Isle Royale and a semi whined on the nearby coastal highway. Out on the placid water one can hear everything as sound travels uninterrupted. Slowly we blended into the lake world, making our own soft noise: paddle blades pulling water and low whispers.

The fog burned off and by noon the solstice sun was beaming down. Just as that brilliant orb reached its summer zenith, hovering above the Tropic of Cancer, we rounded the frontier between Minnesota and Canada at Pigeon Point. The north side is a long cliff that pokes out into the lake, offering no sanctuary except for one marvelous place, Hole-in-the-Wall. A short way down the precipice is a small inlet that doglegs into the mountain, and we hooked around and into the tiny harbor to find a funky old cabin poised upon a flat lawn. The door was unlocked. Someone had left a notebook on the table so Paula opened it and began reading aloud the reflections of past travelers. Not many folks ventured to this remote place, but most who did had something to share: a feast with fresh fish, an escape with a loved one while pinned down during a fall storm, meditations on sacred beauty, rages against the rocks. The journal was completely full, so I dug into our packs and pulled out a fresh notebook and we each wrote down our impressions.

While waiting for our friends we walked the forest. These long skinny points that extend into Lake Superior have their own unique ecosystems; the mixture of cold and humid air generated by the lake creates isolated southern outposts of subarctic flora. Bonsai birch, dwarf cedar and stunted spruce dominated the enchanting grove. All the trees were draped in moss and the forest floor was carpeted with sphagnum, everything a lush, dark green.

Late in the afternoon our friends arrived with another trout, which Tom stuffed with onions and grilled on the embers. After the banquet, Abe decided to make fireworks for the solstice celebration. He walked through the woods and gathered his recipe: sheets of birch paper, moss, balsam needles and dried grasses. He twisted the grass and needles up tightly and wrapped the bundle with a birch bark covering, creating a crackling torch that burned bright and long. Parading up and down the beach he cast weird shadows as the sun went down. He threw the remains upon our beach fire and then leapt over the flames, explaining that we all had to follow suit in order to launch the new season. We obeyed, each taking a good running start and dancing over the blaze, feeling pious and silly at the same time.

Crisp songs of sparrows echoed off the walls in our hidden hole. Nice alarm, I thought. After one last shared breakfast the sailors hoisted anchor and began their long journey home, crossing the colossal lake once more. As we watched them disappear, we paddled up the Pigeon River to check in at the Canadian border. A young woman was on duty and when she saw us walking up the road she looked confused. We explained our situation: Paula was a Canadian returning home; I was a U.S. citizen and wanted entry. Yes, we were together. No, we did not have a car, but came by kayak. No, we had no firearms.

That seemed to satisfy her. She never even asked us our names. We had paddled eight miles out of our way to be legitimate. I planned on spending the next three months in Canada and the immigration officials had no idea I was there.

At the mouth of the river we returned to our temperamental sea where a warm gusty offshore breeze died to sudden calm. Rain clouds broke to sun, cold breezes came and went off the lake. We were surrounded by rock, forest, sweet water and clean air in delicate balance; we were alone for the rest of the day, vacillating somewhere between our human story and the awesome natural world.

We found a beach to camp on in Indian Bay, a small meadow filled with wild spring flowers making a perfect tent site. Kicking about the field, we discovered scattered remains of an old homestead. Here some fisherman from the old country had made his stab at the new world. The cabin was in ruins; the roof had collapsed long ago, leaving the cedar logs to rot and alder brush to grow inside. The poplar forest encroached; within my lifetime all trace of the fisherman will be gone from this isolated place.

The beach had piles of dry driftwood. We relaxed with tea beside our fire listening to the gentle waves lap the cobbled beach. Twenty miles east, out into the vast blue lake, the day's last alpenglow lit up Isle Royale. From the forest a grouse drummed his mating beat and directly before us two grebes displayed a charged courtship dance over one female while two gulls, two loons and two humans watched. Feeling at home, we celebrated the rites of spring as well.

Undoubtedly the best time to paddle on this big lake was in the early morning. It usually calmed down at night and an early launch meant easier miles. We got right into the rhythm, up at 5:00 and on the water by 6:00, rushing back and forth, stressing ourselves a bit while improving our camp skills. As soon as we were floating into the sunrise, however, all tensions faded. Moving slowly and steadily, maybe four miles an hour, we rounded distant points of land and gained new vistas. Steep hills and rugged outcrops rose from the shore forming long headlands that reached into the lake, between them deep clear bays lined with boulder beaches. A velveteen forest clung to the rock wherever it could; lichens filled in the rest.

We passed a chain of islands just offshore: Thompson, Victoria and Spar. They offered us little protection as the afternoon winds increased, but as soon as we outdistanced them we were slowed to a crawl. We labored hard to reach Caldwell Point, just beyond Caldwell Shoals. When we finally reached it, the gales stopped us.

From our newly acquired tip of land we looked west, back towards Minnesota where we came from. We could still see Pigeon Point off in the distance, two days into the past. These big landmarks stay in view for days. Successive ridges and fingers all faded into slightly different hues and green islands and white nimbus clouds floated on the horizon of churned waters. To the northeast we could see into the future: mesa-shaped Pie Island would be tomorrow's camp.

Glancing down the beach I spotted two moose, a mother and her calf walking towards us. I alerted Paula and we both remained motionless, watching. As they neared, a gusty wind carried our scent and suddenly Mama looked up with cautious eyes and trotted off into the thicket, baby in tow.

A duet of white-throated sparrows layered itself into my dreams. The cry of a loon and a solitary hermit thrush reverberated between their notes and woke us. We somersaulted our sore bodies out of sleeping bags. After a cup of very strong coffee, a few stretches and oatmeal, we pushed the boats into another day, the morning endowing us with glassy smooth waters as we glided past Sturgeon Bay and over to Flatland Island. We embarked with our eye to Pie Island, and three miles across open water and halfway there offshore winds stirred. As we reached shore, it got stronger and blew us around the entire island. On the far eastern edge of the island we found a protected beach, literally the last landfall before a daunting six-mile crossing over to Thunder Cape.

The city of Thunder Bay is tucked back into a broad inlet. Even though far from the ocean, it is one of Canada's great ports and ships from all over the globe sail there to load up on Saskatchewan grain and Ontario iron. If we had chosen to enter the city, it would have added some 30 miles to our trip. Instead, we chose to take a dangerous shortcut: six miles straight across the mouth of the bay and right through the shipping lanes. I spent the afternoon timing the ships from when they first appeared on the horizon to when they reached our trajectory across the channel. It took less than an hour, which surprised me. The crossing would take us two hours if weather conditions remained favorable. From my study I concluded that even if we departed with no ships in sight, one could easily appear and cross our course before we reached the other side.

It wasn't so much the ships that worried me though, but the wind. The channel that connects Thunder Bay with Lake Superior can act like a funnel; if we got caught by a sudden squall we could get blown out to sea. The nearest landfall outbound was Isle Royale 20 miles away, and we did not want to go there.

A loud thrashing in the forest woke me; I presumed it was a moose but it was too dark to see. As it tramped off I turned to Paula who was also wide awake. I could feel her trepidation. Outside the world was all silence, which meant there were no waves. I exited the tent and found the calmest waters imaginable—the lake's surface was perfectly flat and without a breath of wind. I looked at my watch—4:00 in the morning—and scanned the horizon for ships. Nothing. I suggested we go because conditions couldn't have been better. For the next two hours there would be no pee breaks so we skipped coffee. By 4:30 we were nestled into our kayaks skimming over dark smooth water guided by far-off city lights. Black water became mercurial as dawn advanced. Across the channel, the silhouette of a plateau came into view, like the profile of a big man lying down. This prominent landscape feature is called Nanaboozhoo, the Ojibwa name for yet another "sleeping giant." As the colors began to bleed over the surface, we moved toward it. For such a monster of a lake, for such a risky crossing, we had the fortune of continuously calm waters.

As we approached the center of the channel, roughly three miles from either shore, we saw on the eastern horizon an incoming freighter, and no matter how hard we paddled it seemed to come right for us. A half-hour later it was so close we could see the deck hands preparing to dock; we paddled even harder, listening now to its captain giving orders over the intercom. Our tiny boats would never register on their radar; we were invisible to them. Even if the captain was kind enough to choose avoiding us, he was oblivious of our existence.

The ship was no more than a hundred yards away and slipping behind us when we realized we were safe. It sliced through the calm channel and by the time its mild wake arrived, we were out of harm's way.

The entire crossing took us an hour and a half. When we finally reached the opposite shore, we touched down on a flat rocky ledge beneath the snoozing giant and with great relief indulged in coffee and a hot breakfast. We had successfully traversed one of the most dangerous parts of our journey. It seemed right to give thanks, so I sprinkled tobacco on the rock and left a small food offering for Nanaboozhoo. "Once in a lifetime is enough for me," remarked my valiant companion.

For several more miles we skirted along the base of Sibley Peninsula, a 300-foot rock wall rising vertically from the lake, its gigantic proportions dwarfing us. If there had been any wind at all, any wave action, it would have been impossible to exit the lake, but the spirits were gentle. We glided all the way to the village of Silver Islet.

In the late 1800s silver was discovered on a tiny island a mile offshore from this hamlet; word spread fast and within a few months there was a little boomtown. In its heyday it was the richest silver mine in the world, a genuine mother lode. Eventually shafts were bored 1200 feet straight down beneath the lake with branching channels spreading out and huge steam pumps installed to keep the lake water out. In one short decade it was exhausted and abandoned and the deep shafts flooded. The old miners' shacks have now been reclaimed as summer cottages. We beached near the end of town and spread our picnic. A chubby elderly woman approached and I feared she would tell us to beat it as this was a private beach. Instead she greeted us warmly and sat down, launching into some scattered history of Silver Islet. That introduction went off quickly into several tangents: her life as a professor, homemade bread, what good wives should be like, her time as a volunteer in the army, kids that left home.

It was all a little fragmented and confusing so Paula asked for some clarification, "Where and what did you teach?"

Her face turned purple and she turned to Paula, screaming, "How dare you interrupt me!" She rolled over, crawled up on all fours, then stood and stomped off to her old shack without ever looking back.

That confused us. She had seemed so bright and friendly until we spoke. Then I realized that neither of us had conversed with anyone else since the bewildered immigration agent a week earlier. Maybe it was us.

We left the beach and began hunting for a campsite. Another six-mile crossing was just around the bend at Black Bay and we hoped to traverse it refreshed the following morning. Just past Silver Islet the black igneous rock gave way to layers of deep red sandstone. At the entrance to Black Bay was a small cluster of islands, an extension of the sedimentary rock. We wove through the islands but could find nowhere to camp, not even on the biggest of them, Middleburn. With a little work we could have hacked something out of the brambles, something big enough for our tent, but the next island, Gravel, seemed more promising by name alone. The problem was that it was three miles away, halfway across Black Bay, and we were tired, having crossed enough open water for one day. Decisions like those were never easy: stay where you are in a lousy spot or move on into the unknown hoping for better. We agreed it was worth the risk and headed for Gravel.

A crosswind blew from within the deep bay making steering difficult. The kayaks wanted to spin around and point out into Superior. Even with the added help of rudders we had to constantly overcompensate to one side to maintain a straight course, quite desirable with a three-mile fetch. In fair conditions we could travel four miles an hour. During that crossing we were slowed to a quarter of that, and the closer we got the stinkier it became. We found not one but two small islands, both large seagull and cormorant rookeries with hundreds of birds all feeling feisty and not at all happy to see us. The stench of dead fish was terrible and with all the chirping and squawking it sounded like raving hell.

We were already halfway into the unplanned six-mile crossing, but as fatigued as we were we had to continue. That meant three more hard miles to Edward Island at the end of Black Bay. Reluctantly we moved out into the growing seas. We tried cheering each other on for another painful hour. The play of the wind switched and grew stronger, but in the end it helped push us into a calm channel. I noticed on the map a small inlet called Horseshoe Bay that looked like the best place to escape the relentless winds. After an incredibly long day of 30 miles with two dangerous crossings behind us, we finally found home.

Horseshoe Bay is shaped like its name. We were back in the Laurentian rock again and this narrow channel looped back into an emerald cove so transparent you could see the bottom of the granite pool. Its shallow water warmed up more quickly than the open lake and a shaft of sun lit the hard shore, giving us time to bathe. Superior continued to churn; blustery winds blew through the tree tops, but we were snug.

QUESTER
Grand Rapids to St. Paul

Down the Mississippi

As we approached Grand Rapids on the Mississippi River, the most obvious feature was the Blandin Paper and Pulp Mill. Just beyond the banks, acres and acres of neatly stacked logs awaited their conversion to fiber. The mill itself was composed of boxy, four-story, corrugated steel buildings, and inside and out the place buzzed with worker bees driving fork lifts, skidders and logging trucks moving among the puffing industrial smokestacks. On the river itself, chains of log booms crisscrossed the river, corralling more logs for pre-soaking.

On the opposite shore of the tree-devouring giant was a small park donated by Blandin to the citizens of Grand Rapids. The second highest waterfall on the entire Mississippi, Pokegama, used to lie between the park and the mill. The 20-foot drop is now contained by a cement dam, which for us meant another portage. Just as Pat and I dragged the boat out of the water a pickup approached and the driver informed us it was company policy to assist canoeists around the dam. The truck was filled and we were deposited downstream, our easiest portage.

The town offered us a chance to stretch our legs. Strolling along we came upon the county museum, most of it dedicated to the clear-cutting of the Great North Woods. We learned that once there had been an enormous swath of centurion white pines covering northern Minnesota. Between 1850 and 1920 the bulk of that forest was destroyed, much of it due to fire from careless logging practices. In reality, the majority was cut down in a few short years at the turn of the century and floated down the river to the mills. Most of the prairie cities were originally constructed from this white pine.

Sewer pipes appeared at the bottom of town; add to that the industrial discharge from the mill and suddenly the small Mississippi became fouled. Up to that point we had naively been drinking from the river, but no more. We bought two large plastic jugs, filled them, and departed.

Between Lake Itasca and Grand Rapids the river moves in an easterly direction, but then shifts course, making a long curving arch to the south like a big question mark. Our latitude changed fast along with the landscape. We departed from the remnant Great North Woods and entered sparse agricultural lands mixed with hardwoods. The farms were small; it's tough growing crops in that glacial debris and about all one could do was graze a few head of cattle and tend a garden.

By early September fall's subtle changes were beginning to show: sumac leaflets turning carmine and maples fading into orange. The last flowers of summer were in blossom—goldenrods, purple aster, pearly everlasting—and we camped in a field of yellow evening primrose. The cool air was fanned by a flock of Canadian geese flying low and a new crescent moon reflected on the twilight mirror.

After dinner I went for a solo paddle, going upstream and then drifting down several times. Floating on the black water I stared off into starry space through the river pane. When I passed by our camp, Pat stoked the fire creating a comet of sparks that burst into the sky and river. The next time I snuck by he was sitting on a log playing his guitar. From his fingers came some of the finest music a guitar can sound: ragtime, blues, a bit of country. I heard Hank Williams while drifting down and some Mississippi John Hurt on my way back up. On the next pass there was Eric Clapton and Jimmy Buffet. They all cast their respective shadows beside the flames as I relaxed in the canoe, held by the melodies, listening to the vibrating strings and voice. When I made my final pass he was working out an original tune, "Well if Jesus walks on water, then I'm bound to meet him someday. 'Cause I've been travelin' out on this river so long, through tempest, hunger, glory and pain..."

A perfectly clear evening, and mosquito-free, we decided to forgo the tent and instead slept beneath the sky. The stars were lustrous, the Milky

Way a wispy cloud. Several times I woke between dreams and opened my eyes to the infinite. With a smile I drifted back into peace while the river flowed silently into the night.

A hoot owl awoke us at dawn. Surfacing to consciousness, I found myself buried deep inside my sleeping bag. I wrestled with the drawstring and poked my head out to find a shroud of frost covering everything—the blades of grass, the beach, every branch on every tree, the canoe, us. With a shiver we rekindled the fire and watched the sun's first light melt it all away.

Meandering through more subsistence farmlands and scattered woods, the snaky river pulled us through a blur of changing leaves, brown muddy banks, black silty waters and azure skies. We approached a section of rapids and found the whitewater mild and playful. Halfway into the run we passed a mink out on a bald rock chewing on a crawfish. In the same instant we all recognized each other and then, just as quick, we were past and moving downriver fast. The mink kept chewing and we rounded another bend, feeling wild.

That evening as I dozed off a pair of black bears came by for leftovers. Pat banged two pots together to scare them away and I began shouting and whistling as loud as I could. It took some time, but eventually Yogi and Boo-Boo got bored with our antics and rambled off, crashing through the night brush searching for another select picnic basket.

The next day east winds stirred. Blue skies turned gray and by noon it began to rain for the rest of the afternoon and the entire next day. Tent-bound, dry and warm in our little cocoon, we sat there reading, writing and sharing thoughts. Between downpours we walked the small beach to stretch our backs and watch the river rise. The forest was saturated, too wet for a fire, so we simply grazed on granola and stolen apples. It felt good to sit in one earthly place for two days with nowhere else to go. Pat summed it up perfectly: "On a sunny day you're supposed to feel good. On a gray day you just feel as you please. That's why I like gray days best."

It was easy to lose track of time while cruising with the river and often I forgot what day of the week it was because it really didn't matter; our clock was the sun and our movements were determined by the weather. When we landed in Aitken, however, we heard bells pealing and knew it was Sunday. As we moseyed through town, we watched the faithful heading into their churches along Main Street. We were in favor of keeping the day holy and decided to join them; the challenge was which sanctuary to choose.

Often while paddling along Pat and I discussed religion, both of us reevaluating our Catholic backgrounds, searching for something vital, something different. When we heard laughter spilling from the Aitken Congregational Church, we looked at each other and nodded.

As we entered, all the parishioners turned their heads to look at the long-haired, scraggly-bearded, muddy-booted strangers. With welcoming smiles they bid us inside and we settled into our pew. I don't know what the sermon was about as I've never been good at remembering them. After the service we filed outside with everyone else and as I passed though the front door somebody squeezed my arm—the minister wanted to invite us personally to the annual church picnic.

When you know you only have an hour or two to share with certain people, it's easy to get to the marrow. We indulged in spirit, mind and belly, all of us. The exchange of ideas between our young hearts and that mostly older congregation was lovely, as if they understood why one would choose to follow the river. We nourished each other while sharing the feast, and as we stood to leave, bowing in gratitude, they bestowed a hefty portion of leftovers upon us. Two well-fed strangers drifted out of Aitken, still questioning but way more satisfied.

It was a hot, sultry September day and we paddled swiftly through the wooded banks, a new moon in the west heaven leading us on. In the afternoon we paused on a sandy beach for another picnic. Between skinny dips we sat naked on our haunches, poised like animals and gnawing bones. The feel of the sun on wet skin, the sound of birds singing, the wind whispering its leafy voice, fresh autumn scents, the moving river of life: it all felt sacred.

Besides religion, philosophical and psychological themes were often part of our conversational soup. I found it easy to meander through life's questions with Pat. How did we ever get to be here? Is life long or short? What is moral? Are we indebted to society? Is it better to be selfless or selfish? What is free will? How should we respond to our own dreams?

On the outskirts of Brainerd we eyed a man and a woman standing in the shade beneath a bridge fishing, and with one wave they reeled us in beside them. As it turned out, the man was a psychologist from Minneapolis and the woman a poet. The psychologist told us, "Interesting people are found under bridges. Remove anyone from the shopping mall and place them here and you'll find someone unique. We all have something to share but it usually takes circumstance to reveal it. Even the dullard would enrich this experience." His theory bolstered my confidence, so I shared my growing list of questions with them. The poet's clever response, "Don't worry. You're going in the right direction," comforted me.

We breezed by touristy Brainerd in the late afternoon and then portaged another dam. By the time we found an island to camp on, it was nearly dark so we threw down a tarp and again slept under the stars. In the morning I discovered we had sacked out next to a patch of *toxicodendron radicans,* commonly known as poison ivy, and as the day wore on red blotches of the incredibly itchy rash began to appear on my body. By late afternoon I was covered head to toe. I took frequent baths in the river hoping to wash it off. Jewelweed is a supposed remedy so I gathered a bunch and rubbed its juice over the worst spots, which felt cool and helped for a while. We passed a general store and I bought its entire stock of calamine lotion and poured it on liberally. It would take several days of excruciating itch and sleepless nights before the seeping sores dried up.

In 1730 a decisive battle was fought between the Lakota and Ojibwa Indians at the mouth of the Crow Wing River. Victorious, the Ojibwa won all the lands east of the Mississippi previously held by the Lakota. At the same site in 1849, the United States built a military outpost to establish a presence in the "wilderness frontier" and the troops then pushed the natives into the prairies. In 1931 at this same historic junction, the Fort Ripley Military Reservation was established as a training ground for the Minnesota National Guard and the post is still there. Floating by the boot camp, knowing I did not have to slug any hardware around, seemed right; cut-offs are more comfortable than fatigues. Under the same sun, beside the same river, other youngsters certainly lived a different reality. The choice between free-floating down a river or training beside it to be a soldier was easy.

Looking for fresh water became an amusing chore. Whenever in a town it was easy to fill the jugs, but between times usually involved knocking on some stranger's door. We were pretty ratty looking and people were a bit shocked at first, but once we explained ourselves and our canoe trip, most warmed right up.

Nearly everyone who lived beside the Mississippi did so for one reason, they liked the river, so most of them appreciated anyone who might undertake a journey downstream past their homes. Some even shared the dream and at times we were invited in for a cup of coffee, or even a meal. Sharing our story while filling our containers was like that shady summer bridge: there was an easy sense of connection.

North of Little Falls we approached one such river home. In exchange for a couple of our favorite tales we received a cornucopia of eggplants, green peppers, zucchini, juicy tomatoes, fresh herbs and ten gallons of clear, cold water. To top it all off, the friendly folks insisted we pitch our tent by their riverside garden.

Sometimes, though, it wasn't so pleasant. Between there and Sauk Rapids we stopped at a wayside farm and I took off with the jugs while Pat tied up the canoe. As I approached the farmhouse, a big, mean ornery dog came peeling around the barn spitting up gravel and drooling and sank its teeth right into my quivering butt just as the farmer showed up and called her down. He did give me water, but after filling up I retreated backwards, limping and scowling.

We were down to our last cup when we arrived in Monticello. There were several bars along its main street and since it was 95 degrees in the shade, we entered the first one, dark and dank. After my eyes and nose adjusted, I saw a crazed drunken man with a very unhealthy glow betting his fellow drinkers that he could eat a beer glass. Nervously the crowd laughed, all anxious to place their wagers. And wouldn't you know, that character put his big ol' rotten brown teeth right onto the top of his stein, paused a moment to survey everyone's attention and then snapped off a sizable shard. With his molars he ground that glass right up until it returned to sand and then he proceeded to swallow it. I figured he must have gotten nuked with a few too many curies from the nearby nuclear power plant. After raking in his earnings, he let out a startling laugh, our cue to exit that bar and town; even though we filled our jugs, I was afraid to drink the water.

At Coon Rapids we walked around another dam—our very last portage. There were still plenty of others plugging up the river downstream, but they all had locks we would be free to pass through. We finished hauling our gear in the late afternoon and then camped just below, sleeping on the outskirts of the Twin Cities.

Early the next morning we wove through the Islands of Peace in suburban Fridley and on the park's southern tip we took a break. Before us was a pair of interstate bridges that spanned the river, the gateway into Metrolandia. No matter how cleverly engineered, they seemed to emanate stress; both were packed with slow-moving rush-hour traffic, drivers afraid to be late honking their horns. We departed from the island and glided beneath the cacophony. We had no schedule to keep, no stop lights, no cops, no bosses or traffic jams. Pausing next to one of the footings, we contemplated all those separate realities meeting at the same time, and then we let go, the river pulling us towards the metropolis.

As the Minneapolis skyline came into view, the feel of the river changed. Upstream it had been buoyant, carefree, but suddenly near downtown it surged into a grownup working river. Barges lined the shores beside lofty grain mills. Towboats, the first we had seen, plied their merchandise. A mile-long coal train fed a hungry power plant. Industrial factories hummed, traffic whined ceaselessly and tall cranes raised new skyscrapers.

When Father Louis Hennipen explored this area in 1680, he discovered St. Anthony Falls. This 50-foot cascade, the largest on the Mississippi, eventually became the impetus to rip the northern forests into lumber and later build a city around the flour milling industry. The waterfall has now been stabilized by a dam and next to it is the river's very first lock, St. Anthony "A," which we approached cautiously.

The sweep of current curled over the lip of the dam and plunged out of sight roaring with white noise. Next to this drop-off were lock gates surrounded by massive concrete walls. Pat had previous experience with locks from his solo journey the year before, but it was my first time and I was nervous. At the entrance was a sign with instructions for small craft and to request a drop in elevation we were to pull the signal cord. Shortly after we yanked it, the lockmaster responded over a loudspeaker that we would have to wait our turn; there was a towboat locking through upstream and another scheduled to go down and they had priority over small craft. Just up from the gates was a floating steel catwalk that we pulled alongside to have lunch and wait. As we lolled in the canoe enjoying the respite, the river beneath us suddenly erupted into a dangerous swirling whirlpool. Evidently they were filling the chamber and we were sitting right above the intake chutes. The catwalk tilted to a 45-degree angle and nearly tipped us over. Paddling madly, whipped around in all directions, we slowly managed to escape the sucking boil and headed further upstream to safety. I was even less confident.

The river calmed back down and the gates opened. Slowly the towboat departed with its empty barge and then another appeared from upstream, moved in and took its place. When it was safely tied off, the lockmaster signaled us in, which surprised me. Between the huge steel barge and the 20-foot thick cement wall was some four feet of leeway and our canoe required three of those. As we squeezed into place a deck hand tossed us a line—something to hang onto. The gates closed; we were committed. I clasped the rope with sweaty palms and a few minutes later realized we were gradually descending in a calm and steady drop with really nothing to fear. We went down 50 feet and then it stopped; hemmed in tight between the barge and the slimy, five-story cement walls gave me claustrophobia. After the gates opened, we didn't wait for further instruction but dashed back onto the river. Never again have I been directed to lock through with a barge. It was a unique introduction.

There's another lock directly below that, St. Anthony "B," and this time our companion towboat went down without us while we preferred to wait our turn from a distance. The gates finally opened to reveal we had the entire chamber to ourselves for the pleasant ride down 25 feet closer to sea level.

Departing from that second lock, we entered a geologically changed river. Between Lake Itasca and Minneapolis the river had traveled through granite, iron deposits, old volcanic flows and pockets of glacial debris. From Minneapolis south to Kentucky it moves through sedimentary rock. During the Paleozoic Epoch this region was part of an extensive warm shallow sea. For millions of years fine sands and calcareous shells accumulated on its floor forming layers of sandstone and limestone. At least four different glacial movements have advanced and retreated over this area since. The most recent sheet of ice, the Wisconsin, is estimated to have been 10,000 feet thick, its tremendous melting runoff gouging out this softer sedimentary rock and excavating a deep valley. Upstream from the Twin Cities the river had flowed just beneath the low banks, but downstream it dropped into a deep crevasse walled in by an ancient seabed that starts just below St. Anthony Falls.

The cliffs banks were steep and heavily forested, shades of autumn washing through the hardwoods. Most of the buildings disappeared from view, giving us a false sense of isolation; if it weren't for all the bridges, we would scarcely have known we were paddling through major sprawl. No other city on the river has so many spans across the Mississippi. I counted 29 on our trusty highway map, the oldest a limestone arch bridge with granite footings. There are wood trestles, concrete arches, steel cantilevers, newfangled straight-line I-beams and even a suspension bridge. Here every design has been tested and the river sneaks right beneath them all.

A few miles past the falls is another lock at the Ford Dam that we went through feeling like veterans. On the downstream side we passed our first major tributary, the Minnesota River. Perched on the bluffs high above the confluence sits old Fort Snelling; hand-laid limestone walls, towers and turrets are joined right on top of Time's own precisely laid masonry. In 1805 Zebulon Pike landed there while searching for the source of the Mississippi. Appreciating the ideal situation for a fortress to protect the wave of anticipated settlers, he made a shady transaction with the Lakota, trading one barrel of whiskey for the prime real estate. Construction began a few years later and soon America had another stronghold in the heart of Indian Country. It's amazing how much this area has changed in two centuries; a couple million people now live in an area that once supported several thousand.

We had entered the commercially navigable waterway and the dredged channel was marked with buoys and regular mile-marker signs on both sides of the river. We were presently at Number 884, which meant we were 884 miles from the confluence of the Ohio and the Mississippi Rivers. The

Corps of Engineers has creatively labeled this section the Upper River. At the Ohio junction in Cairo, Illinois, the Lower River begins and the numbers start all over again, counting down some 900 more miles to the Gulf of Mexico. Getting lost on this federal waterway would be difficult.

Around another bend we beheld the unidentical twin city of St. Paul, leaving our canoe in a park on Harriet Island to walk across the Wabasha Bridge for a downtown stroll. After carousing through a music store, a book vendor and a used clothing emporium, we purchased a bottle of red wine. We walked up to the Cathedral and sat down on its granite steps, leaned against the oak doors and uncorked. An offering was made to the city, the river below us and the shared journey. After draining the dregs, we walked back to the island.

By the time we reached our canoe the sun had set and feeling restless, we decided to give night paddling a try. White, red, yellow and green lights shimmered on the black mirror as we slid quietly through the city. There was no other traffic; the river was ours. On the edge of downtown we entered an area devoid of lights, a welcome ribbon of darkness. We rolled out our sleeping bags and, after one very long day, collapsed in a field.

I've heard that of our five senses the olfactory has the strongest influence on recall. One of my most poignant memories of the Mississippi River is the smell of South St. Paul. The first whiffs that came to us in the morning were from a molasses processing plant, pungent and sweet. Further down we came upon odors from the stock yards: blood, guts and flesh from butchered swine, cattle and lamb. Mixed with this thickened air were diesel fumes from passing towboats carrying scents of corn and soybean. But the most acrid smell of all was the stink that wafted over from Pigs Eye Sewage Treatment Facility, named after the first European trader in the area to set up whiskey dealing with the natives. The confluence of its effluence was a disgusting influence. Impossible to avoid, we slipped through the dirty brown swirls of foam as fast as we could.

A couple miles past the stench, Pat began to complain of a headache that got so bad eventually he had to lie down in the bottom of the canoe and rest. I continued paddling, trying to create some distance. I managed to push us around a couple more bends and then too developed an excruciating headache which drained all my energy and made the veins in my temples throb. I sluggishly beached us onto a sandspit and pitched the tent. We both crawled in and passed out; after a fitful nap I went outside, vomited and then fell asleep once more half-delirious in the warm sand. After a few hours Pat roused and heated up soup which helped revive us. Such sickening air was an outrage. A crude hung-over feeling the next morning only inspired us to push on early. Our river had really taken a beating, and so had we.

FRESH AIRS
Lac la Croix to the Winnipeg River

To Hudson Bay

In the symphony of dawn we were the percussionists. Our wood blades swish-swished keeping tempo and syncopated beats against the canoe hull echoed off the cliffs. Drumming our way through Thursday, Friday, Saturday and Sunday Bays, Herb and I tracked Crooked Lake in tune. After portaging around Curtain Falls, we pitched into Lac la Croix and a short way up the east side came to another collection of pictographs: life-size handprints, moose and several abstract symbols. We camped nearby, tired from a full day's journey of 20 miles. A car would cover that in half an hour; for us, it was a sunup-to-sundown day of voyaging. A mighty good thing we had all summer.

With each passing day we improved our morning routine. I usually awoke first with the early birds and under fading stars I'd start the gas stove and prepare coffee. While waiting for the water to boil, I'd stretch like a waking cat with some slow tai chi, loosening the sore portage muscles and relaxing my back stiff from sleeping on the rocky ground. When the coffee was ready I'd roust Herb, who cooked breakfast while I took down the tent and packed the bags. We ate while glancing over the day's pertinent maps and after washing the dishes loaded the canoe. It all took less than an hour.

On that day we cruised our biggest lake yet, Lac la Croix, so big that for the first time we didn't have to portage. In the late afternoon, as we neared its end, the weather turned and dark clouds threatened rain. There were no legal campsites on our map but we had to find something soon, even if it meant squatting for the night. It began to sprinkle, so we attached the spray skirts. Herb put on his raincoat and since I had lost mine, I donned a plastic garbage bag. Daylight was disappearing fast; we paddled past one point and then another, and just as the last quantum of light faded, we found what looked like a few square feet of level ground. We stumbled through our routine of tent pitching in the dark and crawled into our little home as the sprinkle turned to showers. I was finally in my bag with the candle lit when the storm unleashed its full force.

At the very end of Lac la Croix we came across something new: a mechanical portage; for a modest price a small-gauge trolley hauled your boat up and over Beatty Portage. It was drizzling and we were tempted, but since it really was a short walk we did it the old manual way, believing ourselves purists.

We entered Loon Lake and paddled its length to find at the far end another mechanical portage. A man standing outside in the rain greeted us as we approached. The downpour had increased and since portaging meant exposing all our gear to the weather, we asked how much it cost. When we learned just $2.50, we quickly readjusted our team image. The idea of not having to unload a single item from the canoe except one wallet was irresistible.

The effortless portage completed, the owner-operator invited us into his home for coffee and introduced his wife. Together they ran this enviable business for five months a year. The rest of the time they resided in solitude, reading, writing and snowshoeing. While the kind woman poured, she graciously asked if either of us would like a little whisky spiked into our brew. For the next two hours we sipped on our medicine, warmed inside and out in a wonderful respite. Neither of us wanted to leave and face the cold rains again, but we reluctantly parted from their sanctuary, dressing back up in our spongy outfits and leaving those spirits behind. What a sight we must have made heading out into the foggy waters, zigzagging a little, I suspect. The chilly air sobered us up quickly.

Traveling down the Loon River, we came to a small rapids and opted to line the canoe down instead of unloading all our gear and portaging. To line a canoe means to leave the boat in the water and let the river pull it through while trying to guide it from shore with attached ropes. It was our first attempt at this technique and it could have been the whiskey, or the fatigue, or our cold numb hands, but we failed. The canoe drifted through a standing wave and took on several gallons of water. At the same moment, I leapt to a different foothold to exchange ropes with Herb. The line slipped through my hands and our barge headed downstream alone. We watched in dismay as it splashed through the rest of the rapids and then, at the bottom, drifted out into the middle of the river and out of reach. Without hesitation I dove into the cold drink to retrieve it. After I swam it ashore and emerged my teeth began to chatter. It was the perfect recipe for hypothermia: alcohol, cool air, rain and soggy clothes. I quickly undressed and put on something dry. Herb generously offered to trade his raincoat for my garbage bag, which helped a lot. We got into the canoe and paddled vigorously, trying to generate body heat, but it continued to rain and soon he too was soaked. We picked up our pace, looking for any kind of campsite on the slimy mud-banked river.

Seriously cold, Herb began to mumble. We decided to make immediate camp and pulled the boat onto a mud flat, climbed to a little rock knob and pitched the tent. Herb stripped off his rags, stumbled inside and fumbled into his sleeping bag. He had lost too much body heat and collapsed shivering with fatigue. I recalled from a first aid course the symptoms for hypothermia were called the "umbles": stumble, grumble, fumble and mumble. I knew he needed some hot fluids so I brought our stove into the tent and prepared instant soup and herbal tea. I fished out our gorp, too, so he could refuel on carbohydrates. After a couple of cups Herb fell asleep and I crawled into my bag and within minutes was warm and dozy. With the combination of steady all-day rains and the extra water taken on while lining our canoe through the rapids, all our clothes were saturated. Our food was safe, double wrapped in waterproof bags, and our sleeping bags were protected in rubberized sea bags. But drifting off to sleep, I could only think of pulling on those sopping duds in the morning.

That night I had a very pleasant dream. Herb and I walked over to my parents' house and knocked on the door like strangers. My mother welcomed us in, exuding maternal warmth. She offered us my favorite dishes which we ate with great pleasure. Reveling in her attentions, we feasted while she gathered up all of our wet things and put them into her dryer. I was really happy how she solved all our problems; in the dream I thought how easy it would be now waking up and inserting ourselves into fresh, clean, dry threads. The monotonous, repetitive and reassuring sound of her tumbling dryer gave me profound comfort. Then I awoke to reality. I sat up dazed and disappointed: there was no hot food awaiting us nor dryer warming our clothes.

The air was very cold outside of my sleeping bag and I didn't want to leave its warmth. As I reached to unzip the door for a weather report, an even colder blast invaded the tent. Looking out into the forest all I saw was white; the ground was covered with snow, not much, just a couple inches, but I'd never seen it that late in May. We had to start a fire and dry off so I dressed into my clammy damp rags and went out to make flames. Herb soon followed, scrunching through the snow.

Everything was waterlogged. I gathered some birch bark and dead pine needles while Herb went searching for the smallest kindling he could find. We made our first attempt and could not get anything to burn. Even the birch bark, normally quite flammable, wouldn't ignite. The pine needles would only burn hot enough to evaporate the water on them and then died out. We gathered more fuel, tried again, and still couldn't get any embers. Herb then had the smart idea to whittle small sticks and remove all the wet bark down to the dry heart, so with our knives we peeled away. After adding these to a fresh mix of bark and needles, we finally, slowly, got a response. Whittling away at bigger and fatter sticks, we eventually had ourselves a roaring fire.

Both Herb and I are experienced woodsmen. I can honestly say I'd never before had trouble getting a fire going, but after 24 hours of rain, followed by a blanket of snow, it was a challenge. Within an hour we were standing as close as we could to the heat and smoke, drying the clothes on our backs, turning like rotisseries and watching clouds of steam roll off each other. We cooked up oatmeal and drank pots of coffee. By noon we were finally dry and the sun came out, and so we loaded the canoe and slipped down the muddy banks onto the river again.

On the north side of Crane Lake we officially exited the Boundary Waters Canoe Area Wilderness and entered Voyagers National Park. The difference between these two parks is that in the latter motor boats are permitted. A certain silence was replaced with a combustive drone, but it was still the same rugged landscape.

Both are located in the highlands of the Laurentian Plateau, formed during the Pre-Cambrian era four to five billion years ago and containing some of the oldest rock on Earth. The plateau includes the Great Lakes region and extends to the Arctic, and because it covers over half of Canada, it is often called the Canadian Shield. It was the first part of North America to be permanently elevated above sea level and for that reason is considered its nucleus. During the more recent Pleistocene Epoch enormous continental sheets of ice covered this area, depressing the surface of the land and scouring out thousands of basins. The last of these ice sheets melted 11,000 years ago and the holes filled with fresh water, creating the very lakes Herb and I were paddling through.

Near the Namakan Narrows we saw more pictographs next to a famed symbolic Manitou, or spirit of the Ojibwa world. This Manitou was a white vein of quartzite flowing between layers of gray sandstone, forming the perfect image of a lake monster. It was quite beautiful, really, and easy enough to imagine that long ago it did hold some kind of special significance. Certainly it was important enough for the two of us to get out of our canoe, take a photo and smoke a pipe.

That night we camped on My Island in Lake Namakan. For the first time since departure, our accommodations had a picnic table, quite a luxury, and a large sandbox for pitching the tent. That too was nice, a soft and dry foundation. The other unique feature was an upright log frame used for hoisting food packs up and away from bears. We both knew it would be one of the last "regulation" maintained campsites for the rest of our journey. Once we departed from Voyagers Park, we would mostly have to hack our own out of the woods, creating whatever luxury we could with our hands.

The following day we crossed the remainder of Lake Namakan, passed through the Canadian Channel and then entered large open water, Rainy Lake. It is humbling to gaze over such a void. Somewhere on the distant horizon was our future but we would have to trek a marathon distance to reach it. The water was like a sheet of mercury; our biggest lake yet was also our calmest, the only interruption in the smoothness our own wake extending out from the bow, and, of course, the occasional motorboat. Halfway to the narrows of Rainy Lake we camped on Minnitaki Island.

We were closing in on International Falls, the very first town along our route.

We paddled for 12 hours to reach a pub. Earlier in the day we had met a pair of houseboats on a party cruise and one of the skippers told us about a tavern near the end of Rainy Lake that served legendary hamburgers. We plodded along, hoping to reach it before nightfall. Not every day did we get to retire from a long day's ride, sip beer, and allow someone else to do the cooking. The kitchen grease, stale cigarettes, sticky floor and country music easily impressed us; raucous locals were leaning into the bar and we joined them. One bulbous-nosed regular got whiff of our journey and insisted on paying our tab, behind his roadmap eyes a spark of youthful cheer. Stumbling out of the bar at closing time, we tipped into our canoe and headed over to a small island we had passed earlier. On a flat overgrown lawn next to the ruins of an old homestead, we crash-landed.

My stomach was growling fiercely when I awoke. Herb, snoring like an old man, assured me he was still among the living. I paddled back across the bay with three things on my mind: bacon, eggs and a Sunday paper. The news was disappointing; the food was not. When the aromas wafted over to Herb, he stirred and then lumbered out of the tent licking his paws. The motorboat traffic in the bay was noisy, so after our brunch we departed for a leisurely stroll down the remainder of Rainy Lake.

The shoreline became increasingly populated, a mix of funky old cabins and brand new luxury homes packing the lake's southern edge. Soon we could hear the distant thrum of International Falls with its railway, highway and flyway. A dark cloud hung over the city: belching smokestacks from a pulp plant emitted a stink filled with mercurial toxins, the price of scented toilet paper and shitty newspapers.

It's always risky to approach any city late in the day as potential campsites become scarce. We hedged for a while, debating whether to camp on a nearby island or take our chances and head into town. Stalling near the tip of Birch Point we continued deliberating. The noise of a lawnmower suddenly went silent as some man wheeled the machine back towards his cabin. I suggested we approach and ask about any nearby campgrounds. Once we were within earshot I began the query. The man responded by waving us in. Walking down his dock, he greeted us with a friendly smile, saying, "No, there's no campground on this side of town. The nearest one is ten miles past the city. You can camp in my yard, though, if you want." While we pitched the tent, Doug served us ice tea and explained that he was on his way to International Falls to visit his mother. After that he was driving to Minneapolis, but not to worry. We could use his lawn, his cabin, the shower, the kitchen, whatever we liked; feel free, just leave the key under the rock on your way out, please. Once we were set up he even offered to chauffeur us around town.

At the laundromat we got to wash our cloths in a machine for the first time in three weeks. While letting the agitator do its magic, Doug took us to the post office where we had fan mail awaiting and our own letters to send. Our taxi then brought us to the bank, grocery store, bottle shop, and most importantly, a camping store so I could buy a new rain coat. After all the chores were finished, we drove to his mother's for coffee and pie. She was the grandest of mothers and I wished I could have spent the entire day with her, but Doug had to be on his way. He drove us back to the family cabin and left for the long drive south. We walked out to the point in the front yard to catch the sunset.

Birch Point faces north into Rainy Lake. Way off to the west a system of towering thunder-heads moved towards us, like a mountain range in motion. The sun was setting and illuminating them internally and externally in shades of red, orange and yellow. From within this powerful cell lightening flashed, at times bolts going straight down and grounding on earth, others times moving horizontally between the cumulus. Often the lightening flashed every which way at once. The sun briefly shone through a crack and a faint rainbow appeared; everything was reflected over the subdued lake surface, giving us a double exposure to the extraordinary show. The clouds began to darken after the sun had set and soon just the very summits were lit. They too quickly faded, leaving only lingering flashes of lightening to illuminate the world.

Above us was a clear, cloudless sky and slowly the stars began to emerge. The first, hovering above the eastern horizon, was a lonely cold distant planet. One by one countless other bodies followed as night cast its blanket; then a faint glow appeared, the Milky Way, our galaxy. Another glow appeared which quickly exploded into northern lights. In this part of the continent we are often treated to the spectacle of *aurora borealis.*

Usually they are like florescent green curtains that undulate across the sky, but on occasion when solar activity is especially high, they turn red and purple. During this show they began waving across the sky in that familiar luminescent green, and the darker it got the deeper became their tones. Eventually the sky filled with waves of purple, red and green charged particles, all pulsating towards the North Pole. Grounded on earth, touching the celestial, we were vaulted through the cosmos.

The Rainy River runs between International Falls and Lake of the Woods. We were no longer in the wilderness—on the Minnesota side was a highway and on the Canadian side a railway line. The fast current, the wide river, the tire whine and railway rumbles, the old farmsteads and small villages all seemed familiar. It reminded me of the Mississippi. Both rivers have been used as major transportation routes for millennia, the one connecting north with south, the other east with west. Another shared attribute are Native American burial mounds. There are many along the Mississippi and beside the Rainy River is the Grand Mound, the largest in Minnesota and the furthest north.

This 25-foot high tomb is now protected by the state and after we paid our entrance fee we were given a private tour with an interpreter. She walked us through the historic site, explaining how for generations family after family had used this mound to bury their ancestors along with a few treasures to take to "the other side." Excavations have uncovered copper pieces, ceramics, pipestone and arrowheads, but most things were ransacked long ago. Continuing afield, the guide taught us the local blooming wild flowers: columbines, yellow lady-slippers, Virginia waterleaf, pyrola, buttercups, sweet cecily, purple violets, wild ginger. Rains from a summer shower interrupted our tour, so we all ducked under a canopy of basswood trees for shelter and shared a picnic. As soon as the rains began to penetrate the foliage, the storm passed and we emerged into the bright, damp afternoon.

A little further downstream we came upon Manitou Rapids. The river upstream from there was perhaps a quarter-mile wide; entering the rapids, it became squeezed into a bottleneck of frothing water no more than 20 yards wide, tall standing waves scattered throughout. After our spill at Wheelbarrow Falls we were apprehensive about running the rapids, but we got out to study them anyway. On the left side was a smooth chute that appeared safe to pass through so we tied all the loose items down, fastened the spray skirts and donned our life vests. Flying past boiling cauldrons of cold water with adrenalin pumping, we shouted and laughed our way through without taking on a drop.

In the evening beside a tranquil stretch of the river I took a solitary walk, and as I shuffled along a small object caught my eye. I bent over, brushed some sand aside, and uncovered the bowl of an old meerschaum pipe. I had seen in paintings and drawings of the voyageurs that this was the very style of pipe those first explorers used. I held the rare, delicate treasure in my hands and wondered whose lips had drawn upon it long ago, what aspirations he had guarded, what fears he might have felt while penetrating into this wild landscape. I also thought of the Manitou Rapids and wondered if this pipe had perhaps fallen from someone's mouth as he too hollered his way down the chute, surfacing centuries later for me to find. I brought it back to show Herb and we decided to fill it up, to see if it tasted of another time. We savored a sense of eternity, the smells of the coming summer, the thrill and danger of living on the edge, being outside all day, blending into this sacred country.

Herb had friends who lived on the river near Baudette. When he called the Ronglies to warn them of our approach, we were given directions and informed dinner was at seven. We arrived just in time and mother, father and sons were all waiting for us on their dock. The first impression one got from this clan was their height. An even six-feet tall, I have never considered myself short, but everyone in that family was at least half a foot taller. Marge, the mom, was the exception; I'd wager she's a shade above five-foot.

After introductions they all helped us carry our gear up the steep stairway to the bluff top where they had their home. Theirs was a self-sufficient family; together they had constructed the house, a bountiful garden, the woodworking shop and a wonderful river-view gazebo which was to be our bunk house. After stashing our belongings, we joined them at the table where Marge had prepared a welcome feast.

It was a remarkable stroke of fortune that we landed at the Ronglies when we did. For the next four days it rained non-stop. Instead of suffering the weather we sat in the family fold, watching the wind-spirits dash whitecaps on the river. They were perfect days to read, catch up on the journal, take evening trips to Baudette to shoot pool and drink a few rounds with the brothers, eat lots of Marge's cooking, study upcoming maps and enjoy long naps.

When the storm front finally passed, we were freed. After a hearty farewell we paddled to the end of Rainy River. We landed at Wheelers Point on the shore of Lake of the Woods as the sun was setting and pitched the tent in the growing shadows. It was our last night in the United States; the remainder of the expedition would be in Canada.

As we lay down inside the comfort of our tent, I told Herb the story of traveling to the very same place when I was 16. I'd been working for the summer as a busboy at a resort in northern Minnesota, and when the season was over I had one free week before going home and back to school. After packing a few things in my day-pack, I wandered off on my first hitchhiking trip ever and headed north without a clue to where I was going. It was enough to be on the road. Someone driving to Bemidji picked me up so I went there and spent the night hidden in a small shack at the edge of town. The next morning I got a ride from someone going to Red Lake Indian Reservation so into those flat soggy bog lands I went as well. There was very little traffic in that area and I walked for a few hours just happy to be outside. Eventually someone heading to Lake of the Woods picked me up; I knew the place was somewhere along the Canadian Border and it sounded fine. They dropped me off here, at this exact point, and I walked the shoreline for a while wondering what was on that far shore, fascinated with being so far north and feeling like a bona fide pioneer. It was still early in the day so I continued on. At Baudette I crossed the border and entered Canada for my first time and then headed east on a very quiet, lonely road that ran parallel to the Rainy River. It was getting dark and I was tired; with neither tent nor sleeping bag, I simply lay down in the woods to get some rest, covering myself with my jacket. The mosquitoes came out as the sun went down and I crawled underneath my pitiful protection trying to escape their wrath, but it was impossible. The droning of their wings and their incessant stings drove me mad; I tried to disregard them and sleep at least for a little while, but then it began to drizzle. I was totally unprepared.

I remembered passing a farm house a little ways back and thought perhaps I could sneak into the barn. Anything would be better than remaining in that ditch. I got up and walked back towards it, the swarm following me even in the rain. In the distance a light was shining at the farmstead and I approached cautiously, nervous about dogs. Nearing the house I considered my options: I could sneak into the hayloft and catch a nap, hoping to awake early enough to disappear before someone came to do the morning chores, or I could knock on the door and just be frank. I neared the house and the feared dog began to bark. A porch light went on and the door opened.

I stood there in the light as the silhouette of an old woman appeared at the threshold, just as startled. I suspect she was anticipating a fox, not some scraggly teen. After greeting her with the friendliest "Hello" I could muster, we both relaxed a little. I explained my situation: I was just passing through on a little trip before school started, the insects and the rain caused me discomfort, I would be eternally grateful if I could sleep in her barn. She warmed up with a big smile and I could see now in the light she was quite old. In her own dignified way she kept her gray hair long and braided. Inviting me into her home, she explained how all her children had left long ago for different corners of Canada. Her husband had died; the house was empty and she would be happy to share it for the night. She showed me to the basement where her sons had slept and insisted I take their bed. I crawled in and covered myself with one of her handmade quilts and dreamt like a baby.

In the morning I awoke to her light footsteps overhead in the kitchen. The smell of bacon reached me, then eggs and coffee. She and I sat at her table exchanging a few thoughtful stories. How delightful it was to indulge in her kindness, spreading strawberry preserves over her warm bread, gulping orange juice, having seconds of everything. It was a mutual pleasure as she had not been able to share her table for some time. Showering me with her goodness, this mother really taught me about being generous with strangers, a lesson once learned never forgotten.

I ended my evening tale to Herb with these thoughts: whose path would we cross next, and how could we ever repay all the kindness people had gifted us with while on the road, on the river? My sense is that in some way we reciprocate simply by following our dream. By taking the initiative to follow a river downstream or to hitchhike lonely roads, we brought something important into the lives of strangers. Returning to Wheelers Point made me recognize the circling connections.

Lake of the Woods is another enormous body of water. I woke early and emerged from my cocoon to find the lake dead calm, which was convenient as we had to cross Traverse Bay. By five in the morning we were skimming over the smoothness, witnesses to the birth of another day with its fresh sunrise and riotous chorus of birdsong.

With the coming light we saw something that surprised us both, squadrons of white pelicans flying in their peculiar pattern one behind the other, mere inches over the water's surface. I had always associated pelicans with saltwater and didn't know they could be found in the middle of the continent in fresh water. But there they were, flying right along beside us, landing next to a long sandy spit. The beach was full of bird-life: hundreds of gulls, a few great blue herons, merganser ducks, red-winged blackbirds and even a soaring bald eagle. We stopped to stretch on the far end of the barrier island and I picked the first wild strawberries of the season.

After our restful pause the winds picked up. We plowed through the increasingly difficult boil for another five miles and then beached on Harbour Isle. What we found was a five-star campsite, and even though it was still early we quit. Our new home was actually a pair of islands in the middle of the lake with a small grassy isthmus connecting them—the perfect tent site. On each side was a crescent beach, one for the sunset and another for the sunrise. Breaking waves rolled into one side, while on the other the water was warm and calm and we took our first pleasurable swims of the summer. The two little islands were rocky and made for some fun afternoon climbs. High above, in the top of an old white spruce, an osprey made its nest.

The southern half of Lake of the Woods, or Lac du Bois as some locals call it, dips away from the Canadian Shield into one huge, warm, shallow bay. The shoreline is flat and sandy and forested with mostly hardwoods, while the northern half returns again to the Shield and consists of hundreds of rocky bays. We passed through Nabaskong and Whitefish Bays and returned to the crystal clear, colder waters we had enjoyed in the Boundary Waters. All along the shore were tall granite palisades and our familiar boreal members. We camped on Timber Island next to a small sugary beach.

At the northern end of Lake of the Woods is the village of Kenora. We needed to resupply so we stayed on the outskirts in a pay campground. After we'd finished shopping, we went to the local marina and had an interesting encounter with a man named David Walsh. He also was on a long canoe voyage, attempting to cross the entire continent of North America from the city of Québec to Nome, Alaska, in one summer. It was quite impressive to realize how far he had already paddled. He was doubtful, however, that he could make it all the way to the Bering Sea before freeze-up. He was at a critical juncture and was considering boarding a train, even part way, to expedite his trip. Not wanting to use "mechanized" means to fulfill his dream and at the same time trying to be reasonable, practical and ultimately enjoy the experience, he wrestled his options. I admired him for his vision and was sympathetic to his struggle. We shared a couple of beers, exchanged travel stories and encouraged each other in our separate directions.

When ordering the maps for this trip I had neglected to buy the one that would guide us from Lake of the Woods into the Winnipeg River. I knew that the outlet was just past town, under the railway bridge, and did not foresee any problem. As we approached the bridge, I became confused, for the entrance to the Winnipeg was cordoned off with a log boom. Unsure what to do, we decided to slip over the boom and see what would happen. Quickly our world turned dark as we entered a steeply walled canyon with no way out. We continued cautiously, cornered a bend, and suddenly before us was a six-story hydroelectric dam plugging up the entire slot. It was an impossible obstacle; there was no way to get around it. We retraced our path up against the current and reemerged into the light. Under the railway bridge next to the log boom was a fisherman casting. He looked at us like we were nuts to have run the boom, and then explained there was a portage a couple of miles to the west in Keewatin, which was the only safe way to enter the Winnipeg River. We thanked him and did I feel like a fool.

We had been fortunate the water level was low, for we could have surely been swept to our deaths, sucked into the intake chutes and morphed into kilowatts.

We found the portage and walked over to the Winnipeg River, safely. It had good current and for our first day we had a tailwind that kindly pushed us along through polished granite outcrops feathered with leafy wigs. The Winnipeg is 200 miles long and the first half had no roads leading to it; the further downstream we went the wilder it got. That night we found another deluxe campsite on an island with southern exposure. Moreover, it was summer solstice, so we leapt across a fire and into the new season.

GICHIGAMI
Horseshoe Bay to Sault Ste. Marie

To the St. Lawrence Seaway

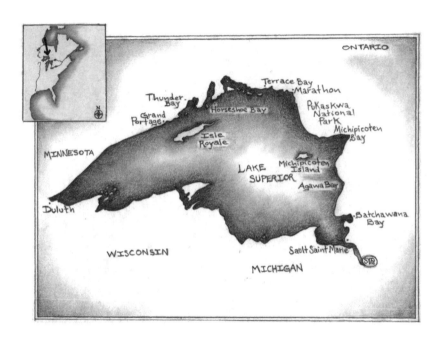

K er-ploosh! At midnight it sounded like someone threw a rock into Horseshoe Bay. Ca-plunk! The second one brought Paula from her dreams. "What was that?" she whispered. I looked outside; two beavers were swimming circles and slap-dunking their tails. I drifted back to sleep and dreamt that Paula had accepted a job as a consultant for an international construction company that dammed rivers. Shis-wis-crik. Something softer, more evasive this time: a deer sneaking around our tent, gingerly tugging greens from the forest floor. I slipped back into the netherworld and found the same multi-national had also agreed to hire and train me as a computer programmer. Desperate and in a cold sweat, I awoke to birds twittering that beckoned me lakeside into the evaporating mist.

Out over the lake the air was cold. When we pulled off onto the black bedrock, it was hot. Fog, caused by the radical temperature swings, wrapped partly around two breast-shaped hills called the Paps, but where exposed their summer green was lit by the sun. Pools of reflected color shimmered all around us and a mother fox appeared, staring off too towards the hills, but only for a moment. Behind her, hungry twin kits frolicked up the shore after her. When our scent reached them, they all dashed into the forest.

Robust headwinds blew constantly the next day and oncoming waves broke over the bows, sometimes pushing us back. Rains came intermittently, forcing us to put on our raincoats and tighten up the spray skirts. Paula was covered in fabric and all I could see were her hands, even her face was tucked into a hood. She looked like an exotic seabird: an indigo crown, a vermilion chest and a tawny bottom that rode the waves. With her hands clutching black wings, she shouldered forward through puffs of saturated air.

A family of four otters indifferent to the weather bobbed along with us, playfully showing off their slippery grace. Equally unconcerned, an immature bald eagle flew from Gourdeau Island and circled above, gliding on the breeze with its six-foot wings. After landing in its spruce-top nest, it eyed us, first from one side of its head then the other. A smooth rock finger protruding from Thrasher Island made a fine camp; Paula prepared tortellini Alfredo in the drizzle under the tarp while I pitched the dome atop a bald knob. Good food and correct tent placement are the keys to comfort. Halfway through dinner it began to pour so we retired into our chambers to preen feathers.

Helen Island was approximately 20 yards across the channel from our camp. When we wriggled out of our nest in the morning, it had completely vanished. In fact, everything had disappeared from view except two boats, one tent and each other. Over a stingy fire we put to council the question, to launch or not? We decided to pack up and grope through the thickness, hoping it would burn off with the sun.

Gliding through a calm back channel we came to Black Wharf, an abandoned fishing camp. Hewn between the rocky landscape and the cold brutal lake was a cluster of cabins, all neglected but one, and peering into a window I observed someone still spent time there. It was clean and recently supplied with freshly split logs. I wanted to stay, build a fire, smoke my pipe, but from Shesheeb Point to Herron Point was a three-mile fetch to paddle.

Because of the gloom we couldn't see Herron Point, but we knew it was out there. We left the protected channel and nosed into the open lake, hugging a rock wall. Within minutes, the calm water turned into a confused sea. Remnant swells from the previous day were simultaneously smashing into the cliff and reverberating back out. It was terrifying, like being in the middle of a whitewater river. Any one of those erratic waves could have easily spilled us. When paddling in fog, instinct tells you to stay close to shore, to keep land within sight, but we had to get away from there immediately and head out into the deeper, safer water, which meant going out into the blind vapor.

Putting the cliff to our backs we fought our way through each unpredictable collision. The rock wall dissolved, Shesheeb Point and Thrasher Island dissipated and everything became gray. I took a reading from my map for Herron Point, and trusting the compass we probed into the unseen, hoping there were no magnetic rocks around. Soon we outdistanced the choppy waters and returned to the steady up-and-down swells. At least we weren't going to tip over. In an hour the opposite shore revealed itself and the waves diminished as Herron Point began offering us protection. The sun finally broke through and the temperature soared. We landed and went for a swim to rinse away the smell of stress.

Our friends Tom and Liz had also planned a long kayak trip that summer. Neither were interested in traversing the dangerous Pie Island crossing, so they decided to start at Silver Islet and paddle around Lake Superior's Canadian shore. We knew they had intended to launch the same day we were passing Thunder Bay. Although we never made plans to rendezvous, we all knew there was a chance of crossing paths.

Halfway across Agate Cove I paused to grab a snack. Paula hitched up next to me and together we took a floating break, joyriding the big swells. We discussed our friends, wondering if they had gotten off safely and if we would ever find them. For some quirky reason I glanced into the cove and noticed a driftwood log at least a mile away, next to it a dead standing tree. Suddenly the tree began to move sideways. "Paula, look, what do you see there?"

She grabbed the binoculars and said with a laugh, "I see two kayaks, one red and one white. And that moving tree, it's Tom!" I waved my paddle through the air to see if he might spot us.

Right then, we later learned, Liz was beachcombing. She happened to look up and glancing out over the bay noticed two strange birds bobbing on the horizon. At first she thought they were swans, but then intuitively knew it was us. Liz grabbed her looking glasses and at the same moment she and Paula spied each other. Tom took his paddle and returned my wave—primitive communication, but it worked. They cruised out to meet us in the middle of the bay, and then we all headed to the next available beach to celebrate. Tom unpacked a bottle of brandy and with our drinks we indulged in a cocktail party, staying up late, hunkered around the driftwood fire and talking up a storm.

Mwaaaa-Mwaaaaaaaaa-Mhaaaa. The foghorn from nearby Lamb Island woke me. First out of the sack, I started the elfin fire; everything was dripping wet, but fortunately I had tucked some dry sticks under a tarp and they ignited quickly. The aroma of fresh coffee stirred my companions one by one. Whether the brandy or the fog, nobody was in a hurry.

A group decision had to be made at Flour Island: take the inside passage through the Nipigon Straight, or veer out to the shorter exposed side. Fifteen-knot breezes coming from the northwest helped make consensus easy. The outer side would be in the lee, we reasoned, and therefore more protected. To get there we had to cross the mouth of the Nipigon River whose strong currents plowed into the lake, which then threw it back upstream in waves. Everything was roiled and with mindful concentration we crept through, swiveling our hips. It felt like riding inside a gimbal.

At the destined point we found a sheltered cranny and the first thing we did was get naked and dive into the crystalline water for a refreshing dip. Like lounging lizards we warmed up on the heated bedrock. It was all very elemental: flesh, water, sun, bread and granite. I stared off into the azure and watched lush green hills swallow white summer cumulus clouds. My breathing slowed and I dozed off into a catnap.

We had been wrong about expecting the lee. After our break we paddled straight into the wind and labored up the length of Flour Island. We were literally blown into our night's home, a pea gravel cove. Paula treated us all to her gourmet camp chili with fresh herb bannock and for dessert we nestled into the pebbly beach to sip jasmine tea spiked with brandy. The sum of our day's movement had consisted in skipping by one island. We had reveled in the morning sun on one end and reckoned its setting on the other.

That night something scraped and snorted on the beach close by. Slowly I poked my head out into the moonlight. Not 20 feet away was a bull moose, pawing away and shaking his rack at me. I noticed Tom was sticking his head out, too, watching the beast in the night. It scratched a few more times and stepped closer. If it charged we could be stomped to death trapped in our bags, or so went my thoughts. By now there were four heads poking out of the tents, which just may have been enough to scare it off, and after a few more snorts it went slashing away through the brush. I could hear a few hearts beating.

The wind died, the waves flattened and the sun burned hotly down. Eager to take advantage of an exceptional day, the four of us launched into Blind Channel at sunrise. A dark purple turned to fuchsia, orange, yellow, pearly white. The fireball winked above the horizon and then pulled itself into the day; soon it was a blinding light that required sunglasses and visor caps. Jackets peeled off and then sweaters followed by shirts. Flat water remained with us all day and skimming the surface was effortless, the water so transparent we could clearly see the bouldery bottom 30 feet down. We were all in a state of ecstasy when we beached for lunch and a swim.

As nature would have it, we awoke the next day to a chilly harsh wind. I had a small transistor radio that broadcast the weather forecast 24 hours a day and a nearby Coast Guard station predicted high winds and scattered showers. It took no convincing; we all agreed to a day of rest in McNab Bay. Liz played with her oil paints, Paula baked camp cookies, Tom went fishing, and I walked down the beach coaxed by the far point.

I scaled the small cliff to the top and before me were the remains of an old bethel, a mariner's chapel. Created first from volcanic rock and then carved by glacial friction, it took eons to build this hallowed place. No mason could construct such durable beauty, only the extreme temperatures of fire and ice. Pillars and arches held the sky, orange lichen was stuccoed over the sturdy buttresses. A more recent addition was the cloister, a large cauldron filled with drilling stones. The tapestries were alive; green sphagnum moss threaded with purple flowers marked the aisles. I found my pew in the nave, a driftwood log, and sat there all morning, feeling the earth's age beneath my bare feet.

Closing my eyes I was washed with more color: rose, amethyst, emerald, gold. Like the sunrise, like the rocks, like the backside of my eyelids, those tones were ever present. The breeze blowing from the forest was fresh with buds growing out of last year's rot. Small wavelets and a swarm of hidden mosquitoes made music, a pileated woodpecker hammered away at a hole. Then a laugh brought me back—Tom was waving a northern pike in the air. Nearing camp I smelled black beans and corn bread. Amen.

The forecast was lousy but Paula and I were anxious to continue. In no hurry, Tom and Liz chose to spend another day in camp. After one more shared breakfast my pal and I launched our kayaks into questionable conditions, but fortunately the wind remained calm and we island-hopped past Ignace, Simpson and Vein. At Little Lake Bay, on Wilson Island, we made camp. As soon as we beached, the sun came out and the temperature swung again so we could bathe in the intensely cold water. Even after the quickest of plunges the frigidness left our bodies aching.

Just beyond Wilson Island towering bluffs rose from the lake for several miles. There was no safe refuge until Terrace Bay, so once again we were committed to the touch-and-go cruise, and again we were lucky. Hustling over the smooth water, we easily passed the headlands. At the base of Schreiber Point we crawled onto a small ledge to stretch our legs, the kind of place that only a kayak could reach in a calm; few others had ever stood there. At the end of the day we visited our first real town in several weeks.

Terrace Bay sits high on a bluff overlooking a long crescent beach. We dragged our boats into the woods and walked up the hill to civilization. After many days of stepping on nothing but rock and duff, our feet touched asphalt. The air was bad; between the sun-baked roadbed and the pulp mill it stank of rotten eggs and hot tar.

Our supplies had dwindled since Paradise Beach, so the butcher, the grocer and the distiller all profited. Back on the beach we set up camp, organized the booty and relaxed with a cocktail.

Two strangers pushing bicycles through the sand neared us and we could see they were travelers, their rigs loaded with gear. Wolfgang and Werner from faraway Germany introduced themselves. For several years they had schemed of a trip around the world and were now two months into their journey. From home, through France, a ferry ride to England, a flight to New York, halfway across North America—these guys were moving. The plan was to fly from Vancouver to Japan, hop another ferry and then bike home through Asia.

I wanted to hear more stories and enticed them with rye. After they pitched their tent, we all joined the fire. Right after the first toast I noticed another stranger pushing a bicycle up the beach. We stood to welcome Coh from Tokyo, pedaling east to Newfoundland. Another whiskey was offered and soon we were five strangers traveling different directions, watching the moon come out of the lake. We each had our chance at global storytelling: there were geography lessons on Europe, Asia and America; Catholicism, Buddhism and Protestantism were compared; politics had its turn, along with family and fun. Despite our different upbringings, two Germans, a Japanese, a Canadian and a gringo had a lot in common: all homeless, unemployed and feeling good about it.

In the morning I made coffee, Paula cooked a bucket of oatmeal, Coh contributed sweet rice cakes, Werner donated homeland cheese and Wolfgang dried sausage. Just as quickly as it started, the fabulous encounter ended. We all felt that nomadic restlessness. Paula and I departed with the wind at our backs as they rode up the hill and onto the distant highway, heading both east and west.

The Coast Guard issued a small craft advisory: 20- to 30-knot winds with two- to three-meter waves, but there was not a whisper of wind and the lake was flat. We carefully slipped into another aqua day and headed to Neyes Provincial Park, winding through the dome-shaped islets, knowing we could pull off anytime. Along the way we watched an osprey circle above a river mouth, then fold itself into its wings and plunge from the sky like a rock directly into the water. It resurfaced from the deep like a bobber, and freed from the lake's tautness flew away with a fish.

As we rounded a small point, a shaft of light beamed through the cloud cover and revealed a discouraging sight. Two miles away, tucked into Neyes Park, were dozens of recreational vehicles shining like light bulbs. After all our isolated campsites over the past few weeks we both wondered if we could spend a night in a place like that. Technically, when entering the park it was required to register and pay—something we wanted to avoid. It was also still early and very calm so we decided to ignore the formidable weather forecast and bypass the roundup. We dug in with our paddle blades and felt more relieved with each lick, until once again everything abruptly changed.

We saw the wind before it hit us: downdrafts pounded the lake into a rough texture, filling it with whitecaps that advanced quickly and washed through spraying us. We looked at each other and smiled. It was only an insignificant squall that we could handle. The wind blew stronger and each wave got higher and steeper, some spilling over the decks. Within a matter of paddle strokes it became so riled we were stopped. As hard as we tried we couldn't inch forward, and without a word turned around. The gales shoved us into Neyes beside the tin can alley.

A man had been watching us in our struggle and when he noticed us turn and head towards the beach, he walked down to give us a hand. As we landed, he yanked our boats out of the surf one at a time. We had surged right into the life of Jim, who insisted we go to his trailer and wait out the impending rain, explaining that his wife had just baked some cookies. And to think that earlier we had done our best to avoid these campers.

As it turned out, Jim was the director of all the provincial parks in the Terrace Bay region, from the Sleeping Giant, Nanaboozhoo, of Thunder Bay all the way to Lake Superior Provincial Park. He was an open book of information and a good story teller. We got the one-pot history.

On an nearby beach the prehistoric inhabitants excavated several mysterious pits; by removing boulders they scooped out a series of holes of whose use no one is certain. There are theories that these "Pukaskwa Pits" were designed as foxholes for hunting caribou, utilized as foundations for lodges, or maybe were simply fire pits. What is certain is that they were created by humans thousands of years ago. Much later the Ojibwa occupied this bay, traveling smartly in their birch bark canoes and were here when the French fur traders arrived in the 1600s. As boat travel throughout the Great Lakes increased, a chain of lighthouses was constructed, with one nearby. In the 1880s, railway workers utilized this beach as a base camp while laying track for Canada's first transcontinental line, bringing many Scandinavian families who then fished commercially along the coast. Loggers followed, mowing down the pine. During World War II the Canadian government erected a German prisoner-of-war camp here, and towards the end of the war it was converted into a Japanese interment camp. Now it's a recreation area.

The storm howled for two more days, pruning trees, scattering wildlife and driving sane people indoors. The lake was agitated; huge pipeline waves pummeled the beach. We were thankful to have our feet on the ground. Between the rains we went for sprints through the sand dune forest scavenging for blueberries, raspberries and wild mint. Beside our crackling fire we brewed tea while calico soup simmered.

While everyone else was asleep, we packed up and returned to the lake—the wind had died and the storm was over. We skipped past the place where the wind had halted us and continued on to another Caldwell Point. Once around it we entered a five-mile channel between the mainland and Pic Island. Aggravating winds blew against us the whole way, creating a painfully slow ride. Stroke after heavy stroke we were drained of strength, and on the far side we turned north past Detention Island. When Neyes had been a prisoner of war camp, the high-ranking enemy brass was held there. Surrounded by all that ice cold water was as good as being surrounded by hungry sharks. No one escaped.

Rugged cliffs rose 600 feet from the mainland. Once you have experienced the lake's sudden violence, it's scary to pass through an area like that. We cut across the swells, cautious to keep away from the wall. By early afternoon Paula and I were both exhausted. We diverted our course and headed for Red Sucker Cove, hoping for a campsite. They were difficult to find in this environment; few places were accessible by boat. As we got nearer we both knew it was a dud, a boulder-bound beach. Desperate, we disembarked anyhow to see if we could find some minimal place to throw our tent. There was nothing that even resembled a flat spot so we were forced to continue. As I entered my kayak, two freak waves broke into the cockpit. Not only was I fatigued and hungry, I was now wet.

We doggedly bounced through the waves and entered a big bay along with another difficult decision: go even further out of our way to a promising camp in Sturdee Cove, or follow the straight line to Ypres Point where we had no idea what we'd find. Either way we had to travel another six hard miles, two long hours. We decided to gamble on the more direct path, knowing full well that if it didn't pan out we'd have to paddle five additional miles to reach the town of Marathon.

Typically, just as we made our decision, Nature stepped in to redirect us. The wind stiffened and without hesitation we altered course for the surer bet, the safety of the cove. The beach was private and sheltered—another prime campsite. A thunderstorm was brewing so I strung a tarp over our kitchen area. After we finished eating, the temperature dropped and the heavens spilled, but it didn't matter. At arm's length was a pile of driftwood and tea was warming in the billy can.

The moon shining through our tent fabric woke me at two in the morning. I went outside and the combination of my sudden movements along with the bright light startled a warbler into thinking it was dawn. It sang a few tentative notes, not sure if it had overslept or been tricked. Realizing that it was still night, the bird turned silent and drifted back to sleep. Not me, though. The lake was calm and the scene inviting. I rustled Paula and suggested we try something new: a moon-cruise. We left our safe harbor and serenaded the late eventide. Constellations burned in the heavens and reflected on the undisturbed water. The moon was brilliant, and at that hour we were Argonauts traveling the island universe.

Fragments of color lit up the high cirrus and then percolated onto the lower clouds, onto the land and upon the lake. When the sun peeked out, we were beside the town of Marathon. Surrounded by the wild and beautiful hinterland, this once pristine bay was now filthy. Another smoking pulp mill at dawn: we sailed on by.

Near the entrance to Pukaskwa National Park we snacked on a marble-cake isle, veins of quartzite swirling through the pastry-rock. It was a calm, creamy day. Along the main shore were chunky highlands and slivered nooks with sugary beaches.

The park headquarters was far out of our way, so we skipped the formalities. Throughout the park, campsites have been developed along various beaches. Each site was provided with a sandbox for the tent, a picnic table, a bear-proof cache and an outhouse. Hiking trails connected them all with spur routes branching off into the back-country. Between the canoe and the walking shoes, it would be a great place to spend a summer.

Behind Otter Island, on the quiet bay side, the Cascade River spills directly into the clear lake. Its water felt warm compared to Superior and we played there all morning, wading between the temperatures. On the front side of the island is an old beach, a leftover from when the lake level was higher, chock full of round boulders and a large collection of Pukaskwa

Pits. At first they're hard to see: two feet deep and maybe four feet wide; orange, black and green lichen colonies cover every stone. Once our eyes adjusted, however, we recognized them everywhere.

We continued along a rock face for a few miles and then camped in a stunning bay. Big hills covered in dark green forest loomed all around us. This was not an official site so it felt even more isolated. I noticed on our topographical map that few features were named—lots of *terra incognita*.

In the morning we passed the mouth of the Pukaskwa River and left the park behind, laboring all day through headwinds to reach the Grain Bin. From a distance, this landmark beach looks like a field of wheat because of its golden color. There are very few sandy beaches on the rocky north shore and this exception has been a popular layover for centuries. Julia Creek empties into the lake and provides a warm stream for bathing and brook trout for the angler. The sand makes a comfortable bed, driftwood is plentiful, the southern exposure allows you to view both the sunrise and sunset, it's protected from the open sea. After a marathon paddling day, the French fur traders would rest there while smoking their meerschaums and singing chansons about Julia, I imagine. Our routine was similar.

The weather was worrisome and the winds gnarly, so we pulled off to rest beside more pits. A squall was passing down the shore, packed with powerful gusts and driving rain. We watched it turn farther out to sea and leave us alone. I sprinkled some tobacco into one of the hollows and we cautiously set out, and in answer to my offering a gifted tailwind blew us away. The waves built within the hour and at times it felt like flying as we surfed the following seas, even getting scary as we cruised at record speed. As we passed Pilot Harbor, it died but the swells kept pushing us on for another hour. Then headwinds throttled, mixed with rain, blowing everything back at us. When the rain ceased and the air calmed, we were close to shore where black flies descended on us, flying into our ears, up our nostrils, into our eyes and, if we smiled, right into our mouths.

Michipicoten Island was off to our starboard, 15 miles out to sea. In times past the natives canoed there to mine copper. They dreaded the journey and little wonder, for it wouldn't take but one squall to upset everything. Whoever falls into Lake Superior has approximately five minutes to live—swimming won't help, hypothermia will get you. But malleable copper was precious and beads, fish hooks and tools were pounded out of the pure chunks. Looking out to the island I was certain those were brave men. Our map showed steep headlands and unfriendly shores ahead, leaving a lingering fear.

Even though it was still early, a strong breeze flapped the tent walls and lying on the ground we could feel the thunder. Outside the beach at Floating Heart Bay melted into the fog which saturated everything but the inside of our burrow. A day of rest—we lounged all morning in our sleeping bags with tea and books. In the afternoon the wind switched and the sun came out hot; I dove head first into the transparent combers, and plunging into the surf I could still hear thunder. As the viscous fog moved further out a nasty thunderstorm emerged heading right for us. The storm cell was full of electricity and a veil of heavy rains trailed behind. We ate a quick meal, buttoned up camp and then dove back in the tent. When it hammered into our cove, torrents of rain fell, soaking everything but us; the sky exploded and the earth vibrated and one strong gust sent a nearby birch tree cracking to the ground.

Another storm rolled through in the night; lightening jolted me awake, the flashes shattering the darkness and illuminating the bending forest and breakers fanning the beach. We anchored fast and slept little.

The fog was back in the morning, thicker than before. During our second round of coffee the sun broke through and despite the waves and poor visibility, we moved; before we even got out of the bay, though, the sun disappeared again. We stayed close together and inched our way forward into the big lake, into the most violent seas we'd seen. Tucked back into our bay we had been deceived into thinking that the swells were coming from the northwest. In reality, they were coming straight from the west, careening off a hidden reef and a sheer wall. The water became more and more agitated and there were no distinguishing features like an island, bay or point. Navigation was hopeless. Our wish was to travel six miles to the next tiny harbor, but we knew we could easily miss the entrance because we had to keep away from the cliffs. Feeling disoriented and frightened, we did something new: we turned around. There were too many odds against us.

Safely back on shore, we watched the whitecaps grow and felt genuine relief. Backs to a log, we sat marveling at the moody lake when suddenly a woodland caribou stomped out of the forest and onto the beach 20 feet away. It was a healthy, dark brown bull adorned with a velvet rack. Once he saw us he leapt off the ground with all fours and after landing shook his body from antlers to buttocks. Loping down the beach he kept looking back at us, casting a wary eye, and then cantered off into the woods. That was the gift for returning: our only sighting of a caribou.

The next day we reluctantly departed Floating Heart. The water was calm but we were nervous; a thunderstorm brewed on the southern horizon and fogbanks hovered nearby. There was also an eight-mile stretch of cliffs ahead. Before entering, we idled in a place called the Flats hashing out the risks. Frightful and magnificent, the solid wall rose 500 feet vertically out of the icy water; stony points jutted from the precipice base and we skipped from one to the other. It always felt important to make an offering during those potent situations—a pinch of tobacco and a song kept us in good grace with the fickle spirits that seemed to watch from every angle. We were granted safe passage all the way to Dog River, where at its mouth we met a guy from North Carolina kayaking solo around the lake. The three of us grouped into a flotilla and shared lunch and stories. He was a teacher and would no doubt have interesting lessons for his pupils when he returned: geography, climatology, astronomy.

I inferred from the map that the surrounding scenery was beautiful, though we didn't get to see much. The towering palisade remained a mystery. Somewhere on top was a forest and a sky, but here there was no horizon, the shore a blur. All I could see was Paula, my point of reference, and without her I would have tipped.

Scattered rock islets remained mostly invisible, but we could sure smell and hear them—they were all seagull rookeries. Oily fishy gull feces permeated the air along with a constant shriek. As soon as they noticed us, the first sentinels would cut through the nebulosity and dive bomb us; follow-up help came quickly as several others tried to ward us off, winging a few inches above our heads. Whenever we got too close to their perch, the entire island exploded into screams and flying feathers. The only ones left behind were the fledglings who watched us indifferently. As we pulled away and into the blindness again, the quiet would return.

Time itself becomes distorted when you are floating on the water in fog, and memories sweep closer. It could be anytime, anywhere as I flashed back through the shroud: marooned on a Mississippi sandbar all day alone, beach-bound in pea soup; in Mexico, crossing over a mountain pass, socked in a dark cloud, the bus driver nearly rolling off the edge; on California's Lost Coast, the cold saline mists swirling around a campfire; crossing over to Newfoundland in a ferry, the combination of big waves and dark brume scaring everyone; walking the streets of New York, skyscraper lights absorbed by the weather and smeared into the heights. Inevitably, a sentry gull would shatter the daydream, swooping down to remind me to keep moving.

At the entrance to Michipicoten Bay, the fog lifted briefly and gave us a grand view of the lighthouse. For about 10 minutes we could see all the way across the bay, but then the curtain fell again. By compass we traversed its three miles and waves breaking on the opposite shore announced we were close. The Michipicoten River was high from thunderstorms and we ferried across the brown current that tried to sweep us back into the bay. A foghorn broadcast the obvious: more frightening cliffs just down the shore.

At Old Woman Bay, the Trans Canada Highway touches the shore. Conveniently a wayside rest provides auto tourists a rare opportunity to view Lake Superior. We hadn't really seen much traffic since leaving Minnesota a month earlier. The parking lot was full and someone had his radio turned up loud, as if he didn't want to listen to the waves, the rumbling thunder, the whispering trees. A semi idled its diesel engine as the driver napped, but children had better sense, laughing and running barefoot down the beach.

A small river emptied into the bay separating our camp from the pull-off. We settled down in a field next to the old woman's decayed homestead; I never learned her story but she left clues. The small plot that used to be her garden was now full of wild flowers: buttercups, raspberries and wild roses. The cabin logs that had protected her through long winters and violent storms were now covered in moss and decomposing—something to nourish the future forest. A rusty stove pipe, a few cans and an enameled wash basin were scattered around. Perhaps she is buried there, her bones in the cold ground.

I tried to sleep but the thought of upcoming Grindstone Point kept me stirred, the name alone worrisome. This abrasive point extends out into the lake and creates a shallow, inhospitable 14-mile stretch of shoreline. Thousands of reefs peppered the area beyond the point, some visible while others lay submerged. With any breeze these obstacles can turn the indifferent lake into deadly turbulence. There was no place to exit safely and avoiding them is impossible: if you enter this area, you have to commit to the entire stretch, a three-hour cruise.

We awoke to a glorious sunny morning. At first a slight breeze pushed us along the cliffs, but, praise be to the old woman or local windigo, when we reached Grindstone the wind died. The hours passed slowly as we lightly threaded through the sharp rocks, not wanting to wake the napping giants underneath. We held back words, even slowed our breathing, and the calm continued. At the far end of the hazard we disembarked to give thanks.

The next prominent landmark was Cape Chaillon. The nefarious underwater ogres were still at rest so we boldly crossed five miles of open water to reach its tip. Sounds and smells from the forest dissipated as we entered the big bay, each drifting into our own silence. During those extensive crossings we had so much time to just think; two hours filled with sky, water, a smoky distant point and our own internal thoughts. Paddle rhythms along with exquisite pools of changing light hypnotized us, and the cape that had seemed so unreachable suddenly loomed.

The difference between those quiet solitary hours in the exposed bay and the next stretch of shoreline was remarkable. Tugboat Channel was narrow, intimate and filled with sights. Instead of everything fading into the far horizon, here you could touch the Earth. Slabs of rock protruded from the water at sharp 45-degree angles, creating enchanting islands that over eons the lake has carved and polished into unique sculptures, some small and gritty bare rocks, others covered in green moss and yellow and purple wild flowers. Caves have been carved into a few and one rock reminded me of a machete, ready to decapitate someone. The most famous is the Devil's Chair, which is shaped like an oversized Lazy-Boy tilted back for a better view. It is said that long ago the Ojibwa guardian, teacher and trickster Nanaboozhoo jumped clear across Lake Superior to here from Thunder Bay, landing in this very chair and playing his trickery on this side for a time. Fortunately he was absent now so we felt free to climb his throne. Beyond the Devil's Chair is the Devil's Warehouse, an island where under lock and key malevolent supernatural powers are rumored to be guarded. I was certain, though, I'd already seen a few looming about in the fog.

The "wild" gradually faded as we entered a sparsely populated shore, but ironically the forest was the most primal we'd seen, especially in and around Superior Provincial Park. Founded in the early 1900s, this is one of Canada's first preserves and is inhabited by grandad white pines, cedars and spruce, the tallest pines rising over a hundred feet. Between lightening, high winds and heavy snows only a few select limbs survive, like thick arms that stretch in different directions and lend each tree a personal shape that reflects its particular lifetime struggle. The slow-growing cedars are the oldest, some going back 500 years, and although not so tall, they have the biggest girths, requiring a small crowd to embrace them. The spruce grow straight as an arrow and their crowns are dense and heavy.

Lake Superior's northern shore used to be covered with these titans. Since the beginning of our float, everything else we had paddled through had been logged off at one time or another. Even Pukaskwa, which is still quite pristine, was harvested in the '40s. While gazing at the old ancestors, we were thankful for those who had the vision to protect them. The sense of being surrounded by something untouched caressed virgin territories in my soul. It was a rare chance to see the forest as the natives witnessed it, the same one the voyageurs viewed and what the white settlers eventually cut down.

As we rounded a point, a canoeist suddenly came into view and we all saddled up for another over-the-water encounter, eager to share information. Jerome, a young Frenchman, had paddled solo from Montréal and was heading to Norway House. His plan was to follow the international boundary from Lake Superior to Lake of the Woods and then go north through Lake Winnipeg, basically the same route Herb and I had taken. Unfortunately he was going to have to take a few detours because he had no U.S. tourist papers. In Sault Ste. Marie, American immigration refused him entrance to walk four blocks around the locks, informing him he would first have to go to Winnipeg, a thousand miles away, for a visa! It had taken Jerome six weeks to travel from Montréal to where we met, much of it upstream. Paula and I would gain the current's advantage and the news encouraged us—it was possible to reach faraway Québec before winter.

The legend sings the feat of several Ojibwa warriors who canoed across the mighty Gichigami for three days and three nights seeking retaliation against their enemies. By the time they landed in Agawa Bay, they had paddled over 200 miles from home. To honor their safe passage they painted their red story on a granite wall.

They knew the best place for their brush was on a protected rock face, beneath an overhang on the shady side: no sun, no rain, no lichens. Several cliffs in Sinclair Cove offered perfect conditions. The main one, which most tourists see, is large and covered with the symbols from that feat: a large war canoe, three suns for the three days of travel and a water serpent with sharp breakers protruding from its spine, ready to capsize any boat. Mixed in among them is also what appears to be a horse. That would date at least some of the paintings to post-European arrival. Beyond the narrow viewing ledge there are several more vertical slabs accessible only by boat, painted with more arrows, handprints, animals, manitous, and memories of other crossings.

After admiring the collection, we crossed an eight-mile fetch to the Montreal River, for nearly three hours gliding over glassy liquid, thinking about the warriors who had paddled for three full days.

At the river we checked into a private campground, the place a little run down with everything in need of repair, with Mom trying her best to maintain the joint. Her eldest daughter half-helped as a waitress. Her oldest son, not sure how to help, smoked constantly while playing pool and listening to Alice Cooper. Her youngest son seemed a nice enough kid, entertaining us while we drank our first cold beer in five weeks, followed by a burger and fries.

To get to our tent site we had to paddle a short distance up the river. The strong current slowed us to a crawl and inch by inch we struggled up the bottleneck. Just as we reached the calm back water, applause erupted from the RV section and an older couple from Holland came by to greet us. With a look of nostalgia, the gentleman told us that during the Second World War he had built kayaks out of Norway Pine for a little extra scratch. After the war he and his wife emigrated to Canada and now farmed near Georgian Bay. When he said, "I haven't touched a kayak since the war," I offered him mine. Shaking his head, he replied, "No, I'd rather watch you two."

The nice-enough kid bicycled over to our tent site. He sat down next to Paula, and when he thought no one was looking pocketed her wallet. She was keen, however, and caught on right away. She kindly told him, "If you want to keep friends you have to be honest," and he begrudgingly returned it.

Public phones had been far and few between and I took advantage of the campground's to call my eight-year-old daughter Lana back in Minnesota. She asked me if we'd reached Canada yet. I told her we'd already been there for a few weeks.

Then she asked, "But are you where you're going?"

"No, we still haven't gotten there."

Since leaving home 500 miles back, we'd stopped to rest wherever we pleased. The beaches had been ours to explore, the islands uninhabited. As we neared Sault Ste. Marie and civilization, "No Trespassing" signs began sprouting up beside all the prime real estate. Typically, after two hours of paddling our bladders were full and we needed to stretch. On the morning we departed from Mica Bay we paddled for three hours into frustrating headwinds until we found a beach. The map showed there was a house beside it so we tried to lay low. As soon we landed, a dinner bell chimed and we joked about who would be inviting us to lunch.

Instead of an invite we got an out-vite. An ornery man stomped towards us waving a machete while launching into a tirade, "Get the hell out of here! This is private property!" We were startled, but having no choice we ignored the old sot and drained our bilges.

Hardly refreshed, we climbed back into our boats. I paddled near him to apologize, "Sorry, eh? We meant no harm. Just wanted a little break."

The grump shouted, "That's all right, just keep going. And don't come back!" He turned away and busied himself in meaningless chores, clearing brush away from his "Keep Out" signs.

The wind died, the seas calmed, and the day grew hot. We trudged on and after rounding a few more points entered Pancake Bay Provincial Park. Diverting off course a few miles we finally found a place to rest. At the far end of the park on a long sandy beach, we reposed in the shade of a pine. There was a hiking trail behind us and a few curious campers dropped in to visit, their cheers reviving our flagged spirits.

On the far side of Pancake Bay we left the Laurentian Shield behind and entered brown sandstone shores—a leap from Pre-Cambrian to Paleozoic in one bay. Instead of the familiar evergreens, we were now surrounded by yellow birch, maples and oaks, the lake transformed from cold and deep to warm and shallow.

Exposed to the blazing sun, we continually sponged down shirts and heads to keep cool. The miles drifted slowly, as did the day. By 5:00 in the afternoon we were still afloat, long past our usual quitting time, with nowhere to camp and nothing promising on the upcoming map either except a hotel around Batchawana Point.

Patio umbrellas advertising Labatt's swayed over the outdoor restaurant of The Salzburger Hof Lake Superior Resort and we deserved a beer. What we discovered was a quaint Austrian lodge run by a very friendly family. When I asked for permission to camp on their beach, the owner welcomed us.

That night after setting up, Paula and I went out on a date. The house specialty was rague, a delicious beef stew. Dining on the deck with a cold beer, overlooking the long shore we had just paddled, our smiles returned. Necessity and perseverance had pushed us a long distance; we had burned through two maps and covered 30 miles struggling in wind and doldrums. There had been fatigue, hunger, refreshment and feast. We laughed about the unhappy churl back on his private island, contrasting him with this family who fed us the best meal this side of Paradise Beach and gave us camp.

As we neared the end of Lake Superior, our days became full of power swings. At dawn we began the six-mile crossing to Goulais Point, with a bit of a tail wind pushing us into some blessed calm. Feeling refreshed and strong, we glided to the far shore, but at the tip of Rudder Head Point a headwind clobbered us. Forget momentum; every stroke was like starting over from a complete standstill.

Wearily we navigated past point after sandstone point whose bays were packed with cottages. Wherever there were no cabins the steep beach rose to greet an impenetrable wall of brushy forest. Big crossings, strong winds, heat and populated shores all played with our moods.

After our second lunch we agreed to camp in the first available spot. We passed up a couple of poor options before reaching the end of Goulais Point and the end of possibilities. I managed to level a flat spot on the rocky beach big enough for our tent and the establishment of our home brought mixed relief. A fresh gravel road led to the tip of Goulais, a stone's throw away, and along both sides were survey lines marked with bright orange flagging and real estate signs. Everything had been subdivided into lots and one big "Sold" was nailed to a birch near our tent.

We could see Gros Cap off in the distance; after six weeks of paddling on Superior, the end was in sight. Beyond that blue point was Sault Ste. Marie and the St. Mary's River which would take us into Lake Huron. A 1000-foot ore ship emerged from around the Cap. I watched it with binoculars as it headed out into the great lake indifferent to wave or storm. I turned on the weather radio for an update which warned us that the winds were expected to build to 20 knots the following day.

Strong gusts of wind began to throw waves onto our beach and a few even licked the foot of our tent. I looked out into the night, confused by all the white noise, and watched with horror as a series of erratics tipped over the boats. The beach was gone, completely washed in foam. The surge began to flood the forest and then an ebbing flow swept our kayaks into the lake. Feeling trapped and helpless, I screamed, but the roar stifled my voice.

It was a dream but the noise of crashing waves was real. Aiming the flashlight towards the lake, I noticed we still had a narrow berth between the waves' highest reach and the forest. The boats were safely tied to a tree so I dozed back to sleep, returning to the same dream.

Come sunrise the wind was blowing hard and the rascally lake did not want to let us go. Departure implied a four-mile crossing to the mainland. We both wanted to move, to close in on Sault Ste. Marie, but venturing into the unprotected bay was risky. Just in case, the boats were packed and ready to go. When a lull came we launched a bit stressed into warm headwinds, a dense and humid haze over the surface making the far shore barely visible. The waves were strong and we crashed through several, others brusquely picking us up and then dropping us down. With the spray skirts tight the breakers washed away from our decks. It was a lot of work, but I found it thrilling to be out in all that nasty power. The water had warmed considerably so we were not threatened by hypothermia, and our skills had been finely tuned. The waves softened as we neared the end and sweet forest aroma invited us even closer. Looking back across the bay, we could see those green waves we had sliced through while big drafts of air pawed the surface, coloring it black.

At Red Rock the rain began, millions of droplets striking the lake at once forming a continual chaos of rings. The biggest drops seemed to bounce right back out of the elastic surface, stretching the lake up. The dazzling show lasted for several hours. A family of loons played with us for awhile; they all popped up on the right side of the boats, sang a few tremulous notes back and forth and then dove under us to reappear on the other side. We felt like birds gliding over the water through the weather, occasionally holding our breath, too.

Just off Jackson Island we found our roost for the night: a little beach with a few cabins off to one side, on the other a patch of ledge rock big enough for tent and tarp. There was no place to hide — we could see the neighbors watching us from inside their homes. I felt like an intruder, but we had little choice. The rain had lost its charm and we needed to get off the lake. Underneath the tarp, sipping tea, we waited for a break. When a short pause came, we dashed, pitching the tent, tossing all the dry bags inside and tucking in the boats. It only lasted a moment; stronger showers drove us back under the tarp where dinner was waiting. Even in the rain we could rekindle and find an ember inside.

The forecast was terrible. In the evening the wind was supposed to shift out of the northwest, reaching speeds of 15 to 20 knots, the waves growing from three to six feet. A small craft advisory strongly urged everyone to immediately find safe harbor and people on piers and beaches were warned to stay clear. Fog horns from two passing ships blew loud and forlorn as the waves picked up.

Around midnight the tent began to shake, fierce 30-knot winds blowing out of the northwest trying to lift us off the ground. We had pitched it as far from the surf as possible, behind a small rocky jag protruding into the surge. The waves were pounding hard very near our heads and the ground was uncomfortable, but we were safe. It blew all night and by morning 10-foot swells were rolling down the lake towards Gros Cap a mile away.

We couldn't go out on the lake. The hardest part would be launching into the surf, a wet maneuver. The end of Superior was so near, and we were stuck in a crowded alcove. Frustrated, neither of us wanted to just sit there all day. The map showed a road leading into Sault Ste. Marie, only 15 miles away; we could walk that far if necessary.

The gravel road was quiet, and all those pounding waves and gusts blended into a far off lake noise that grew fainter with each curve. Walking felt good and the forest was refreshing. An hour passed before we saw a car. Paula had never hitchhiked before so she extended her thumb. A lone woman driver, someone just like your mother, stopped. Although she had never picked up a hitcher before, Lorain wanted to meet us.

I woke up looking for the familiar nylon mosquito screen, and instead found a white stucco ceiling. Freshly brewed coffee tickled my nostrils and I remembered we were at Lorain's. After breakfast she shuttled us back to our kayaks. We found them where we'd left them, safely tied to a tree. The seas were still churned up, but the waves were steady and tolerable. Under sunny skies and over gentle swells we dipped our blades into Lake Superior. Those last miles after so many hundreds were a joy, knowing the entire north shore was tucked into our memories. Around that last rocky point and the locks, a different scene awaited.

The St. Mary's River was flowing fast.

BLUFFING
Red Wing to Davenport

Down the Mississippi

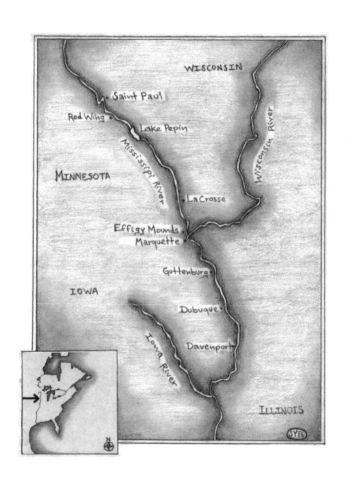

The name of every town along the Mississippi tells a story and through them the exploration and settlement of the valley can be read like a history book. The first inhabitants certainly left their mark: Keokuk, a chief; Natchez, a tribe; Cahokia, a city. When the French came to trade with the natives, they built their outposts: Prairie du Chien, St. Genevieve, Cape Girardeau and New Orleans. For a brief time, Spain possessed the waterway and left such reminders as New Madrid, Gonzales and DeSoto. With the Louisiana Purchase development along the river exploded. Some of the new towns reflected a nostalgia for the old world: Memphis, Warsaw, Scotlandville and Venice. Others responded to the more immediate environment: Goodview, Waterproof, Little Falls and Fountain City. The majority, like Hastings, Clarksville, Vicksburg and Boothville, simply honored their founders.

Many of these new settlements became commercial centers for the farmers, traders, loggers, miners and fisherman. Up from New Orleans came supplies and down from Minnesota came the lumber. With the construction of the railroads the importance of the river as a transportation route began to fade and for most towns the boom was short-lived.

To walk the cobbled streets of these relics is a trip into the past. Red brick store fronts from the 1800s line the quiet streets; a touch of Colonial, French, Spanish, and frontier architecture all blend in design. Tall church spires mingle with mansard roofs, widow-walks, hand-wrought balconies and rustic fieldstone cabins. In the background the golden bluffs rise and in the foreground the river flows.

Red Wing, Minnesota, is one of those old remnants, its downtown full of historical buildings. Proximity to the Twin Cities helps its economy; many commute there while others find it more convenient to work at the nearby nuclear power plant. Ambling through a town always felt good, to get out of those canoe positions and stretch. After our tour of the county museum, the grocery store and the local café, we camped on a nearby island. Since there was now a highway and a railway hugging both shores, islands were the best. Freight trains, towboats and semi-trailers all cruised under the gathering Canadian geese.

In its infancy between Lake Itasca and Lake Winnibigoshish, the Mississippi passes through a series of lakes; 250 miles later there is one more, the only other natural lake found on it, Lake Pepin. For thousands of years, deposits from the Chippewa River have created a sandbar that backs up the Mississippi into a 20-mile by three-mile pool filling the valley from bluff to bluff, from Wisconsin to Minnesota.

At the beginning of the lake there was a long sandy spit and near its tip we set up camp. The view was excellent: a sun setting over the expanse of blue water hemmed in with tall limestone bluffs carpeted in autumn tones, a crescent moon on the surface, and, slowly, the stars.

Come morning the view was similar, but with one difference: we were heading into the panorama. The sun rose over becalmed water, a good day for traversing little seas. At Lake City, about halfway down, the wind began to blow from behind. At first it was mild, but throughout the day it continued to build. Gales and waves both sent us sailing towards the outlet. We traversed the 20 miles easily, making it our farthest day's paddle. Near the end we began our challenging search for a camp, but between the steep bluffs, the railway and the highway, we were having no luck. The sun set and lights shining on the Minnesota side seemed our last hope: a commercial campground. With neither permission nor admission, we squeezed our tent into the darkest corner, hiding between a tribe of Winnebago campers and the iron-horse tracks. Tired to the bone, we drifted off to slumber.

The first train was the worst. Literally shaken from sleep, we realized just how close it was; a couple dozen feet is little distance between speeding tons of steel and idle flesh. The mile-long monsters rolled through hourly and their noise was deafening. It was a restless night filled with absurd dreams of sleeping out on the river, floating around in my sleeping bag trying to find peace. At first light we were rocked awake one last time and then snuck away unnoticed.

Past Pepin we found the flowing river again and the valley spread even wider. Along both sides scattered tributaries joined the Mississippi, each with their own dell framed by more steep cliffs. We had entered what is known as the Driftless Area, so named because the last glacial movement by-passed this region of southwestern Wisconsin and southeastern Minnesota. Since there was no glacier, there was no chance to deposit glacial debris, or drift. The bluffs are more disintegrated and rugged, hardwood forests skirting their base and alpine meadows facing their peaks. Seen from the river the 400-foot promontories are impressive, like fortress ruins from a past civilization.

The Mississippi's main river channel serpentines its way between the valley walls, the rest of this five-mile wide crevasse filled with lowland forest and sloughs. These backwaters are some of the most prolific aquatic resources in the United States, and in 1924 the Upper Mississippi Wildlife and Fish Refuge was established by Congress to preserve them. The refuge begins at Wabasha, Minnesota, and extends all the way south to Rock Island, Illinois, covering over 240,000 acres of marshes and wooded islands, including the entire flood plain between the bluffs. Nearly 300 miles long, it passes through Minnesota, Wisconsin, Iowa and Illinois.

Despite its protected status, the sloughs are filling in with sediment. Basically the causes are twofold: farming and dams. The practice of fall tilling leaves the ground vulnerable to erosion: five tons of soil are lost each year for every cultivated acre in the Midwest and it all eventually ends up in the Mississippi. Under the guise of "flood control," the U.S. Corps of Engineers has crafted several dams which have converted the river into a series of reservoirs. Instead of allowing the current to carry the suspended solids away, these slowed waters can only drop their silts, along with industrial waste, to the bottom. Every spring before the construction of the dams, the flood waters would rinse out the sloughs and carry away the sediments in a perfectly natural cycle. Now the river can only bring in polluted mud to deposit, and it keeps building up.

Not only are the sloughs silting in, but also the main river channel. The Corps has responded by maintaining a dredged nine-foot channel to allow the barge traffic through. Often these spoils are deposited in the backwaters, further damaging the fragile ecosystem, for without these rich wetlands there are less feeding grounds for all the wildlife.

The Mississippi is one of North America's major bird migration routes. Every fall flocks cruise down the valley in waves, each with their own distinctive flight pattern and each with their own peculiar destination: herons, loons and geese go to the Gulf of Mexico; warblers and hummingbirds to the Mexican highlands; finches, vireos and the hermit thrush fly deep into South America; the arctic terns winter in Antarctica.

As the ducks start passing through, the hunters prepare their blinds, grass, willow and reed huts or forts perched over the shallows. When everything is readied, the hunters dress in camouflage, set out their decoys and wait for the flocks.

One morning we quietly passed one such blind; a group of mallards flew by low, and suddenly all hell broke loose. The roof of a blind hinged open and up popped four hunters in fatigues blasting round after round. As several ducks dropped from the sky, a golden retriever leapt into the river. The opening day of hunting season.

On this working river the towboats were busy. They do not tow anything, but rather push flotillas of barges lashed together up and down the river, the biggest capable of moving a 40-barge raft, equal to five acres of steel and cargo. Peavey, Cargill and Bunge transport grain while Sheily hauls gravel. These are two of the more benign products; barges often carry hazardous materials like chlorine, anhydrous ammonia and hydrochloric acid; add to this all the petroleum goods and the river becomes very frail. Many were heading down to New Orleans, where their loads would then be transferred onto ships destined for every corner of the world.

From mid-river we heard the familiar blast of a towboat's horn. There was one coming down and another heading up. Downstream tows have the right of way, logically enough, taking at least a half mile to stop. One toot means the towboat heading downstream will pass on the left, two means a pass to the right. Whenever we heard their warnings, we got well out of the way of the buoy-marked channel. Swelling up to six feet high, the wakes these behemoths leave extend for miles. At first they intimidated me, but eventually I grew to enjoy them and on calm days we would divert ourselves just for a little thrill on the fluid roller-coaster ride.

Nearly every town along the river has its grain elevator stockpiling wheat, corn and soy beans, waiting to feed the barges and the world, many exporting grains for over a century. For us these cement structures were like guideposts and we navigated from one to another. La Crosse, home of G. Heilman Brewing Company, had several scattered along its shore, assuring us there would be plenty of beer in the near future.

Near La Crosse the bluffs rose 500 feet above the water, the highest along the Mississippi. The surrounding autumn forest was ablaze; the hard maples were orange, the oaks vermilion, the ashes yellow and the lowland soft maples still green, giving us a kaleidoscope of color. We settled on another island and enjoyed a fiery sunset. It was a warm October night so we slept in my favorite place, under the stars.

The following day we entered Iowa and left Minnesota behind, Pat now back in his home state, a reality which implied we would soon be parting company. Long before I had decided to continue alone once Pat debarked. The experience of slipping down the continent together, immersed in the outdoors and enjoying every freedom, had left its impression. Around a few more bends everything would change and we both felt nostalgic.

In 1673 a Jesuit missionary named Marquette and a fur trader named Joliet were sent on an expedition to search for a passage to the Pacific Ocean. At that time, many believed there was an undiscovered route across North America that led directly to Asia. China, with its silk, tea and spices, was a long way from Europe and if the supposed shortcut could be found it promised great wealth. It was rumored that a big river existed somewhere beyond the Great Lakes flowing west to the Orient. Hernando de Soto had actually seen the river in 1541 while looking for the famed Seven Cities of Cibola, but more than a century had passed and no one was really sure. So the missionary and the trader traveled through the Great Lakes and then worked their way onto the Wisconsin River. From there they continued downstream and eventually reached the Mississippi near present day Prairie du Chien, their hopes high as they followed the mighty river. It took a while, but by the time they reached Arkansas, they realized they were not on a passage to the orient but on a river going very fast, very south. Foiled, they turned back.

Today close to where those intrepid voyageurs first sighted the Mississippi River is the town of Marquette, Iowa, which lies tucked into a safe hollow notched into the surrounding bluffs. Just a few miles upstream perched high on a cliff are some ancient Indian burial grounds; the people who built them had already vanished by the time Marquette paddled through. They are called the "Mississippians" and all that remains of their culture are their uncommon burial plots. There are many other mounds throughout the river valley, most low rectangular hills or cones, but here they were raised into the shapes of animals—bear, turtle, snake, frog, bird and panther. It is believed that these effigies symbolized different family clans. At the edge of the cliffs overlooking the river that gives and takes life, the view for the dead was magnificent.

That evening we camped near the celebrated junction of the Wisconsin and Mississippi Rivers. Day after day we searched for a unique passage, a unique kind of wealth. We discovered that with a full belly and a small fire, a trusty shelter and an old canoe, good friendship and earthly rivers, we were sated.

When we pulled into the marina at Guttenberg, Iowa, it was high noon and an enthusiastic man marched up to us and asked what in the world we were doing. As it happened, he was the reporter for *The Guttenberg Times* and wanted to write a story about our journey. As an enticement lunch at the local café was included. He guaranteed our story was headed straight for the front page and promised to send our families a copy. I definitely liked the idea of my parents reading headlines about their errant son via a respectable fish-wrapper from a small town in Iowa.

We set up another camp at the outskirts of Dubuque, Iowa's oldest town. It started to drizzle and neither of us felt much like cooking, so instead we walked into the city for a hot meal. The smell of hops, neon signs lighting up wet streets, gusts of wind blowing through sidewalk trees all sent us into a tavern. Sipping whiskey, feeding the jukebox, playing pool—last call came fast.

Tail winds blew strong during our last couple of days. We paddled well together and moved quickly, gallivanting from Iowa to Illinois. Whenever we passed an island, we stopped to stretch our legs, and time. Our ultimate camp as paddling partners was just below Albany; beside the fire I conjured up the memory of our first moment on Lake Itasca, and Pat told me about the lower half and the story of his final takeout in New Orleans. The current slithered by into the night. We had become like the river: continually on the move, always changing and yet always connected to where we began, like a dance, like a circle, always connected to where we end.

The Quad Cities of Iowa and Illinois are Davenport, Moline, East Moline and Rock Island, where in 1853 the first bridge to span the river below Minneapolis was constructed, part of the transcontinental railway linking Pacifica with Atlantica. The bridge crossing utilized "The Rock," a strategically located island that lies in a narrows. Near that important bridge crossing, that profoundly transitory place, we beached Pat's Alumacraft canoe for the last time. He had completed his river journey. From that point forward mine would continue solo.

Pat's oldest brother John lived in Davenport and we spent two more days together at his house celebrating the end of our shared trip. My mission was to locate my own canoe and replace some other gear Pat was taking with him. I found an outfitter in Davenport willing to sell me a dented used Grumman for a hundred bucks. I bought a plastic cooler and filled it with food, a tarp, an extra paddle and an Iowa state highway map. I was as ready as I could be.

Living and traveling side-by-side for two months with Pat had stirred up all kinds of waves and currents for us both. Before we began, I was young, confused and seeking direction; now at least I had direction: downstream, exactly where I belonged. The idea of launching alone down the rest of the river was a bit frightening. I knew I'd miss my friend.

CHARACTERS ALIVE
Winnipeg River to Pigeon Point, Lake Winnipeg

To Hudson Bay

The Canadian government has constructed several hydro-electric dams along the Winnipeg River. There are no locks so each one requires a difficult portage; upstream the shore is fenced off and downstream the water trace is boiling whitewater. These massive dams back the river up into *lacs,* or reservoirs, wide open flat-water. The Winnipeg flows basically due west. The winds blow predominantly due east, which Herb and I battled the whole way. We'd watch the gusts approach, ruffling the *lac* into whitecaps, and then brace for their arrival. The smaller ones blew us to a stop; the stronger ones backwards. Usually they breezed through quickly, giving us a chance to regain our momentum before the next one.

Generally at night the air stilled and the lake settled. To compensate for the windy waters we arose even earlier to take advantage of the precious calm. Our habit was to be afloat by 5:00, and what magic there is at that hour. The first strokes would be in relative darkness, and slowly we entered into the penumbra between day and night. Then the sun would rise, brilliantly illuminating our world. The first red clouds reflected upon the glassy liquid, creating a double sunrise, high and low. We cast mighty shadows; reaching out with our paddles, we could touch the distant shore. It was easy to treasure those moments, knowing that with the sun's full force the struggle would begin anew.

Halfway down the Winnipeg River we exited Ontario and entered Manitoba. For the remainder of our trip we would be paddling through that province, first to Lake Winnipeg and then north to Hudson Bay.

After one long 30-mile day we reached the dam at Pointe du Bois. It was hot, 96 degrees, and we were parched by the time we finished the portage. Herb suggested we walk over to a nearby store and see about some ice cold beers. Sitting in the shade beside the dam, we let the afternoon cool down before continuing.

The store clerk informed us there was a free campground just downstream from the hydro-plant, and so we launched into the turbulence, relieved to be on the downstream side again. When we reached the boat landing, we staked our territory among the other campers and after dinner liberated our second six-pack.

A funny, toothless, wild-eyed, tobacco-spitting Irishman named Neil brought along his own sixer and ended up partying with us until midnight. He was fascinating, a genuine gnarly rapscallion who lived primarily to hunt, fish and drink aplenty. Work came and went depending upon the season and his mood. He looked rough, really, but had a heart of gold and we both enjoyed his farfetched tales. The following morning he invited us over to his camp and introduced us to his extended family. His wife Ann prepared venison sausage and eggs for the entire clan. Neil and Ann lived downstream in Great Falls and insisted we stop on our way through. It was Sunday and all the campers slowly disappeared, leaving us alone beside the rushing river. What we needed was a day of rest; we were in bed well before sunset, ready for another early morning cruise, praying for calm.

Our library included many titles from north woods writers: *People of the Deer* by Farley Mowat, *Portage into the Past* by J. Arnold Bolz, *Open Horizons* by Sigurd Olson, *Rainy River Country* by Grace Lee Nute, *Survival of the Bark Canoe* by John MacPhee. Not only were these books great rainy day companions, but they sometimes opened unexpected doors.

Fresh Water Saga by Eric Morse is a collection of canoe stories, different voyages the author took throughout Canada. The design of his trips was always the same: spend a month exploring a different watershed, a different region of the country. His forays into the wilds were unique because his guest list included foreign diplomats, leading scientists, environmentalists and academics. The group size was usually eight people in four canoes and they paddled from remote arctic rivers to the rugged north shore of Lake Superior, from the desolate regions of Labrador to the pristine rivers of

Manitoba. They were well organized and traveled hard, encountering all sorts of adventures and misadventures.

One particular chapter recounts paddling the length of Lake Winnipeg, a tale of special interest as we were quickly approaching that sizable lake ourselves. I read with fascination and fear about the rigors they faced while cruising the 250 mile-long eastern shore, from Lake Playgreen to Pine Falls. Because the western shore abuts the wide Canadian prairies, the wind pretty much always blows over shallow Lake Winnipeg, turning the surface into difficult choppy water.

Halfway down the lake near the Berens River, a fierce storm blew in from those empty plains. Their timing was awful; as they crossed a bay, three miles from land, the front caught them by surprise. Hastening to shore, they landed just as the full force winds hit from the west. Morse describes the canoes being blown down the beach and out of sight, trees being uprooted, others snapping in half. They were quite lucky to make landfall because the crashing waves could have easily drowned them, but being on shore was a near-death experience in itself. When the storm passed, they spent the rest of the day recovering their drenched gear, their dented boats and their frayed nerves.

Meanwhile, since this was another of his high-level diplomatic trips, the Royal Canadian Mounted Police immediately began searching for them, flying up and down the east side but finding no trace, and it was feared they'd been swallowed by the storm. One of the guests on that trip was a renowned Canadian nuclear physicist, Bill Mathers. He'd had a very difficult time deciding whether or not to join them as his wife was eight months pregnant. This was not his first trip with Eric Morse; he had gone on several others and loved nothing more than a month in the wilderness. His wife encouraged him to go, convincing him she would be fine, but the very day the storm struck the canoe party his wife went into labor. She knew about the storm and had already heard rumors that the party was missing. Of course, they did eventually pull themselves out of the wasteland of storm debris and the next day were spotted by a plane. They finished the trip shaken but alive, limping into Pine Falls at the bottom of the lake.

When I finished reading this story, I shared it with Herb, figuring we might as well be prepared for the worst. We were both nervous to say the least; a storm like that would spell trouble on any body of water, in any forest.

The next day we portaged around the Slave Falls dam and forged into headwinds to a tiny town called Pinawa, home of the Whiteshell Nuclear Research Facility. That fact intimidated me, but we were thirsty so we hove-to for refreshment, beaching next to the town park. An older man sat at a picnic table dripping wet, having just come out of the river from a hot day's swim. His eyes lit up seeing us and he asked where we came from. When we explained to him our route he smiled and told us that he, too, had paddled many of the same waters we were cruising. He had a cooler on the table and invited us to a beer.

It was always gratifying to meet someone who shared our passion for paddling and for voyaging through the wilds. As we sipped, we all swapped stories. My journey down the Mississippi impressed him. He told us that when he was younger, he had paddled through several different regions of Canada. One summer he had paddled through the Boundary Waters Canoe Area, our backyard, and another time he had traveled around the entire north shore of Lake Superior. Now we were really listening. "Yes," he said, "I'm quite familiar with where you're coming from, and where you're headed. Once I even paddled all of Lake Winnipeg, and nearly died. You'll have to be careful there."

A little surprised, I asked, "Have you ever heard of Eric Morse?"

He laughed and answered, "Yes, I know him, and had the privilege of accompanying him on several journeys, Winnipeg among them."

Had he read *Fresh Water Saga*?

"No, I've never heard of that one."

I ran to the boat, dug for the book, and quickly returned.

"What's your name?"

"Bill Mathers," he responded, extending his hand.

"It is you! I read all about you just last night, and your travails with a storm on Winnipeg, and your wife even delivered a baby that night while thinking you were lost forever."

He laughed again and reached for the book. While he chuckled along with the text, Herb and I looked at each other shaking our heads, not sure if this was real. I was reading about this very same character the previous

106

night, and now in a tiny town in the middle of nowhere he's sitting beside us sharing a beer and reading about his own life, not even knowing events in it had been published. We were all a little stunned.

Bill closed the book and sat for a moment staring into the water, remembering no doubt all the emotions buried in that terrific event. He then looked at us and insisted we have dinner, meet his wife and son. We walked to his home where he introduced us to Beatrice and Christopher, born during that storm long ago and now a young man. Here were the rest of the Mather characters, popping right out of the pages.

After dinner Bill grilled us; he wanted to know more about our specific plans, like what route we planned to take from the end of Lake Winnipeg to the ocean. There were three options, the huge and dangerous Nelson River, the small and chancy Gods River, and the less traveled, smaller, treacherous Hayes River. I told him we were undecided between the Hayes and the Gods, but that we had maps for either route. He seemed pleased with that information. What he most wanted to know, however, was once we reached our goal at York Factory on the shore of Hudson Bay, how indeed were we going to get out of there and ultimately back home?

York Factory is at the mouth of the Hayes and Nelson Rivers, but it's still 150 miles away from the nearest town. Paddling some 50 miles up the Nelson River to a railway crossing was our planned option, but the currents are powerful and it would be too difficult, Bill thought. The other choice was to paddle the shore of Hudson Bay, passing polar bear dens all the way to Churchill, close to suicide. Bill informed us that at York Factory there was a radio phone and suggested we simply call for a float plane when we arrived, which could fly us up to Churchill where we could catch the train back home. It sounded like the safest and easiest choice, but we explained to him our funds were limited and we hadn't budgeted for a private float plane. He looked us over, pausing, and then said he would feel much better knowing we were going to be returned to our homes unmaimed by bears. He would arrange for the plane and pay for it and we could repay him when we got home.

Was this destiny, serendipity, divine intervention or what? Looking back in hindsight, we would have had a hellish time trying to get out of York Factory without his wise and welcome support. He had made all the difference in our journey and we would be forever grateful.

The following day Bill invited us on a private tour of the Whiteshell Nuclear Research Facility, where he worked as a resident wizard mathematician and physicist. This facility at which the Canadian government carries out much of its research in nuclear power is also where they store spent rods from some of their nuclear energy plants. I wasn't sure I wanted to enter; the very concept of the place scared me, the sight of it even more.

Upon entering we immediately drew many odd stares. Herb and I were dressed in our typical uniform—cut-off shorts and ragged tee-shirts. It was pretty obvious we weren't from around those parts. Bill, however, was quite eccentric and I felt that somehow we were acceptable because we were with him. We approached some high security doors and Bill handed us both a white smock, white slippers to put over our shoes, and a white shower cap. Now we looked like everyone else. Passing through a radioactive detector, we got a green light and proceeded down a long well-lit sterile hall. At one end was a window of 12-inch thick leaded glass. We observed two employees manipulating robotic arms as they poured off spent plutonium into supposedly safe tubes. Bill explained that these containers were stored a thousand feet below us in the thick Canadian Shield bedrock where it would be safe for at least 500 years. At that point they would have to be "repackaged" unless, of course, we found a better use for this incredibly hot stuff.

On our way out of the high security area we had to pass through the detector again. I went first, got the green light, and waited for Herb. As my buddy was passing through the light turned red and a loud siren screamed while blinding white lights flashed on and off. His face went gray; my heart rate tripled. Bill just laughed, assuring us that the machine was temperamental and that he should go through again. I immediately thought of Sharon Silkwood and imagined my friend in the scrub shower, later diagnosed with leukemia or some other cancer. I needed Herb. Enough! "Get us out of here," I pleaded.

Herb did get a green light. After one more swim together, we said our fare-thee-wells out in the sunshine on a dock over the river. The past two days had been full of surprises and different realities. None of us could really name what had brought us together, and we were content to leave it at that. We were ready to cruise away, and I could tell Bill would have loved to join us too, but his was a different path now.

That night we camped on an island just outside of Lac du Bonnet after a filling pub dinner in town and many lively conversations with the folks. Herb realized it was our seven-week anniversary together as buoyant comrades, so we toasted to success and future fluid happiness. We were two days away from Lake Winnipeg, and a little anxious.

Our gnarly Irishman's home was a short day's paddle away. Neil had given us good directions and it was early afternoon when we arrived. Surely we must have been surfing on a good karmic wave because just as we walked up and over the river bank, crossing the quiet highway, a car turned the corner and entered their drive. It was Neil and Ann coming back to their house to gather a few supplies, like a cooler full of beer and moose steaks, for the "Great Falls Summer Picnic," to which we were invited.

Temperatures that day set records all over Canada and it seemed the town had a mighty thirst. We mingled with the villagers: the town cop, the high school principal, the carpenter, the doctor, the county mental health worker, the gaggle of kids, the slippery woman, the local poacher and all the dam employees. We were introduced only once and after that were considered part of the local stew. There was live music, tubs of beer, several pits for barbeque, homemade salads and diverse pies — a veritable banquet.

The next day it seemed the entire town was in convalescence; I know I was, sleeping until noon. In the afternoon Neil took Herb and me over to meet his father-in-law, Ben. We sat in his tin-roofed garage while passing summer thunderstorms unleashed their furies, listening to the soft-spoken gentleman relate his stories. He was a full-blooded Cree who had grown up in the bush and still spoke his native language. According to his version, Canada got its name from an encounter between two Crees and a party of French explorers who met in the forest one day. The Frenchmen were traipsing about lost and asked the natives if they knew where they were. They responded, "Quananda," that is, "On a walk, going nowhere."

While hanging at Ben's, other folks dropped in for the hair of the dog. One man named Gary told us that he worked for a local shipping company whose fleet transported cargo up and down the shores of Lake Winnipeg and presently were hauling timber from a logging camp on the eastern shore about halfway up the lake. He informed us that the following day an empty boat was going north and if we were interested, we could probably hitch a ride. It was tempting.

That night Herb and I discussed the new possibility: we could be on a boat the next day motoring up to the middle of Winnipeg and save ourselves a lot of flat water paddling. Herb, suffering from carpel-tunnel in his right hand and apprehensive about any further abuse those constant winds and waves might cause him, was drawn to the idea of shaving off some difficult miles. As for me, I wasn't so concerned with the purist notion of traveling by canoe to the sea; rather, I was open to whatever options presented themselves. While canoeing down the Mississippi, for example, I had hitched a ride for a while on a sailboat and later on a yacht. Those short spells had afforded me unique experiences. The important thing was to float downhill from my home to the sea. The canoe was the chosen vehicle for many reasons: it's quiet, seaworthy on river or lake, can be easily portaged, and besides, I simply enjoy paddling. But if an opportunity was presented to board another vessel, I was game. The bottom line was, we concluded, that we were on this journey to enjoy ourselves—there was no need to suffer if we could avoid it.

The next morning we phoned Gary and told him we would definitely like to take a boat ride. He said he'd call the captain, who'd ultimately decide. A half-hour later he called back with the news; the boat was leaving at 6:00 p.m. from the town of Pine Falls, 16 miles downstream. If we were there on time, we could board. He generously offered to drive us, explaining he had to go there anyway, but we preferred to paddle the rest of the Winnipeg River; we had until 6:00 after all. Gary then offered to at least haul our gear to lighten our load, an irresistible gesture.

As a send-off present Neil and Ann gave us a frozen Canadian goose, along with a sack of their own hand-harvested wild rice. After we waved goodbye, Herb and I cruised light and fast to Pine Falls and the end of the Winnipeg River.

We arrived just as the Kinnaird was tying off. Gary was there, waiting to introduce us to the captain. The tug was pulling an empty barge north and we were instructed to secure our boat upon it. Gary helped us load the rest of our gear inside before departing.

110

The captain and deck hands made us feel right at home. We were given our own bunks and told dinner was at 8:00. One thing they know how to do at sea is eat; we had steaks while heading north towards the Narrows. Sometime in the middle of the night the weather turned sour and we were tossed around like a bobber. The empty barge behind us was tugging violently on her lines, jerking us even more in the rough seas. Poor Herb got seasick; all he could do was lie aft and hold on to his stomach. We chopped through the night at eight knots per hour, twice the speed we could paddle even in the most ideal conditions. The waves were crashing up and over the barge and Captain Howard told me they were at least 10-foot swells. My depth of vision was slight, for our lights did not reach far. What scant light was available illuminated nothing but dark waves colliding all around us in the middle of the lake, filling me with both awe and dread. I began to worry about our canoe that was invisible now in the blackness behind us. I mentally retied all the knots I used to secure it, trying to convince myself I had got it right and the boat would still be there come sunrise. For me it was a sleepless night; I spent most of it with the captain in the pilot house and later down in the galley writing scribbled letters home. It was an exhilarating experience just to sit and watch the miles go by, even in the stormy dark.

At first light I climbed back up to the pilot house and was relieved to see our red canoe still there. Shortly thereafter we rounded Pigeon Point and entered a calm bay, the tug tied off at the logging camp and a separate crew began loading up the barge. We thanked everyone on board for the ride and unloaded our belongings. It certainly felt strange to get into the canoe again, now halfway up Lake Winnipeg. A bright sunny day awaited, and we were ready to move on under our own muscle power. We crossed the small bay and as we rounded a few protective islands we realized the bay had been deceptive: the lake was still violently stirred up, and we were not going anywhere. We landed on a big island and set up camp, knowing it was impossible to enter the windstorm.

HURON
St. Mary's River to Georgian Bay

To the St. Lawrence Seaway

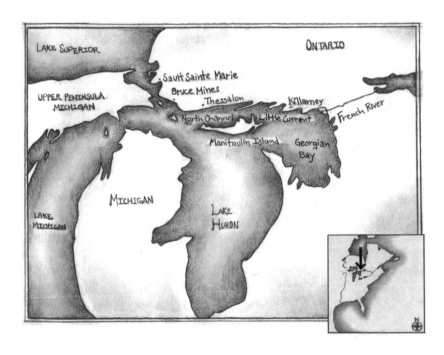

As Paula and I nosed into the St. Mary's River, a 1000-foot ore ship inched out of the Sault locks. Barely idling, it chased us to Island Number One. The juxtaposition of that eight-story ship passing beside our 16-inch high kayaks was impressive. Way above us, its pilot house was filled with radars, sonars and computers while the only instrument we had down below was a compass. The ship's engine consumed tons of fuel while we required a few cups of oatmeal. Where we left a slight wake and no trace, its prop stirred the river muck. All boats can be sunk, however, so we got well out of its way.

The land was flat and the frigid water swirling over sandy rippled bottoms warmed up fast. All of a sudden there was vegetation in the water, seaweed below us and combined bulrush and cattails along the edge. Superior was so cold that little plant life could grow in it but here there was life everywhere, both in the water and atop it: hundreds of seagulls and terns fed off the ship's prop wash, ducks winged through the islands, an osprey perched atop a navigation marker took flight as we passed. There were quite a few humans, too; cabins lined the shore and the islands. We entered the intersection of Lakes Superior, Michigan and Huron and the boat traffic was heavy. Another ship came upstream in Neebesh Channel and we gave it plenty of berth, while sailboats breezed along with several large pleasure boats.

At St. Joseph's Channel the river slowed and rocky islands, traces of the Canadian Shield, returned. Most were occupied with cabins but we found a vacant one for our camp, sharing it with two bald eagles. Lying as low as possible, we tried not to disturb them. I took my first swim in Huron and felt the tension of Lake Superior melt away.

We'd only been on the water a short while before the sun rose. There were no clouds, just sky turning into deep blue. Between two small islands we spotted a cedar canoe and diverted course to make sure our trajectories crossed. Inside was a mother and her son who had also paddled out for the sunrise. They lived in California but since 1905 their family had summered on a nearby private island, Encampment d'Ours, and they invited us for coffee.

Spread out over the island was a cluster of cottages built by different relatives in their own idyllic ways. Pagodas, cupolas, and palapas were all connected with footpaths. Hammocks swung over every deck—the place defined "laid back" and we sat on the "sunrise" patio with cappuccinos.

Later we wove through the numerous islands of St. Joseph's Channel and then reached the North Channel of Georgian Bay and its picturesque scenery: boreal forest covering Laurentian rock which met clear emerald waters. Old money found the attraction of this place long ago, and for good reason: three of the five Great Lakes are in your back yard. The shores had many dream homes, some quaint, neat and tight while others overflowed with ostentatiousness. It was a fantastic play land and everyone had a boat.

Our first camp on North Channel was right beside Bruce Mines on one of the few undeveloped rock islands we could find. Clean bald rock had become our favorite type of campsite; the self-supporting tent was pitched on the solid knoll so that if it did rain it would all shed away, leaving us dry. There was no sand to grit our food nor was there mud to drag into the tent. Walking barefoot was very comfortable; in fact, being naked was easy. There was always a small ledge for diving off into the lake and the water was warm. In the world of all these summer camps ours was priceless, that is to say, free.

On our island was an old stone fire pit and around it were boulders arranged as chairs, a place where stories had been thrown to the wind. A six-foot quaking aspen grew from the ashes, giving enough shade for one blueberry bush. Next to the pit was an ancient white pine which became my seat of choice as I settled in with my back to the trunk. Right beside the rock-bound twisted roots was a pine sapling growing slowly; I gently clasped it and considered what survival meant. The winds were gusty and the majestic pine swayed, whispering songs in another old, creaking language. Across the rippled water over on the mainland, we viewed the ruins of Bruce Mines, where the buildings had been abandoned when the iron ore was depleted. Deteriorating cement walls and rusty beams rose with the forest canopy. Above a red-tailed hawk soared and down the shore a carrion bird was happily picking something apart.

Thessalon was a dusty town, a remnant of the logging industry with a sawmill and a gravel pit but not much else. All the stores were closing and crooked "For Sale" signs swung from the doors. A few teenagers were hanging out on the steps of one abandoned shop next to a different sign that read "No Loitering on the Steps." The baker always seems to be friendly in any town. We licked our fingers; the pastries were good, and with nowhere else to spend our pesos, we departed.

Beside Thessalon Indian Reserve Number Twelve was a group of enchanting, undisturbed islands. The smaller ones, polished every winter by the lake ice, were made of clean pink granite, while bigger ones that escaped the scouring were covered in gray, blue and green lichens. Some rocks were even big enough to sustain a few handfuls of soil which supported small bonsai groves with cedars, spruce, birch and pines. Little purple and white flowers grew in the cracks and wispy grass stalks held the fringes together, dark green moss finding the shady interior. For me each was an exotic garden. We nestled in beside one on an island that looked like a petrified egg. As we watched the sun go down over Huron's North Channel, a mallard swam by with 18 ducklings in tow, all pulling hard to keep up with her. They landed on their own islet nearby and also settled in for the night. Waves breaking on the reefs and cricket chirps blended in the darkness.

Just as the sun rose we slipped onto the North Arm and headed due east with the wind. Reds and oranges tinted the hot August day, watery tones turning to soft gray and white as the sky brightened. Since we were moving with the breeze, we got to look at the backside of the luminescent green waves; white water frothed from some as they collided with submerged rocks.

The shallows were littered with hidden reefs; on our map each one was depicted as a tiny cross and there were hundreds in the area creating a burst of stars, so many it was impossible to keep track. All we could do was look for them by reading the water, paying attention to where the texture turned rare and the water seemed to boil. We cautiously negotiated them all morning; a few waves did catch us by surprise, breaking beside us when we thought we were safe. Inches below our hulls we could see the ridge of rock, but fortunately we never scraped and the spray skirts kept us dry.

By early afternoon we had danced through them all and the lake opened up again. Hardwoods began to mix with pines and cedars creating a more diverse forest, but the shore was still crowded with homes making camping difficult. We searched hard and finally found an empty cove on Nicollet Island. Waves washed us along to the music from breezy pines, tattling maples, rioting locusts and warblers. The bed of soft spongy moss on the hard bald rock felt good to my tired bones.

We awoke to rain and found it easy to turn back over, though as soon as it let up we hopped into action, eating and breaking camp. By now we had the procedure down so well that it was effortless. Drizzle continued on and off all morning as we coasted into Whalesback Channel; Johns Island, at the entrance, does indeed look like a five mile-long whale. Serpent River Indian Reserve was along the north shore to our left, the channel marked with buoys for the numerous yachts and sailboats that come to this pleasure craft heaven. Even though the lake shore is rugged, plenty of safe harbors are scattered between the islands.

The La Cloche Mountains came into view, at first smoky blue, but when the sun shone through a cloud break they became illuminated into a mass of white rock. I had been told they were made of quartz. We stared at them for the rest of the day, watching shadows shift across their faces. When we finally found our private rock in a tiny bay, the same hills were awash with the day's last light.

A radiant new moon pulled us into a dawn cruise and with the wind to our backs we bobbed along through time. A group of Native American men camping in a cedar grove stirred beside a fire. When I waved they all nodded, each in his own subtle way. The sun rolled over the horizon and splayed light over remnant volcanic islands. Ruins from Fort Cloche, an abandoned French outpost, came and went. Slowly we slipped beneath the base of the mountains: Round Hill, the Notch, and White Mountain. We followed the shadow line cast by their bulk all the way to the Rous Islands and leapt across a geological threshold; where the Precambrian meets Mesozoic, cooled magma meets sedimentary. The La Cloche Mountains are the remnants of a billion-year-old range worn down by glacial activity, wind and rain; much more recently a warm shallow sea lapped at their shores, forming limestone. On West Rous, I discovered a few fossils, seashells cemented in the past. At the town of Little Current on the north tip of Manitoulin Island, a narrow channel separates the two distinct periods in rock formation. All these passings reminded me that our own history is always unfolding—time was set in motion by the strength of a paddle blade, every stroke propelling us into some future.

When we got to Little Current, the first thing we did was package up 25 pounds of unnecessary gear: extra clothes, tools, books, spent maps and wet suits. Soon we would be departing Lake Huron and entering the French River, with portages ahead. After shopping and dinner we lounged at the marina, chatting with the sailors and sharing water stories. One fellow told us about a good campsite on nearby Bird Point; by the time we departed it was late afternoon so we checked in. The place was really the local's "party spot," but the good news was that it was Wednesday and the only fiesta was ours.

Watching the ever-changing shore from our kayaks allowed us to slowly take it all in: the warm breeze, the forests, the singing birds, the sculpted rocks, dawn's jumping fish, the temperamental water, our place in the weather. But such meditations were frequently interrupted by motorboats, from little runabouts to immense luxurious yachts that zipped or puttered by. The latter were immense gas-hogs and sitting upon their towering helms their captains steered powerfully through the bays, creating nasty wakes that could tip a canoe over.

At the channel entrance to Killarney, Paula spotted another kayaker who stopped to wait when he saw us. Role was on his way home after spending a week alone in the nearby islands and we all paddled the last stretch to town and a shared lunch. Our conversation was mostly about ancient boat forms and the simple life out on the water. Few understand the beauty, but this fellow who reminded me of Herb was an exception.

As we left Killarney's calm channel we nosed into Georgian Bay proper, our first big waters since Superior. It had taken only a week to forget what vast meant: that endless expanse to the horizon. Three-foot waves bounced off granite walls generating unpredictable chop. Feeling a little overwhelmed, we ducked into the first available bay and what we found was ugly.

On the shore, only a few feet from the lake, was an eight-foot by four-foot steel pan placed over an open fire pit, its outside coated with a thick layer of tar, the surrounding bedrock covered by huge piles of cooled sludge. It all stank of creosote and a film of oily residue shimmered scary rainbows over the water, contaminating the entire bay. This small but highly toxic operation was right on the outskirts of Killarney. Neither of us knew what this nasty business actually was, but our best guess was chemically treating logs to be used as pier timbers. Whatever was being concocted certainly ought to be illegal there at the water's edge.

We had to get out of that dreadful place—neither storm nor swell could keep us there. Returning to the agitated lake, we labored around a few more points, distancing ourselves from the spoiled area. It was hard and frustrating but with a reward: Dufois Bay, perched on another pink granite knob, tucked back into a calm bay. The setting sun illuminated the La Cloche Mountains again; still within view, they had become old companions.

In northwest Georgian Bay there's a galaxy of tiny islands called the Chickens, hundreds of rocks protruding from the lake swirling in veins of black, red and white granite—a wonderland for paddlers. We could venture out into Huron's open blue waves or sneak inside the cluster where the water was a calm transparent green. The islets ranged in flora, with incredible natural bonsai bosquets. Everything was caressed with water, the rock polished smooth and the ride enchanting.

One particularly interesting sculpture made for a picnic spot. The island's surface, a granite plane about the size of a football field, was gouged with parallel lines like bowling lane gutters, 12-inches wide and six-inches deep. When the last glacier moved through here, it ground boulders through this bedrock creating these scratch marks. They all pointed straight into Huron, changed angle with the water gradient, and then disappeared toward the bottom. Between the striations were curvy ponds each holding a different color water. Those nearest the lake were clear, refreshed whenever the lake kicked up. Baths further from shore, however, changed from light green and yellow to a peaty brown and black. Beyond the waves' reach, those puddles could only recharge with the rain and snow. The further from the shoreline the riper they became and the furthest away seemed to re-create the primordial ooze we all come from.

We constructed our last camp on that Great Lake among the Chickens on our own rock island coop. A canoe with father, son and daughter slipped by and we watched as they took turns casting. When the girl got a bite they all cheered. Three local men in a runabout motored by, greeting us with a slight nod. After dinner I unfolded the next day's chart; the mouth of the French River was in the middle of the map, a short paddle away.

Long ago, the Native Americans discovered a shortcut that connects Lake Huron with the St. Lawrence Seaway, eliminating hundreds of miles. Instead of traveling through the remainder of Huron, the entirety of Lake Ontario and all of Lake Erie, they diverted inland here through the French River. From there they ascended to Lake Nipissing, portaged over a small divide and then descended the Mattawa River to the Ottawa River and finally the St. Lawrence. When the French fur traders learned about this shortcut, they also used it to travel between Montréal and Grand Portage, as we would. Except for the 100 miles up the French and another 50 around Lake Nipissing, the rest was downhill.

The French River unbraids itself into several different distributaries as it empties into Lake Huron. Studying the map, we tried to determine which of the many channels to take. It appeared the first, Voyageur Channel, would be the quickest.

NOT AN ISLAND
Davenport to Cairo

Down the Mississippi

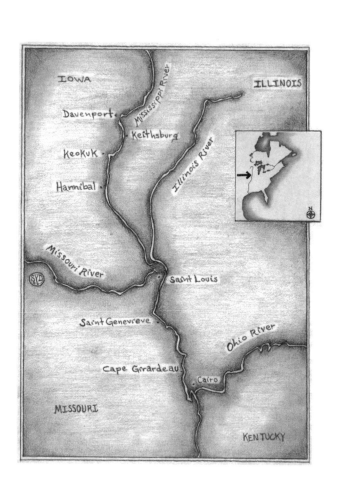

On a cool, gray day I left Pat standing beside the Mississippi and began my solo voyage. The weather was unsettled and gusty winds blew from upstream filling the river with whitecaps. My first concern was to cross over and lock through Davenport's dam. It seemed logical that the downstream side would be calmer since it was protected by the dam. There would be current again and I figured it was worth the struggle just to be moving on. Placing all my gear into the bow to help trim the canoe, I kissed the wave's first spray. With every oncoming gust my boat tended to rotate back toward the shore, and Pat. Steering was difficult; what I really needed were two more strong arms.

A lot of water sloshed into my canoe during that short crossing. When I summoned the lockmaster, he looked down at me with an incredulous look, thinking I was insane to be out on such a nasty day. Reluctantly he opened the large gates to give me passage. I entered the empty chamber feeling vulnerable, cold and wet. I sank as the chamber slowly emptied; the gates opened, revealing my uncertain future.

Where I had expected the current's calm strength, I found instead huge boiling waves breaking in every direction and careening off the hard cement walls. It was a frightening mess and there was unfortunately only one way to go: into the middle. I fastened my life vest and got down on my knees better to brace, thinking, "I could spill here," then entered the violent froth. One stroke forward and one surging wave backwards, I was lurched up, slammed down, punched aside and twisted around while chilly winds showered me. The dam loomed behind me and I had to get away from its hydraulics.

Adrenalin moved me forward, five muscle-packed strokes to the inch. I knew any horrendous wave could upset everything. My life depended on my strength, my ability to fight the dam's grip, the breakers and unrelenting wind. Surviving from one moment to the next, I concentrated on balance and power. I've rarely been so scared.

I finally made the shoreline and trembled onto the muddy banks. The first thing I noticed was a volunteer marijuana plant, which gave me a good laugh. With a cup of tea, I rekindled my fire—my initiation with solo paddling had been tempestuous, but somehow I got through.

Come morning still waters reflected Davenport. Anxious to verily move on, I left the city behind, riding the smooth swift current into the country. Weaving through islands, soaking in the Indian summer day, I let go of some fear. Paddling alone in a two-person canoe wasn't a great idea: not enough weight or thrust and hard to control in the wind. The dam had taught me my limits and I would have to be more cautious.

Autumns shades were exploding throughout the valley. When I had passed through the Twin Cities, the colors were beginning to peak; a month later, in central Iowa, they were still at their climax. I discovered that as I moved south down the continent, I was actually surfing on the wave of changing leaves. My paddling pace of some 20 miles a day seemed the same rate Fall descended toward the Gulf of Mexico. That brilliant transition and my motion agreed.

Slicing through the calm morning waters, a motorboat diverted course and headed for the canoe. A commercial fisherman cut in beside me, shut the motor, and offered up a cup from his thermos. Flopping around in the hull was the morning's prize, a scad of carp and catfish. When I asked what else could be snagged, he told me on rare occasion he'd caught the primitive and elusive paddlefish, which like the shark has no scale or bone. And a few sturgeon—his biggest had weighed 160 pounds and was nearly seven feet long. Sometimes he'd net a bowfin or a gar, ancients as well, but mostly he was after catfish.

As we floated together sharing a second cup, I was able to tell him about the beginning of this river, how it starts so small and shallow and

126

two months later grows into this. Even though he'd spent his entire life on the river, the old man had never been beyond Davenport. For him the Mississippi was 50 miles long and one mile wide, and he knew it well. I shared with him my discovery of the new sport—fall color surfing—and he laughed approvingly. We shook strong hands before letting go of each other's gunwales and drifted apart on the same river.

Upstream from Muscatine I found my private beach and dove into camp chores. Now I had to pitch the tent, gather firewood, cook supper, clean the dishes, make house and provide my own evening concerts.

When Pat had canoed south the previous fall, he camped at the junction of the Iowa and the Mississippi Rivers. His first night beside the big water he slept in a cozy wooded campsite. One year later I was blown into the same place, pinned down by strong winds and forced to hang out. Between walks through the hardwoods I read *Siddhartha* while tending a fire.

Being a fan of map names, my curiosity was piqued when I discovered there was a town called Keithsburg up ahead. I arrived one early morning and walked to Main Street. It was small with not much to it, but the café was open and inside I found a veritable museum; all available wall space was plastered with old photos and maps. It was the owner's collection and she was well-versed, explaining images of floods, steamboats, early settlers. I asked about the village's name: it was founded by one Robert Keith in the early 1800s.

"Ha!" I exclaimed, "That's my dad's name." I ventured these two Robert Keiths must be related and that I had discovered my old river tribe. I felt like a prodigal son and the greasy eggs were free.

Living out all those days and nights alone was a new experience for me; a sense of loneliness was always present but I also found the solitude enjoyable. In a little canoe out in the middle of a great river, the world comes down to you. Personally, I can think of no better way for young adults to discover their backyard and their inner selves than following any river downstream. The moments are filled with tranquility, surprise, danger and joy: all part of the same fabric. There was so much silence, too, all day letting the mind wander, undisturbed, never speaking. Contact with humanity wasn't far away though; most every day a town, or a cabin, something to remind you that you're not that alone.

One afternoon nearing the end of Lake Keokuk, I searched for my camp. The shore was populated with cabins and the sun was getting low. At the end of the lake was another lock and dam which I didn't want to pass through in the dark. I was beginning to get frustrated when I heard voices hollering from the east bank on the Illinois side. A small group was out on a dock, jumping and waving at me.

As I neared, one of them hollered, "Are you hungry for some fresh catfish?"

"You know I am."

"Well, get on out of that bucket and come on in while it's hot!"

Smokey and his wife had invited some friends to their cabin for the weekend. They were sitting down to eat when he noticed me paddling in the twilight. Curious, they all got up from the table, walked down to the shore and hailed me in.

Once my canoe was secured, they led me up the stairs and into the shack. Someone grabbed an extra chair and plate and then we filled ourselves with fried fish. The idea of floating down the river made their hearts leap a little. Smokey and his friends were too old to canoe the Mississippi, but that evening we shared the journey together. One of them said, "Do it while you're young," which was followed by, "Be young while you are."

After dinner the cards came out and eight senior citizens and I played "blitz" until the bewitching hour. One of the couples, Paul and Hilga, lived on the other side of Lake Keokuk and shortly after midnight they rose and prepared for their drive home. On the way out the door Hilga gave me a hug and invited me to canoe over to their house for breakfast in the morning.

I was deeply impressed by the kindness of these people. Imagine your parents inviting a hairy, total stranger into their house for dinner, much less a bed. That night I drifted off to sleep on a couch listening to the lullaby of old folks snoring.

Early in the morning those bright-eyed friends walked me back to my boat and I departed with the rising sun, skimming over to Paul and Hilga's in Iowa. They were waiting and we had coffee on the dock. After breakfast as I prepared to leave, Hilga presented me with a farewell gift: a bottle of their homemade wild raspberry wine.

Past the Lake Keokuk dam lay Missouri, my fifth state, a big billboard next to the river announcing the event. A short distance beyond the welcome sign was a wonderful bar called the Purple Cow. It was Sunday and, according to custom, there was a cauldron of homemade chili free for the eating. A local minstrel entertained the crowd with folk songs and everyone danced. I felt right at home sliding in and out of people's lives. We knew we wouldn't see each other again, but it didn't matter—for one afternoon we were many friends, and that is a vision of truth.

Alone in my tent that night, I savored the memories of river humanity, sipping raspberry wine in a steady rain.

If Mark Twain were to return today to his hometown of Hannibal, Missouri, I'm sure he'd guffaw. The setting for his classic tales *Tom Sawyer* and *The Adventures of Huckleberry Finn*, Hannibal was a place where youthful dreams were realized, where discrimination was painfully transformed into suffrage and where lies gave way to truth. Now, I imagine, the town would inspire a different novel, not about stirring the imagination of children, old and young alike, but rather how to make lots of money from tourists. Walking through the streets I felt as if I were in some plastic theme park with all of its nostalgic kitsch capitalizing on a literary legend. Tom Sawyer this and Huckleberry that! I laughed cynically at the proverbial white-washed fence. Indeed, if I were a young fellow living there today I am certain I'd play hooky and float right on out, which I promptly did on the same river that pulled Huck and Jim south, returning to the place where imagination doesn't cost anything.

Today Lake Michigan is artificially connected to the Mississippi River via the Illinois River, the link made in Chicago where they cut a canal. This major city now has access to the Gulf of St. Lawrence and to the Gulf of Mexico. I noticed an increase in towboats when I passed the Illinois junction. The water didn't look too good either; a constant rebounding of wakes kept me on constant alert. Not far downstream the Missouri River also dumped in, adding yet more barges. With this surge, a bottleneck has formed at Alton Lock, Number 27. The Corps always wanted to expand this facility to allow for more and bigger barges to pass through and ease the strain. Opponents fought back because they simply didn't want an increase; the bottleneck acts as a traffic control. The result, however, is that the Corps is getting their way.

I had been warned that I should expect to wait several hours before allowed through at Alton. I was even prepared to portage around it, but luckily they locked me through immediately. The outskirts of St. Louis were near; wanting to avoid the sprawl I camped early, nervous about so much city.

The next day I studied my map for a city campsite and found a good prospect, a patch of green on the east side called Lewis and Clark State Park, directly upstream from the convergence of the great Missouri and the mighty Mississippi, two of the world's biggest rivers. It seemed an appropriate place, so I paddled hard trying to reach it before nightfall. The darkness caught up with me but I continued into the night, knowing I was close. The profusion of city glow melded onto the river and gave me sufficient light to navigate, barely. When towboats pass you in the dark, it's a little frightening—you never know for sure when their wakes will hit, nor when they'll end. It's time to lower your center of gravity, get down on you knees and rock steady.

Hugging the park's shore, I spotted a campfire and laughter drifting from the blaze pulled me closer. Whoever it was, they had a canoe right on the beach and I'd found my home for the night. Gently I glided in, yanked up next to the other boat and crawled out, stretching wearily. Approaching the fire, I startled the dickens out of two guys cooking up a kettle who hadn't expected company coming off the river so silently at that hour.

These two fellows were also canoeing down to New Orleans. They had started in Fountain City, Wisconsin, a month earlier and now our two ships were beached together for the night. We took turns adding driftwood to the fire and sharing adventures. They both thought me a bit odd for doing the trip alone and I, at times, felt the same. The fire dwindled and I unrolled my sleeping bag and crashed on top of a picnic table.

Where the Mississippi and Missouri meet is a tremendous mixing of water as they blend into one new dangerous current. During Twain's day, the stretch just downstream from this confluence was aptly called the Graveyard. Submerged rocks and sunken ships lay underneath the surface waiting to rip hulls apart. Today the Chain of Rocks Canal bypasses the rough waters and all traffic goes through that ditch. At the end is one last lock and dam, and beyond it the river runs unobstructed to the sea. I arose early the following morning just upstream from that junction, anxious for town. I hopped out of my sack and went to my canoe for breakfast. As I rummaged through the food pack, I noticed my neighbors' boat was gone. Their tent was still pitched, though, which seemed bizarre. At first I thought they had simply gone fishing, but when I heard the sound of bodies wrestling to wake I knew I was wrong.

Shocked, I told them the incredibly bad news: their canoe was missing. They leapt out of their tent and ran down to the beach to see for themselves. It was gone just like that! Two fine lads living out one of life's great adventures and, in an instant, all thwarted. They both turned pale and even cried. I felt sick.

When I had pulled my canoe onto the beach the previous night, I must have nudged it up that extra foot. We all figured a towboat wake must have come and pulled theirs away because the level of the river hadn't changed. And we all knew that if a canoe were set free on the river at this junction it had only one direction to go, toward the Graveyard. It must have been pulled through the rapids.

The three of us paddled in my boat over to the island that separated the calm channel from the turbulent river and walked along the shore for an hour hoping to find some trace. There was nothing, not a scrap. Next we paddled into the canal and flagged a passing boat whose skipper radioed the nearby lockmaster and asked if there had been any sightings of a lost canoe downstream. Not a word. The lockmaster radioed all downstream tows to keep an eye out, just in case. We drifted for awhile, waiting for good news; eventually, the lockmaster responded again, but still nothing. It was decided we should go back to the campground and if there were any sightings they would be contacted there.

They weren't too far from home, so perhaps some kin could bail them out and get them back on the river. There was really nothing more I could do, so I left them to their own destiny, to be honest relieved to still have my personal journey together. Paddling through the canal, I kept thinking about fate and my dumb luck. Life and the river can play vicious tricks on us—it could have so easily been me stuck back at the park. Instead, I locked through for the last time, and there before me across the river was the world's tallest arch, the famed gateway to the West.

St. Louis has historically been a shifty place. First the lands around this river junction belonged to the people we call the Mississippians, who built mounds nearby. When Hernando de Soto raged through, it was the Missouri and Osage Indians who called the place home. Of course, the Spaniard claimed the valley for his king, and a little over a century later Marquette and Joliet floated by and claimed it for their French monarch. After the Treaty of Paris in 1764, France ceded its holdings on the east side of the river to England. Twenty years later, after the French and Indian War, the Americans gained possession of the English holdings. In 1803, a desperate Napoleon sold the French territory on the west side to the Americans by way of the Louisiana Purchase. The United States itself once became divided by this river, cut in half by the Civil War, and when that conflict was over, they controlled the entire valley and this confluence. The place where the great rivers meet became the threshold for western expansion, and that historical epoch is symbolized today by the Arch, which was within striking distance.

I had to cross the river to get there. When I was out in the middle I noticed a very distinct contrast of colors. The Mississippi water was blue compared to the brown silty Missouri, a visible line created where the two currents met and seemed hesitant to mix. As I paused on that line, I noticed just how fast I was moving and it scared me: it wasn't the same river I was used to.

The downtown river front was lined with retired paddle wheelers, a few barges parked above them and beyond that open shore, which seemed the best place to land. Mostly I just wanted to stretch my legs, stroll through town, and then move on to the far side. As I neared the uppermost barge, I powered hard for the revetment. Halfway across the width of that parked barge, I realized I'd gone too far. The river was going to sweep me into its bulk before I would make shore. My timing was way off; back-paddling furiously, I tried to reverse my mistake and get away from shore. I damn near made it.

The powerful current whacked me broadside into the unforgiving tank. I was inches away from clearing its front outside corner when my aluminum collided with its hardened steel over the rushing river. With my arms I braced myself against its wall, trying to push out a little further, but the canoe was wedged in place and slowly listing. The river was winning and water was leaking in gallons at a time. I had to jump. It was inevitable—the canoe was tipping and I sure didn't want to get sucked under. Fortunately the barge was full, which meant it was low to the water. I grabbed a steel cable hanging from its deck and hoisted myself up just as the canoe completely flipped. I was safe, but right beneath me the canoe was upside down with all my unlashed gear inside, locked tightly in the river's grip. The stern was still sticking out into the main current. I hung over the deck and, with one hand on the cable, I was able to reach the upturned hull with my feet. With little adrenalin-powered shoves I slowly kicked the boat out and finally freed it. Released, it was whisked away downstream upside down, quickly and without me.

There was only time to react. I pulled myself back on deck and ran down the length of the barge trying to catch up. Just as I was gaining on it, the barge ended and I dove straight into the river, pants, jacket, boots and all, planing freestyle over the scummy water and catching up with my darling. After rolling it upright, I was amazed to find all the half-drenched packs were still there. Now that we were together again, we had to get to the shore which was flying by.

With mustered might I began dog-paddling the full canoe towards the river front, and for every foot gained towards dry land I was swept downstream a dozen. "Throw me a line! Help!" I shouted to a group of men sitting on the stern of a paddle wheeler. They all sat motionless, surprised at the sight, and before anyone moved I was already out of reach.

I quickly became an attraction. Several people saw me flogging in the river, and one even alerted a policeman who hopped into his squad car and raced down the cobblestones to attempt a rescue. I watched as he followed me with sirens and cherries, the waves of tourists turning to stare. Finally I managed to pull myself into the eddy behind a boat. I reached the calmer waters exhausted and completely waterlogged. As I swam the last strokes, the cop arrived on the scene. It was really quite hilarious; the chubby fellow rolled out of the car, untied and removed his shoes, folded up his pant cuffs and then waded into the first few inches of dirty water, extending his hand. I was shaking and my teeth chattered. That had been way too close; the entire day since awakening had in fact been a close call.

A crowd formed a circle around me and I answered a hum of questions. The cop helped me spread my gear. One of the steamboat owners loaned me his dryer and a place to store my canoe and another bought me lunch. One guy, Mike, insisted I meet him later for a tour of St. Louis. Cause and effect: because I had tipped over I was received in red carpet fashion. Although the largest metro area on the river, it felt like small-town treatment.

I did meet Mike in the early afternoon and we started with a walking tour of downtown. Then we got into his car and took the bridge over to East St. Louis, Illinois. There were some ruins I wanted to see, remains of the largest prehistoric nation north of Mexico. Long before the so-called discovery of the New World, roughly between 800 and 1400 A.D, a thriving urban center of at least 20,000 people lived in Cahokia, the religious and administrative center of a chain of fortified town-temples spread throughout the river valley from Minnesota to Louisiana. Hundreds of earthen mounds were raised, the first in the valley to be constructed for ceremonial rather than burial purposes. Monks Mound is the largest, rising up a hundred feet and covering 14 acres.

It seems the priests understood astronomy, considering five different celestial observatories have been found, similar to Stonehenge in design except upright logs were used instead of rock. This agricultural society cultivated corn, squash and beans like their Meso-American neighbors and developed a far-reaching trade network. Copper ornaments from the Great Lakes region, pipestone bowls from the Minnesota prairie, conches from the Gulf of Mexico, tortoise shells from the Atlantic, mica from the Appalachians, flint and grizzly teeth from the Rocky Mountains have all been unearthed. The Cahokia culture ended before we ever got to meet them; it's believed climate change with a depletion of resources led to their decline. In the 1830s, the scattered few who managed to survive were marched off across the Mississippi River with the Five Civilized Tribes on the "Trail of Tears."

From the top of Monks Mound we watched the sun sink beyond the Arch: two monuments built by two different tribes during two distinct eras. It would have been a fine way to end the day, but there was a party in North St. Louis. After enough music, food and cheer, I finally retired from that incredulous day, better understanding the blues.

Departing from St. Louis was like running a slalom course; the towboat traffic was heavy with barges from as far away as St. Paul and Chicago, Kansas City and Cincinnati, New Orleans and Memphis. To avoid them I had to weave from bank to bank, often crossing the main navigation channel. One particular towboat, the *Leviticus,* gave me a good scare as it headed upstream pushing a dozen barges lashed together. The current was fast and it had its throttles wide open. Even from a distance I could see that its wake was bigger than usual, so I diverted my course towards shore. As the rolling waves neared I swung around to take them head on, when suddenly 10 feet away one of the swells began breaking. The following wave was also breaking and I had no choice but to go straight into the combers and hang on for the ride. I crashed into the first six-footer and immediately took on several gallons of water. All my packs were floating around in the bottom as I steered into the second, taking on even more, and with my canoe half-filled I wallowed to shore to bail out.

I hadn't had much difficulty with towboat wakes before. I guessed the reason this one was so lively was because the wake and I must have met over a submerged object. When a seemingly harmless wave passes over something shallow, it will break and there's no telling where the submerged objects lie until, of course, it's too late. I remembered then that I was on the edge of the Graveyard; somehow, I felt certain, it wouldn't be the last time I got wet.

With the recent marriage of the Mississippi and the Missouri, the river wasted no time. I paddled 50 miles easily one calm day, still surfing the autumnal crest, and was alone on the face of the Earth, on the river of life. Besides the few towboats, there was no one else around. Right before sunset I stopped to camp on a sandy island, pitched my home, prepared a hearty meal and stoked my companion fire. When all the chores were done I plucked my guitar and spoke aloud for the first time all day.

The oldest town on the west bank of the Mississippi is Ste. Genevieve, Missouri. Originally it was a French trading post built in 1735. Today it has the most extensive collection of French Colonial architecture in the U.S.; its Catholic church dates back to 1756. I arrived the next morning and made the rounds of the old city.

It was getting late and the river grew dusky. As I sought another night's home I noticed a campfire in Missouri. Fond of fires, I checked it out and once near the beach could see the silhouettes of two men squatting by the light. I'd learned it was dicey to sneak up on people so I banged my paddle against the hull to alert them, and once they got over their initial surprise they offered me a beer. They were just beginning to cook supper; roasting over the coals was a fresh raccoon. I had never eaten such a dish before and its dark meat went well with canned ale.

Here were two characters living the good life beside the river. They both had their own story of growing up on nearby farms, but their greatest joy was to wander along the shore, camp, hunt and trap. Neither of them worked much; when they did, it was only to earn enough to restock their grub stake and then head back into the woods. I found it interesting that neither had any interest in actually getting on the river though. By now it was huge and like most folks they were intimidated by its force. I told them I had paddled from the source, a place where even into a headwind you can spit across the river. After my story of swimming in St. Louis, they were convinced I was a fool. In the morning, after a bellyful of leftover coon and a cup of chicory joe, I disappeared into my sunrise and they marched off on their own search.

Near Cape Girardeau the bluffs that I had been traveling through since Minneapolis ended; the rock foundations gave way to an alluvial flatland: the start of the South. Thousands of years ago, the river mouth was located here; dumping its suspended solids into what was then a shallow sea, it slowly grew the continent. Today this delta is a hundred miles wide and stretches from southern Illinois to southern Louisiana. As the river slithers through the mud, it constantly alters course, looping into enormous bends; eventually, these curves grow so long they begin to cut through themselves at the shortest point, creating oxbow lakes. The process is then repeated—the river carves another bend in the opposite direction and eventually cuts that one off.

At the southern tip of Illinois next to the town of Cairo, the Ohio River merges with the Mississippi. If the form of a river can be compared to a tree, then Cairo is where the main trunk begins, all of the higher tributary branches having now joined together. Most of the raindrops that fall between the Rockies and the Appalachians eventually drain past this junction. It could rain in Pittsburgh and a few weeks later, on a calm sunny day, the river rises down here. It could rain in Montana, Ohio or Minnesota and a month later the water will surge. It could rain everywhere for a few days and then this place becomes inundated.

The combination of the flat landscape and increased volume of river water converts this lower trunk into a flood plain. Every spring before we began to attempt control, the river naturally flooded out into the delta and deposited its rich soils. You couldn't find better farming anywhere; the natives and the first Europeans knew it, and they cooperated with Nature by building their homes on stilts, suffering the wetlands every spring while appreciating the fertilized plots.

As settlements grew, however, stilts were no longer adequate protection and thus the construction of levees began. Beyond Cairo continuous earthen embankments were eventually mounded up on both sides of the river all the way to the Gulf of Mexico; the idea was these ridges would contain the river and keep it away from the population. Originally they were constructed by slaves shovel by shovel. In the mid-1800s powerful floods burst through and the federal government stepped in and delegated authority to the Army Corps of Engineers to wage full scale war on the river. Their plan of attack was to construct higher and longer levees, presumably to contain the river at all levels, but there were more floods that prompted even higher ones. This has been going on for over a century.

These levees are not foolproof. A muskrat hole or a crawfish tunnel can cause a sand boil, or a break, and when they do break flash floods sweep everything in their paths. In 1927 there was a big gusher just upstream from Greenville, Mississippi, and more water moved through that crack alone than the total amount flowing over Niagara Falls, devastating the town. Then the Corps decided to change its war policy; levees alone were not enough, dams were needed.

The theory was that if all the main tributaries were dammed up, the lower trunk, from Cairo to New Orleans, could be controlled. They spent astronomical sums to completely dam the Ohio, the upper Mississippi, the Missouri and many lesser streams. It can be argued that in the short run these dams have been helpful. But as mentioned, the reservoirs behind them are steadily silting in and losing their capacity to contain water. In addition to the dams, the Corps has piled up rip-rap along the banks to help stabilize them and thousands of smaller wing dams have been installed to send the water out into the main channel to help scour the bed. They have woven together huge cement slabs and carpeted the river in the most serious erosion areas. They have cut through several sharp bends to shorten its length and excavated spillway channels in Louisiana to help divert the floods. And of course the levees were raised even more: some are over 40 feet high and as long as the Great Wall of China, and growing. Flood control is a misnomer; we cannot stop the rain from falling.

The junction of the Ohio and Mississippi Rivers has always been a coveted stronghold. In 1757, the French built Fort Ascension there to protect its claim over the river valley; a few years later the stockade was enlarged and the name changed to Fort Massiac. In 1794, the Americans occupied Massiac in an attempt to quell the conflicts between the Spanish, the French, the British and the Native Americans. In 1861, the Union army constructed Fort Defiance at the confluence to gather troops and supplies for its invasion of the Confederacy. It was at the time their southernmost stronghold, and from there General Grant launched several decisive battles.

Out on that strategic point where the two mighty rivers meet is a park commemorating Fort Defiance; its perfect location along with its flat lawn makes for an irresistible campsite. I dragged my canoe through the mud and up onto the rock revetment. Once my encampment was established, I sat back satisfied and watched the sun sink over the Mississippi and the full moon rise from the new Ohio.

The following morning I was awakened by the sound of a car door slamming. Still half asleep, I heard footsteps approaching the tent so I unzipped the door. Standing before me were two men, one a cop. My first thought rolling out of the tent was: busted for camping in a public park. Instead the policeman asked with a slight southern accent, "Are you by any chance the owner of a canoe with an Iowa registration?"

"Yes. Why?"

"Well, this here fisherman just found it four miles downstream floating away. I thought maybe the owner would like to know."

"What are you talking about?"

It was the fisherman's turn. "The river rose last night and took your canoe with her. You're lucky, son, I found it floating right-side-up. Would have never seen it otherwise."

I glanced at the place where I had left my canoe the day before. After my experience at the Missouri junction, I always pulled it far from the river's reach. I clearly remembered sliding it onto the rock revetment, but that same place was now under eight feet of water. Looking back towards the fisherman, sure enough there was my canoe tied onto his boat trailer.

The river had stolen my canoe in the middle of the night. A fisherman found it at dawn. It was brought back to me by early morning. A canoe lost, found, and returned all while I was asleep. I promised the fisherman to never again leave my canoe untied.

LAKE LIMP-A-LONG
Pigeon Bay Island to Norway House

To Hudson Bay

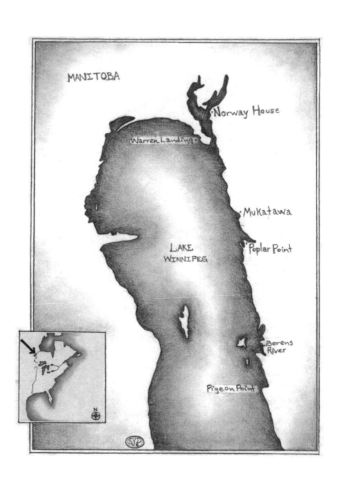

W indbound. That was a word we came to understand. Some folks tell of being pinned down on Lake Winnipeg for up to 10 days. Herb and I were forced to sit still on our small island for four. There was no fighting it, nothing to be done but try and enjoy the respite. Our first day we roasted the goose Neil had given us, wrapping it in aluminum foil with margarine, onions, garlic and mint, then placing it on a bed of embers. It was a big bird and required several coal changes, and with the last one we stuffed it with wild rice and nuts. A good bottle of wine was the only missing ingredient.

It was easy enough to sleep in the following morning. The wind had been whipping our tent all night and the sound of the waves breaking on the rocks below had been constantly in my dreams. We ate leftover goose with eggs and then I set out to explore our island. There was a private beach where I swam in the surging waves, and while beachcombing I found a collection of wooden floats from a fishing net. After I returned to camp and showed them to Herb, he had a sudden illumination: he grabbed his knife and began to carve a round ball out of one of them. Then he went on his own walk around the island searching for something. An hour later he returned with a crooked walking stick and meticulously peeled off its bark and tooled the knob on the end into what looked like a handle. Pulling out our trash bag, he withdrew two old tuna cans and buried them in the ground. I was beginning to get the idea—the first "Winnipeg Invitational Wilderness Golf Challenge." There were only two cans but they were easily relocated to provide us with an authentic 18-hole course. Herb was unbeatable.

Those were also fine moments to read from our library and I appreciated having an entire afternoon to absorb myself in a book. Pausing frequently, I would look around and listen, smell and feel the very place where we had landed. It was easy to reminisce about the past and realize that these very moments were already becoming memories, and then dive right back into the other world of my book. Writing letters home was also a good way to fill a day; not often do we have time to dedicate an hour to someone we love, to share some creative moment over the distance. It didn't matter that I couldn't actually send the letters for another week or two.

One afternoon for diversion we both decided to shave off our beards. I had been growing mine since we departed; Herb on the other hand never shaved his beard. For as long as I had known him, I'd never seen his naked face. What a shock! Its whiteness alone was blinding. I felt like there was someone new stranded on the island and Herb had disappeared. We were glad for the laugh.

Day after day waves pounded the shore, on the third day reaching their crescendo. There was another smaller island next to ours perhaps 12-feet high, and from time to time a wave would wash up and over the entire islet. I'd never seen bigger waves and such tremendous power. We were thankful not to have chosen to camp there. Pigeon Bay Island was safe enough, but we moved the canoe and tent to higher ground. The winds kept threatening to blow the tent hither, so during the day we loaded it up with stones. At night our own bodies became the ballast as we held fast to turbulent dreams.

Sometime late at night a strange sound awoke me. I stirred, trying to recognize it: silence. Herb noticed it, too. The wind had died, the waves had calmed, the storm had passed. We applauded with a shout and dressed quickly, ate and broke camp. Even though it was still dark, we had both had our fill of being sedentary and desired to get in motion.

There was a large bay to negotiate: 20 miles around the curve or five across the open water to Berens Point. We were unanimous, but very apprehensive. This was, after all, where Bill Mathers had nearly died. A mile into the stretch the sun rose and the winds began to blow again from the west across the entire lake. Damn. We discussed the option of returning to our safe island, but we fastened the spray skirts, tightened our life vests and took our chances. I was seriously concerned for our safety, but we were, at least we convinced ourselves, seasoned by now. Quickly the waves grew to four-foot swells. Some came as steady smooth rollers nicely spaced apart, but most were very erratic, bunching up together and colliding against us one atop the other, breaking over our gunwales. The canoe would have filled without the spray skirts.

Nervous sweat stinks; I was scared, and so was Herbert. If we tipped over out there, no one would rescue us and it was a long swim to shore. Every moment was heightened intensity; every move, every thrust, every hip movement calculated. Even as we pushed ahead we continued to debate turning back, always that question rolling in the back of our head. In an hour we were halfway across with the distant shore in focus. I dared joke, "What if our mothers could see us now?" A little humor pushed us ahead and lightened our fear, and we reached the distant point. As soon as we maneuvered around it, we were greeted with a tailwind that surfed us right onto the beach in front of the tiny Berens River.

The largest building there is the old Catholic mission, since converted into a fly-in fishing resort. When the owner spied us, he came marching out the front door extending his hand and true to northern hospitality invited us in. Once we were seated in the dining room, he placed full plates of bacon and eggs before us and pulled up a chair. At one point in our conversation he asked if either of us had heard of Eric Severeid.

"Yes," I responded, "I read his book *Canoeing with the Cree* when I was in high school. It inspired me."

The story is about Eric and a buddy paddling from Minneapolis to York Factory in the early 1930s. Our host explained that when they got to the Berens River, they spent the night at this very place. There have been some changes since then: the Catholic mission has been decommissioned, float planes and motor boats have been introduced, generators light the bulbs, and you can call home. But outside the lake remained the same unruly body of water, the same challenge. He told us that in all his years he had seen few canoe parties pass by, but whenever he did he invited them to share his table. It was an honor to be included in his dining club.

All day we paddled beside one long pristine beach backed by sand dunes. It was devoid of humans, not a house, not a road, not a light, not a power line, stretching uninterrupted to the horizon—the type of beach a travel agency would use to entice weary January dreamers. We got out several times to stretch and swim, surfing in the waves.

Trees were getting smaller the further north we went. Just past the sand dunes, great expanses of bog were interspersed with tamarack, black spruce, willow and the odd birch. Wild rose, beach peas, evening primrose and fireweed were prolific. Along the shore pelicans flew by in great numbers, always upsetting the local seagulls and terns. I even saw my first pair of sand-hill cranes; we were paddling close to shore when two of them leapt into the air and cawed their husky rattle.

Catnaps made a difference. If the weather was good after one of our snacks, we'd both doze. We were fast asleep once when suddenly a powerful wind snapped us awake, as if someone had flipped a switch from relative calm to turbo-gust. Within minutes it strengthened and the waves grew to impossible heights, making it clear we'd been checked: there would be no more paddling that day. Bivouacking behind a copse of speckled alders, the only protection we could find, we set up camp.

The French Voyageurs called windbound days *dégradé:* frustratingly trapped, motionless, suspended without pay. They loathed them. We too suffered our own degradations, wanting to move forward but forced to sit still. Hard to beat the view, though; cornered between a sand dune and the lake was all part of the odyssey.

In a dream a masked woman appeared with long, flowing hair and breasts showing through a gauzy dress. She approached me, gliding erotically over some liquid surface, stood in front of me and removed her disguise, revealing nothing as she was faceless. She then turned around and became Lisa, mother of my daughter Lana. I watched her pick from a pile on the floor, weeding through a heap of old books, furniture, paintings, broken vessels, discarding one thing after the other. Lana appeared and began to gather fragments and piece them together into a puzzle. It grew into a beautiful mosaic whose center piece was a shard of stained glass streaked with indigo, coral, crimson and amber.

Outside in the fading night I put on the coffee and prepared for another paddling day. We were on the move by 4:30, observing the last of the stars. High above wispy cirrus clouds turned indigo blue then orange on red over amber yellow. I drifted along between dream and reality — in the first hour they're easily confused.

That picture ended at Big Stone Point. For many miles it had protected us, but nosing around we encountered more impossible wind and waves coming at us. Forced back, we returned to the leeward and found an excellent campsite: a long protected harbor carved out of the beach, a flat grassy area for our tent and a stand of balms de Gileads for shade. On the other side of the dunes was an immense grassy swamp, the strong winds whistling through the tall reeds producing the oddest whine-hum-buzz. The Cree attribute this noise to the voices of "the little ones." Well before sunset they were lulling me back into fancy dreams.

Somewhere along the eastern side of Lake Winnipeg we got misplaced. Our first thought was that Poplar Point was beside us and the Big Black River a couple hours away. Skimming over the smoothest waters we'd seen on Winnipeg, we made excellent time all the way to the supposed mouth of the Big Black. We went around a point and encountered a series of buoys marking a river channel. We also saw humans, our first in several days, zigzagging about in motor boats. High on a hill in the background were a few microwave towers. It was all very perplexing because on our maps there was no town on the Big Black River. Lunching over the problem, we humbly concluded we had overestimated ourselves and were just now approaching Poplar Point.

Setting out again, we became pretty sure. Along came a yawl steering straight for us and a curious fisherman pulled in beside us and cut his outboard. A native Cree who had fished these waters all of his life, he confirmed that indeed we were at the mouth of the Poplar. He seemed genuinely concerned for us being out on this temperamental body of water in such a little boat and not knowing where we were. We respectfully reassured him about the canoe, but I think he remained unconvinced about our navigational skills. I showed him our Canadian Geological Survey maps, which he studied carefully, having never seen the likes. His own map of the lake was in his head: personal knowledge gained from a lifetime of storms, peaceful places, long winters nights, spring eruptions. The old fisherman's eyes, even his hands, seemed like a map, cartography in motion. The water, the dunes, the ridges and lowlands were all part of his chiseled face, reflecting this moody landscape. Studying his upturned palms, he informed us that the Big Black River, along with a store, was another ten miles north.

Past Poplar Point the shoreline changed, the long sandy beach replaced with tongues of Precambrian rock extending into the lake. Threading our way through smooth, bald granite islands, we discussed a possible diversion up the Big Black River, or as our Cree fisherman had insisted the Mukatawa. It would mean paddling a few extra miles, but what was that to us who had already paddled so many? Besides, stores always had their charms, like chocolate bars and potato chips. Even though we were tired, the promise of treats gave us extra vigor.

It's curious paddling up a river in the middle of nowhere searching for a town that's not on the map. We wouldn't have known it lay hidden a mile upstream if not for the old fisherman. But after negotiating the fast current we rounded a bend and there it was, Mukatawa, a Cree word meaning Big Black Bear, a funky rustic fishing village with a dozen houses, a fish factory and one small store.

Resting on a bench and eating our snacks, we noticed the whole town was a flurry of activity. A fellow named Ingmar came over and sat with us and when I asked about the hubbub, he explained this was a fishing camp, open one month every summer; the employees were cleaning the last of the catch and packing up to prepare to go home. The commercial fishing season had ended the day before and a boat was coming in an hour to take the inhabitants back to Grand Rapids on the western shore of Lake Winnipeg. If we had arrived here a day later, we would have discovered essentially a ghost town. Would it be possible to camp, perhaps even buy a pickerel? Of course we could camp wherever we wanted, and yes, they had plenty of fish.

He led us into the fish house and introduced us to John Bear, who was deftly wielding his razor-edged knife. He chose two beautiful walleye for us and within seconds had them perfectly filleted; then he pointed to his house on the edge of town and insisted we take them over to his wife, saying, "She'll fry 'em right." That sure was nice, but I'm not one to insist on any stranger cooking my supper. Noticing our hesitation, he walked us over to the house himself and introduced us to Ann. She lit the stove, breaded the fish, warmed up baked potatoes and hot bannock, and we gorged with pleasure.

Soon after our feast, John Bear returned with a liter of some unidentifiable white drink. Grinning widely, he explained that it was "Moose Juice," some leftovers from their farewell party the night before. He filled our glasses while describing his secret recipe: raisins, canned peaches, potatoes, sugar and yeast mixed in a 55-gallon drum and fermented for at least three days. In other words, whatever they sell in the store mixed with yeast and fermented for as long as you felt like waiting. In remote areas devoid of alcoholic beverages, this is how one enjoys a drink. Several other villagers came over and one, Lawrence, invited us on a boat ride.

We boarded his 20-foot yawl. For Lawrence there was no such thing as idling, and as soon as the lines were released we rocketed full throttle back down the river to the lake. At the mouth were thousands of granite islets and hidden reefs. Lawrence smiled as he maneuvered between them, knowing we were scared out of our Moose-Juiced brains. The closer he got to a reef the louder he laughed, steering sharply away at the last second, lurching us from one side of the boat to the other. Only half-frightened, I believed our pilot knew these waters like the back of his own hand. Once we reached the open waters of Winnipeg, he slowed down so we could watch the sunset. That's when he began to share his story: growing up as a Metis Indian in remote Poplar Point, days and nights of drunken stupor, several near fatalities, a wife who left him, and ultimately "smartening up" and going sober. He proudly told us he hadn't had a drink in five years. With the money he used to waste on alcohol, he had saved to buy this very yawl and now he was a member of the local fishing co-op and doing well. Sure he missed the party, but he was never going back to that hell, and I believed him. He was a man with conviction, and at least now he seemed in control of his own recklessness. It seemed important we know this. We returned up the river mouth in the twilight, plotting fast between deadly rocks.

While we'd been away, the ship arrived and the villagers had begun loading up. One by one they embarked, all heading back to their own private worlds. Like old buddies we waved goodbye. Lawrence, who lived in nearby Poplar Point, was remaining behind along with a couple of others to close up the camp and he invited us to stay at their house instead of pitching our tent, a welcome invitation as night had descended. We crossed the river to his cabin and were introduced to the stragglers: Raymond, Clarence, his wife Nadine and their young son David, the only remnants in what had been a bustling village earlier that day.

Raymond, the president of the co-op, had also grown up in Poplar Point one of the few whites. For most of the night he entertained us with stories of his time in the bush, a hermetic life to which he seemed disposed, never marrying or having kids, a very solitary character as well as a gifted sage. It seemed the farther one got into the hinterlands, the more important story-telling became. His last tale before going off to bed was about a balancing rock somewhere down the shore — with just one finger you could push this massive boulder and make it wobble. It appeared to me that Raymond was just like that rock: an old piece of the landscape, solitary, weighty, tough and yet easily moved by small gestures.

Clarence and Nadine were "Treaty Indians," with dual citizenship in Canada and the United States. They had grown up in Canada but were taking advantage of scholarships to study at the University of North Dakota. Nadine was working on her master's degree in wildlife management and Clarence his doctorate in linguistics. He spoke several languages, including English, French, Lakota, Ojibwa and Cree.

It rained all the next day; listening to heavy drops splashing the window panes from my soft bed, I felt cozy, protected and lazy. Nadine announced it was Canada Day and then served us Canadian bacon and eggs. We lounged around all day conversing. I had never had the opportunity to sit still in one room with Native Americans, passing the pipe as it were. Herb had grown up on a real working farm, I had grown up in the epitome of suburbia, Raymond in a tiny north woods village, and Nadine, Clarence, Lawrence and David on their own treaty lands. Despite our different backgrounds, we all sat there as friends discussing everything from Cowboys and Indians to religion, politics to fishing, canoeing to bannock, and ultimately the language of love. It was a refreshing, open and honest exchange. The kid said it best: "It's good to make friends while it's raining."

During our two weeks of traveling on Lake Winnipeg we had only one day with steady tailwinds to ride that sea monster's back, our last. We appreciated the send-off gift from the water gods. While surfing along easily, I let my mind wander. With Herb at the helm, my part was easy: all I had to do was keep time, paddle along in our rhythm, unconcerned with our direction. The effort is so repetitive and thoughtless that it becomes meditation in motion. A shout from Herb though brought me back to the present: "I see it!"

There's a lighthouse at Warren Landing at the very end of the lake and we paused there to give ceremonial offerings for safe passage and continued fortune. After one more bath in its waters we left that lake behind with mixed memories. The long beaches were beautiful and the inhabitants exceptionally generous. Winnipeg had been a body of contrasts, a gorgeous gem and a terrible beast; paddling into its constant winds was very tiring and every mile gained was a strenuous chore. Herb's carpel tunnel syndrome had become serious, his wrist inflamed and irritated. What we needed was a day off and Norway House was just around the bend, on the far side of Playgreen Lake.

Afternoon rains were threatening so we quickly made camp on Kettle Island. Since it was the Fourth of July and we were feeling celebratory, we uncorked the last of our whiskey and made our Declaration to Genuine Independence: to a world where canoeing down the streams of everyone's dreams becomes reality; to a community of all races joined in a shared wealth of all things essential, a chance to honor our ancestors with a shared pipe, a place where children are nurtured with hope—a place to come in out of the rain. And it did rain, all night.

We awoke to a bright cheerful morning, ready for travel at 4:00 a.m. and the crossing of Playgreen to the old town of Norway House. The sun rose while we were afloat, but a dark wall, a very dark front, moved in and our cheeriness quickly diminished. Foggy fingers reached into the bay, reached across the entire lake, reached into our hearts. We pulled out our rain gear, fastened the spray skirts, and slouched down for the wet cold. The drizzle turned to light rain; showers followed and never let up, but at least there was no wind. We found our way to Playgreen Point and entered the Jack River. A house, a dog barking, the slam of a car door, radio broadcasts, a chainsaw, the scream of a child, another house, another dog. Our pace picked up; we were on the outskirts of Norway House and treats, contacts, a mailed food-drop from Sonja, perhaps a beer.

Norway House was initially a fur-trading outpost, the Hudson Bay Company having built the original settlement here in the early eighteenth century. Like Grand Portage, it was used to help supply the interior with trade goods and as an exchange place for pelts. There are many of these outposts scattered across Canada and most are still quite inaccessible. Norway House, however, has a gravel road leading to it now so it doesn't really feel that remote. The real plus was a hotel, the Playgreen Inn: after the day-long saturating rains we indulged in long scalding showers, washing out the last two weeks of smoky fires from our hair and clothes.

That night in the tavern, Herb and I discussed our possible routes from there to Hudson Bay with some locals. The word was that the Gods River was low and the Nelson too dangerous; most people agreed the Hayes was our best option, but to get there required a 10-mile portage. When a fellow named Jerry offered to take us over the portage in his pickup, we bought him a couple rounds.

RESCUE PARTIERS
French River to Mattawa River

To the St. Lawrence Seaway

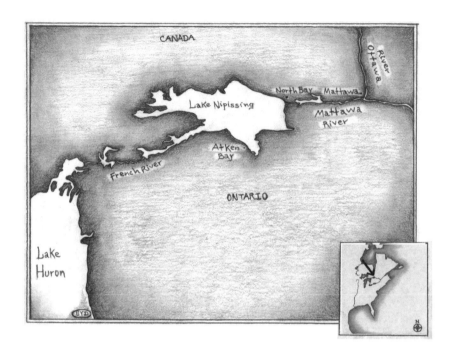

Awakened by guttural heron talk, Paula and I jumped out of bed and excitedly broke camp, anxious to enter the French River. We launched onto Lake Huron once more, waggling through the last of its rocky islets. Out on the tip of Grandine Point we cheered an Ojibwa man as he constructed his new winter lodge, having chosen an excellent location, accessible only by boat and right where the waters met. Leaving him behind, we entered Voyageur Channel.

The world slowly, intimately closed in upon us. Warm forest scents replaced the cooler sterile lake breeze and the water's temperature rose, too, its hue turning a transparent brown. Along the shallow riverbanks birds flew in and out of wild rice; on our left slabs of smooth polished granite slanted out of the water, while to the right were huge, broken chunks of stone hewn by time. Peacefully we slipped up the canyon.

We followed the channel carefully, anticipating the first rapids, and when we arrived at the place where our map indicated whitewater we found only a shallow slow-moving river. We laughed off the few scrapes and continued toward the next marked rapids whose approach was through a six-foot wide slot. We slipped in, cornered a bend and entered a slack-water box canyon: a dead end.

It takes a bit of energy to move a kayak and the last thing we wanted to do was backtrack. As we sat there hemmed in by three walls, we tried to ascertain what went wrong, where our channel was. We methodically replotted our course from the beginning and in the end concluded we were indeed on course, but the river itself was so miserably low that the channel had shrunk and the rapids and falls disappeared. We noted high-water marks along the walls overhead, darkened stains that told of flash floods and spring runoffs, but for us there was nothing but a fetid pond. We decided to portage over the dry falls and plod the upper pool, and a quarter mile later we ran into another dead end, another dry waterfall. By then we knew that we should have entered the Main Channel or Canoe Channel, but it was too late. Up and over we hoisted the gear and slipped into more shallows. On the plus side since there was not much current, paddling upstream was so far easy.

By day's end our minuscule channel had merged with another and we had deep water and a current. Digging in we slowly moved our way up looking for the eddies, keeping to the inside when possible. The thick forest grew right up to the river's edge and campsites were scarce. It was late when we finally found a vacant beach.

That night I lit our first fire since Old Woman Bay, way back on Lake Superior, and we realized we'd never had one on Lake Huron. Those rock islets seemed too sanctified to disturb with fire; their fragility required every stick of wood remain untouched, every piece of organic material left to foster life. Here there were piles of driftwood and it was a comfort to be fireside again. I felt right at home on the river, so close, narrow and touchable compared to the limitless lake horizon.

Not a whisper of wind, the water a black mirror reflecting a crescent moon and fading stars. Inside her kayak Paula looked like an interstellar windmill, all blades spinning at once. Except for the fish, we were the only wake breaking the surface. It was prime paddling, playing the river at dawn, and soon a light breeze stirred, changing the flat plane into an intricate pattern of tiny bouncing wavelets. As the sun rose the breeze freshened; all morning the wind velocity increased and by noon it was hot and gusty. Fortunately it was all coming from behind; we had gained the rare tailwind and the steep canyon created a wind tunnel that further increased its force, eventually becoming so strong it actually pushed us upstream even when we weren't paddling. Scattered along the free ride were three sets of rapids: leaning into paddle blades against the rocky bottom, we poled our way through the first; the second series was light enough, 10 minutes of hard stroking popped us through the top; the third, Recollect Falls, we had to portage.

There were many old cabins in the area, the basic simple shack with a 16-foot Lund tied to the dock. Mid-August was peak summer vacation time and they were all occupied, but we found one snug hiding place on Lost Child Bend beside a little beach shaded by a lone white pine. The wind was howling up the river but a few feet back into the woods it was calm, and that's where we settled.

Powered by paddle blades and shoulder blades, we angled our kayaks through Crooked Rapids. The next section of whitewater, the Devil's Chute, lived up to its name — it was way too fast and dangerous for us. Instead, we lined the boats from shore, pulling them with rope. A third unnamed rapids took everything we had to navigate; the way was smooth, steady and sure until we hit the final throat where the river bottlenecked, and at its narrowest part there was a visible uphill lip. Paula was the first to reach it, but as soon as she entered she stalled, unable to go beyond the water break. The bottom half of her kayak would not let go of downstream. I was behind her and shouted, "You're right on the edge. Push harder!" From somewhere, she found a little more muscle, gained that extra inch, and slipped into the slower upstream waters. I stalled in the same place and then flailed hard and fast; it took a moment, but soon I was right beside Paula. In the previous two months we'd become very strong paddlers, but in those rapids we came to know our limit. At Little Parisienne Rapids the French River was squeezed into a six-foot crack, but there was a portage and we used it. Next to the trail was a fine campsite complete with a soft whitewater orchestra.

We continued the next day, portaging Five Mile Rapids and then paddling slowly through Double Rapids. Hauling against those choked waters, we moved past two old men from Pennsylvania standing on the rocks. "Lord, lord, you two are impressive," one called out.

All morning we had been anticipating Little Pine Portage, which looked like the perfect place for lunch and a swim; we worked hard to reach it but when we arrived we were disappointed. Across the crowded little bay was a large resort and its numerous smelly motorboats were out fishing.

Determined to swim anyway, I stripped naked and cannonballed into the river, spooking both fish and fishermen.

On the cusp of friendly tailwinds we entered a wide channel dotted with islands; there was no discernable current and we sailed along easily. Off in the distance I spotted a canoe and when we neared it, we heard a man shouting, "I'm looking for Keso Point. Do you know where I am?"

Luckily he found us when he did as the misplaced fellow had already paddled through strong gusts a mile past the point. We turned him into the right direction; we were heading there ourselves. At Keso there was one last portage from the French River into Lake Nipissing. It's a half-mile long, and since it was late afternoon we decided to camp at its base. By the time we'd settled in, our lost friend stumbled through.

The adventurous older man gladly accepted our invitation to tea. Recently retired after 35 years of teaching, he had long dreamed of canoeing for a month in the wilderness and now finally had his chance. At that point he was half into his solo journey that looped through the French River channels. I noticed he had chosen a very difficult route with many long portages. It was pretty clear he was a poor navigator, too, but I sure admired him. There was plenty of room in our site for another tent so we invited him to camp with us and stay for dinner, but he declined, wanting to push on a little further.

Both Paula and I looked at his pile of packs and plastic canoe; he had a lot of weight to carry, so we offered our help. He and Paula gathered packs and paddles and I hoisted his tub onto my shoulders, amazed the old bloke had already lugged it so far. We trotted up the trail and at the end, when we finally plopped everything back down, he said, "That's the best cup of tea I've ever had. Thanks."

I responded, "Maybe when I'm an old dreamer like you someone will carry my canoe." He was nearly my father's age, after all, and I'd portage a canoe for him anytime.

Our journey the next day began on foot, portaging boats and gear out of the French River and into a long arm of Lake Nipissing. We passed several islands, each with its own posh lodge, homes you can't fold into a bag. The closer we got to the main body of Nipissing the bigger became the waves, and by the end of the day we were pushed by 25-knot winds and four-footers. As we rounded Frank's Point, the wide open expanse of Lake

Nipissing spread before us and the shallow lake was roiling. We could go no further, but fortunately there was an empty beach.

Little morning showers kept us tucked into our warm bags. When we got a break between the rains, we launched onto smooth gray waters. How quickly things changed—four-foot waves one day and becalmed the next. There were no more islands to shelter us, just straight open coastline. A few little bays offered some sanctuary, a place to exit in an emergency. Slight west breezes started to blow, quickly backing around towards the east and growing even stronger. One sudden gust blew my cap off, not a good sign. Paula fished it out of the lake and brought it over to me, a worried look on her face. The skies were getting dark and we wished we had stayed in the tent, but a small bay on the other side of Cross Point looked hopeful. When we got there, we were saddened to find it filled with cabins. And then it began to rain.

We rafted up together wondering what to do—should we continue to the next bay, two risky miles away, or simply idle where we were until the rains let up? There was another option: head over to the cabins and plead permission to camp on their property.

As we floated in our boats debating, the weather got worse. The sky thundered and a few lightening bolts struck nearby; snotty winds grew stronger, sending thick raindrops at us horizontally. We had to get off the lake.

Landing next to the first cabin, we approached and knocked. The door creaked opened and a giant appeared, filling the frame.

"Can we camp on your beach?"

The man, Christopher, never gave us chance to explain, instead forcing us to sit at his table and eat scrambled eggs. His wife and four children all just sat there smiling while gusts of winds slashed through the trees and growing waves pounded the beach. More lightening and thunder and rain, but a warm fire sparked from the hearth and we sat beside it sharing stories.

It was really Christopher's father, Dinty, who owned the cabin in the bay. Dinty Parks, a.k.a. the Golden Boy, had been a professional wrestler in the '50s. He and his brother Herb became famous for their tag team wrestling with a bear named Gus and together they made a small fortune from their sport. One day, however, Gus finally won the match; the bear figured out how to take off his protective booties, which enabled him to claw the dickens out of Herb's chest. At the height of his career, the Golden Boy, who was really from Florida, married Barb, the Snow Queen of North Bay, Ontario; thus our jumbo friend was born from regal stock.

In the afternoon when the rains subsided, Paula and I established our camp behind the cabin. After we finished, Christopher invited me for some male-bonding, asking, "Maybe make a little firewood?"

He cut and I hauled, but I couldn't keep up with him, so every once in a while he'd turn off the chainsaw and help. As I watched him drag half a tree away, I was reminded of a skidder. Side by side we worked up a sweat and when the boss said we were finished, we both dove buck naked into the bay, body-surfing in the waves and giving the girls a show.

By the time we got to the evening bonfire, we were all good friends. Paula and I even concocted a nickname for them, the "Rescue Partiers." They had welcomed us warmly, saved and fed us. Even better, since they all lived in North Bay, which was along our future route, we were expected to visit them there, too.

The clouds thinned and the sunset gave way to a starry sky, but the winds continued to howl all night. It was a restless sleep: worrying about trees falling, boats blowing away and the tent ripping. The breaking surf awoke me at dawn, and outside the air was cool, like fall was moving in. We weren't going anywhere.

The Golden Boy was due to pick up the Rescue Partiers at noon in his cabin cruiser and then take them back to his house on Sommerville Island. Nobody really believed he would come because it was way too rough. It seemed we were bound to the beach for another day. We had helped eat up their food supply, so it was our turn to play host. Paula is a wonderful cook and given a real kitchen, she never disappoints. Corn bread came from the oven and hot soup off the range.

To everyone's surprise, in the afternoon Dinty did come, appearing like a specter out of the tempest. Because of the waves he couldn't beach, but instead anchored 20 feet offshore. Christopher carried everyone out to the boat on his shoulders while I helped with the cargo of suitcases and empty coolers. When I arrived with my first load, Dinty fired me a few questions:

"So, you're kayaking? Where you from? Is that so! Do you know how to handle a black bear?"

"Bang a few pots together," I proffered.

"That's right," he responded. "Make some noise. Sometimes that won't work though, so you have to pop 'em one smack dab right on the nose. Ohhh, they hate that!" When Christopher chimed in that we already knew about Gus, Dinty smiled and said proudly, "That was an educated bear."

We said our goodbyes, knowing we would meet again soon, and then they bounced away swaying in the big seas. We, however, were held fast to Atkin Bay, the steady 30-knot winds much too much for us. They'd left the cabin open, insisting we be at home and settle in beside the fireplace.

In one long day we paddled around the rest of Lake Nipissing, but annoying headwinds frustrated us the entire way. The early breeze was from the south as we headed into South Bay. The Gull Islands gave us no protection, the wind finding its way around them all. When we turned east towards Sommerville Island, the wind accordingly switched direction and continued blowing into our faces. On the last long haul to the city of North Bay, the winds turned again; dragging through choppy water, we plodded along the shore and finally into town.

We were exhausted by the time we pulled into the marina. Anxious to get to town, we had overextended ourselves; our stride was too fast and our breaks too few. We pushed hard because we knew the "Rescue Partiers" would be there. I placed a call to their house and minutes later Christopher arrived in his pickup.

North Bay in northern Ontario is the town in Neil Young's song "Helpless." While giving us a tour, Christopher explained that Neil actually lived there as a young man. Deep inside the bowels of a nearby hill, the Canadian military has tunneled in a hidden missile base and a lot of big birds fly across the sky, maintaining vigilance.

Eventually we wound up at Sunset Point and the wind switched once more, hard from the west. How satisfying it was to sit and stare across the big lake, back into the waters and waves we had so recently cruised. Our day that began on the faraway shore now ended with the promise of a bed.

To continue our journey we had to portage over a little continental divide, up and over the hump that separates Lake Nipissing from Trout Lake and the beginning of the Mattawa River. Our struggles with upstream paddling were over; once we dipped into the Mattawa, it was all down hill to Montréal and Québec.

Trout Lake is a deep, cold, clean jewel; Mattawa Provincial Park begins on the far side and from there a small winding river flows into Turtle Lake. Paula was in the lead as we neared its end. I couldn't see anybody but I heard her begin conversing with someone on shore, "Hello...Québec... Minnesota...Yes!"

Danny, Cher and their daughter Julie were camping under a pine grove and as it turned out, Danny was Christopher's cousin. They'd already been told about us and in fact were expecting us. We were invited to join them, Cher waving as bait an ice-cold wilderness beer. They insisted we set up house beside them and share dinner.

In the morning after coffee and pancakes, we moved on through Portage de la Mauvaise Musique and entered Pine Lake on a dead calm day. We flew across its length and then hiked the Portage de la Pin Musique into Talon Lake. From there was a stretch through the Mattawa River whose walls rose a hundred feet above us, closing in our world again. On small Lake Pimisi we found camp, and for the first time in several days we were alone. All our North Bay friends were memories and our dialogue was again with the crickets.

In a six-mile stretch of the Mattawa River we had to undertake six portages, most of the foot paths rough and difficult. The most demanding aspect was the proximity of each one: paddle a short spell, get out, unload, get up, haul, reload, get down, paddle a small pool and then repeat.

The French voyageurs understood the struggle it took to pass through this small waterway and their descriptive nomenclature remains. The first, Décharge des Perches, is where they customarily threw their poling sticks away and picked up the paddle again. Portage de la Cave does indeed contain a small dark grotto. Portage de la Prairie is beside a grassy island at the base of difficult rapids. Portage des Paresseux is the site of a lazy waterfall. Portage des Roches, a horrible rock-strewn path, is a serious ankle-buster. Portage Campion, the last, at last.

Beyond Campion Falls we continued through the steep canyon where the water ran dark. After all those carries it was our reward to finally sit and ride the current, the canyon ending in what is called the Gut. Our camp that night had a welcome feel. Scrounging for firewood, I found a broken arrowhead and not far away was a rusty can along with a mess of nylon fishing line. For thousands of summers this place has been a popular rest stop. The Ojibwa, the French and the Canadians have all taken pause on this rock before or after ascending the canyon, and it felt proper that we should carry on the tradition. Sitting beside the fast waters having a smoke, I felt a connection with my fellow paddlers. An owl hooted over the still water, crickets chirped, a beaver slapped the surface and frogs croaked. It was all something of a dream.

THE BIG MUDDY
Cairo to St. Francisville

Down the Mississippi

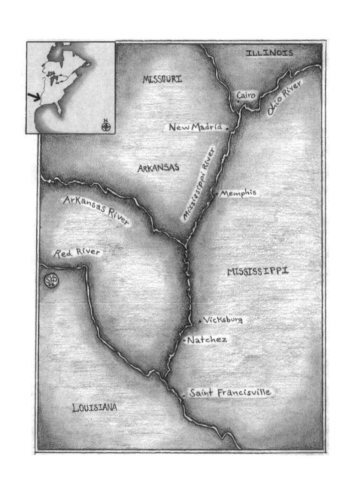

With my lost and found canoe I entered the new Mississippi. The morning was calm but the river was not; the slick surface was pocked with boils that surged up and swirled me around. There were powerful whirlpools, too, their force often shooting me back upstream or out into the middle of the river. Even with a life jacket you can drown if you get caught in an eddy or a boil. Voices of people I'd met came back reminding me of the danger: it's such a big river and you have such a tiny boat.

Soon after crossing into Kentucky, I heard someone hollering at me from midriver. Looking over my shoulder, I noticed a kayak advancing, which turned out to hold an Englishman who'd always wanted to float the Mississippi. He had organized his journey in the form of a fund raiser and a list of sponsors donated dollars for every mile he paddled, with all the proceeds going to the American Cancer Society. His sojourn had begun at Three Forks, Montana, at the Missouri River headwaters. To paddle from there to the Gulf of Mexico, you have technically gone the longest stretch of river on the continent, he explained. A support team followed him; every afternoon he would pull into a predetermined campsite and his tent would be pitched with dinner ready. Banking up the miles he raced away from me, hurrying off to sea, and within a half-hour he was out of sight.

Early Sunday morning I docked in New Madrid, Missouri. Out of potable water, I grabbed my jug and went searching for the spigot; the only places open were the churches and the police station. Since I'd already been to church in Minnesota, I opted for the cop shop; glancing through the door, I saw two men sitting beside a pot of coffee. Donuts and history followed.

In 1811, New Madrid was near the epicenter of a powerful earthquake, among the strongest ever to hit the U.S. In December of that year the earth was split apart and the land visibly undulated in waves; many homes were leveled while others were simply swallowed up, and most of New Madrid slipped off into the Mississippi and disappeared forever. The tremors lasted for several months and left the locals terrified; the larger quakes were felt as far away as the East coast. It was one of the most extensive earthquakes in American history regarding the number of shocks and the size of the area affected. There was no Richter scale in those days but seismologists estimate it was an 8.0, bigger than anything in recent times. The river instantly rose 20 feet and for a while actually flowed backwards; fissures in the land flooded and formed new lakes such as Reelfoot across the river in Tennessee. The fault line is still there lying below the alluvial silts and small tremors are detected even today. An earthquake in these parts is comparable to throwing a rock into a bowl of pudding.

One of the guys at the station informed me that he was actually the town constable's son and it was his responsibility to tend the shop while dad was in church. After the history class he invited me for a cruise in the squad car, so we hopped in and drove down the main boulevard. What a bizarre sensation being in the front seat with all that equipment—I had been in police cars before, but only in the back. We beelined out towards the country where the first of the cotton fields appeared, tufts of white fiber filling the landscape. As we followed the levee back, I realized the Deep South was indeed at hand.

I slid out of town and steeped myself in the river again. The forest was changing, colored hardwoods giving way to greenery. There in the sub-subtropics plants were still growing in early November. I was outpaddling autumn; while Minnesota waters were beginning to freeze, I peeled off my shirt to better feel the warm breeze.

That evening I camped on a large sandbar, my own beach. Everything was still, the river flowed by silently and I was certain I felt a tremor.

A storm developed during the night and by morning the river was filled with whitecaps. I was happy to settle into the small island; the guitar was a fine companion on those days and every time I picked it up I learned something new. And reading: a good day to finish Woody Guthrie's *Bound for Glory*. There was all the time in the world right there, by the banks of the great runnel. Breaking waves inspired a nap, a chilly breeze inspired a walk for dry driftwood, a smoky fire inspired stone soup.

The mile-wide Mississippi flowed faster the closer it got to the Gulf of Mexico. Predominantly, the winds came blowing up from the Gulf, gravity pulling me seaward while strong gusty winds tried to push me back home. These two forces acted against each other and often created difficult paddling. Because of the current's force, the wind-blown waves stalled in place and instead of moving just grew in size, the stronger the wind the higher the standing waves. There was no escaping—the surface of the river was filled with them. To further intensify the situation, there were always erratic towboat wakes that could catch me off guard. On those windy days travel speed slowed greatly.

As I neared another bend, I saw a familiar towboat and I fought to gain the shore as the *Leviticus* headed downstream. That time I felt I could outpaddle its nasty wake, but I was wrong. Just 50 yards from shore the rollers caught up with me. The first few were tolerable as I balanced my way through the three-way collision of wake, current and wind. The fourth or fifth wave lifted me up to its crest and I noticed right in front of me, at the bottom of the trough, a hidden wing dam. Normally these small dams were harmless to my shallow draft canoe, but with that passing wake I was dropped down onto its lip. The aluminum dug into sharp rock, not wanting to let go. The next roller came and broke right into the canoe, half-filling it before pushing me away downstream. I wallowed in the remaining waves and slowly made the shoreline cursing both the Corps and the *Leviticus.*

Once dried out I crossed over to Caruthersville, Missouri. The winds were settling down and by early afternoon I arrived. Vagrancy is generally unwelcome in these small towns, but I discovered that a vagrant with a canoe seems more acceptable. The waitress snuck me a slice of pie. The children laughed at me when they saw me coming. The policeman gave me permission to camp in the town park. The bartender bought me a draft beer.

When cartographers first established state lines in the delta region, they used the Mississippi River as a logical boundary. As the river shifted its course through the alluvium, however, it began to mock their efforts. Tennessee was to my left, on the east bank, with Arkansas on the west for the most part. Since those original boundaries were drawn, the river (and the Corps) has cut several new bends that sliced into both states. The result is that the river has deposited parts of Arkansas into Tennessee, isolating them from the rest of the state. Bends have done the same thing to Tennessee, leaving a part of that state on the other side in Missouri. Today little pieces of Louisiana are scattered across the river in Mississippi, while parts of Mississippi are in Arkansas.

Now and then one still finds a few scattered bluffs in the delta, made not of limestone but clay; the highest and hopefully driest places around, most have towns atop them. On one such rise, Chickasaw Bluff, lies the city of Memphis. I arrived at sunset and camped in a marina downtown. There I met three Minnesota guys who were kayaking down the Mississippi River. I had departed in mid-August and they in mid-September; somewhere in the past day or two they had passed by me unawares. Bob, Scott, Dave and I wandered downtown looking for some Beale Street action, but what was once a thriving musical Mecca seemed shoddy and neglected.

I left Memphis the next day in a shroud of fog; eventually, the veil became so dense that I could barely see the bow of my canoe and was forced to make camp. I stumbled onto a small sandbar in Mississippi and spread out my belongings. Sitting beside my tent with a small fire, I wondered where civilization had gone; at that moment, more than any other, I felt utterly alone, completely socked in my own world. Between walks for driftwood and pots of tea, I read Twain and prayed the river wouldn't rise.

Fresh breezes began to separate the fog in the morning and I slipped through the wisps, listening for boat traffic. From downstream a loud steam whistle pierced the air. As I floated around one still bend, the specter of a paddle wheeler revealed itself through the mist; the *Delta Queen* was anchored fast to the shore. Presumably, it too had been forced to wait out the fog. Even for those radar-equipped giants it can sometimes be too risky to travel; an unseen floating tree would do serious damage to its hull. She let out another whistle and when I got closer, I could see its chimneys billowing smoke as it prepared to depart.

While I drifted by this vision from the past, suddenly from midstream another shrill steam whistle blew; the *Mississippi Queen,* its newer and larger sister ship, emerged from the obscurity with its wheel churning up the river. The *Delta Queen* sounded another greeting and began to play her calliope. I felt as if I had leapt through a time warp, back a century in one foggy river bend. I was the lone voyager in my canoe passing between two paddle wheelers which then both faded away.

Small ripples from the Ozark Mountains reached the Arkansas shoreline covered in beautiful hardwoods—oaks, hickory, sycamores, gums, yellow poplar and cherry trees. The place felt wild as there were few towns or roads. Paddling along one morning, I noticed a trailer house in a small clearing, smoke unfurling from its stove pipe, and since my legs needed stretching I went to investigate.

I knocked on the door and a soft voice bid me inside. I opened it and found a feeble old man in his bed listening to the radio. He smiled and then slowly worked his way up into a seated position. After introductions he reached for the stove and heated up leftover coffee. Alexander had lived by the river all his life. He had worked the towboats and for a while fished commercially and gathered clam shells for a button factory. In his youth he had been a trapper, a hunting guide and a logger. Now he had emphysema in a fierce way and his days were numbered; he could not walk more than three steps without becoming totally breathless, and just getting up to pee was a half-hour chore. When he learned that I had arrived by canoe from Minnesota, he smiled. I had a pair of deerskin moccasins in my pack that I never used and before departing dug them out for Alexander—a gift for sharing one of his last days with me. As he offered his thanks, I thought, "This is a worthy place to die, here beside the river. I should be so fortunate."

When Greenville, Mississippi, was first settled it was located on the main channel, but the capricious river began to shift course and threatened to swallow it whole, so the Corps of Engineers was called in, which responded by slicing through an upstream oxbow and diverting the river around the town. Greenville is now a slack-water port and its entrance a lake. As I headed in, I encountered Bob, Scott and Dave again, heading out. My friends seemed rather blue, low on funds and basically tired of their race downstream. I was in high spirits; my sojourn was nearing an end and there was a new town to explore. Besides, there was no hurry—it was getting colder up north every day.

I ate lunch at a crowded restaurant. Since it was Sunday, the place was loaded with the after-church brunch crowd. After weeks of being basically alone, it was strange to sit in a room full of people talking at once in a riotous chatter that sounded like the constant lulling hum of white noise. Most every table was filled with a family which made me think about the concept of "home" and what that meant to me while wandering down the river. I was feeling very content as the solitary monk drifting in and out of people's lives. Surrounding myself with all of that humanity was comforting, but it was not the place I wished to stay: the river's pull was stronger.

My camp that night was blessed with an excellent star party. Laying on my back, I watched the crescent moon with its companion planet trace across the heavens. A billion stars filled the dark void; the fire crackled; a distant train rolled through and then a towboat all lit up purred by. Lying still, looking up at the firmament, I realized what a marvelous planet we have. Often I despair at what we humans have done to this river and to our only home, but gazing out into the galaxy, out into the past, I realized that as the Earth spins everything changes. All beings, all matter, all forms are the effect of countless revolutions. Every soul does have a place in this procession. Where we're all headed is such a great mystery, but how we got here in the first place is equally puzzling. The universe continues to expand like the concentric circles created by my paddle blade. My hopes are pretty small, and that's all right.

The largest towboat on the river was called, appropriately enough, the *America*. Two erratic waves from its powerful twin screws caught me by surprise; the swells were six feet high and for some reason two of them were spaced quite closely together. As I broke through the second swell, I once again took on gallons of river water and needed another dry-out on the hot asphalt revetment.

That night I camped atop the levee. A warm ocean breeze blew through the cotton fields and I could smell salt. Below me were two magnificent trees. The first was a pecan laden with fresh delicious nuggets and I filled my pockets. Beside it was a magnificent live oak. When given plenty of room, these oaks grow enormous fat branches that extend out and then down and then up again, each branch like a gigantic arm resting on its elbow. It must have been a couple centuries old. Live oaks never lose their leaves, remaining crowned with green all winter as a reminder you're in the South. Back on the levee I watched the sun sink into Louisiana, my last state.

As I paddled up to the docks in Vicksburg, someone hollered, "Hey, you in the canoe, where you coming from?"

Gus had also canoed down the river with a buddy Don. They had left Chicago three months previously, floating down the Illinois River and then entering the Mississippi. Powered mostly by Budweiser and Kools, they eventually made it as far as Memphis where they met a young couple traveling down river in a homemade catamaran. Sadly, the couple had gone bankrupt and were forced to sell their dream and their boat, but it just so happened Gus had a small sum of money and offered to buy it. He and Don tied their canoe behind the sailboat and continued on their merry way, meandering from Memphis to Vicksburg. Once they arrived there Don placed a call home only to find his mother had taken ill; deciding to return home for a short while and pay her a visit, he left Gus to wait in Vicksburg and two weeks later I showed up at the marina. Gus was restless and wanted to move so he invited me to join him aboard the 30-foot *Mythswyth Sarth* all the way to New Orleans.

The catamaran had two long narrow hulls and inside each one were the quarters. The starboard side had two beds and a chart room while the port side had the galley and a storage bunker with another bed. A spacious deck was suspended between the hulls, complete with two captains' chairs. The idea of finger picking the miles away was enticing and I had always wanted to learn to sail. I walked alone into town to mull it over.

Vicksburg is an antebellum showpiece, the historic downtown full of buildings dating back to the early 1800s. In 1863 during the U.S. Civil War, it was the site of a 47-day battle. In the end the Confederate army surrendered the town to Grant's Union forces. A decisive engagement—when the smoke cleared the Union controlled the entire river, which effectively cut the south in half, stranding Texas, Arkansas, Missouri and much of Louisiana. Even so, it still took two more years before the Confederate South fully surrendered. On the outskirts of Vicksburg is a National Historical Monument commemorating the siege. Walking through the park, I found it disturbing to consider all the blood spilled there. All wars are horrible, but I think civil wars must be the worst. The tombstones were all lined up in perfect rows, too perfect and too neat; there was nothing orderly about that chaotic hell and I wondered how anyone could feel nostalgic about it.

Strolling back to the marina, I considered the proposal. For me the real adventure was the journey down the river, not the craft I rode in. The canoe was a splendid vehicle, but it certainly wasn't the only choice. After nearly drowning and several recent soakings, the comfort and safety of a sailboat were attractive. And the river demands spontaneity. In the end I could think of no reason to refuse the opportunity, so I bought a bottle of champagne.

When I returned to the ship, we made a toast to our new joint venture. Whether or not I went with Gus as far as New Orleans remained to be seen, but we would launch in the morning. That night I didn't have to pitch my tent.

In the morning I tied my canoe behind the *Mythswyth Sarth,* next to the one Gus had paddled from Chicago. The captain fired up the outboard and we motored out of the marina and onto the big river. Once we reached the middle, we cut the noise and raised the sheets. One day I canoed into Vicksburg and the next I sailed for Natchez.

Sailing on the Mississippi isn't easy. Around every bend both the current and the wind changed directions; we tried to tack into the wind but the current wanted to push us elsewhere. Because the catamaran was a shallow draft boat, we were able to go outside the deep channel, but still our range was limited. In a canoe you can pretty well go where you please, but with the sailboat we had to be on constant lookout for sandbars, wingdams, buoys and deadheads.

Gus had been born and raised in a Wonder Bread American suburbia, like me. Restless, he joined the Navy at 18 and was shipped to Vietnam.

He shared some awful stories with me and I did not envy his experience. Having survived that horror he returned home, and after a while it occurred to him that floating down the river might help ease his dissatisfaction. It seemed to be working well; he was content out there piloting his boat. We had each taken such different paths to arrive at the same bend and the company was enjoyable. So was the ride—writing, singing, playing, sitting, cooking, conversing, all the while moving at a respectably good pace.

Natchez has long been a port of call for paddle wheelers. At the same time we pulled into its small marina the *Delta Queen* was docking, its steam calliope whistling southern tunes while curious onlookers gathered beside her. We tied off near it and disembarked for our own tour.

Notched into the bluff just below the village is Natchez Under the Hill. Historically, this was the seedy part of town where the river rats worked and played. We went into one of the taverns for a burger and a beer and ended up staying under that hill until midnight. Inside we found a communion of river folk—with the rush of fall, there began an exodus of Northerners heading south in houseboats, yachts and sailboats. Most had New Orleans as their destination, but others would continue to the Gulf of Mexico and eventually island hop in the Caribbean. One fellow, Russell, hailed from my hometown and had spent the past three years constructing his sailboat and was finally on a dream-quest to traverse the Panama Canal and sail to the Pacific Islands.

After the last round we walked out into a thunderstorm. I fell asleep to the sound of rain pelting a watertight vessel.

Soon after we departed from Natchez, we left the state of Mississippi behind, in Louisiana from there on. We were 340 miles from the Gulf of Mexico and moving fast when we passed the Red River coming out of Texas, the last sizable river to empty into the Big Muddy. By now thousands of tributaries had merged to become this deep wide body whose branches reach to within 250 miles of the Atlantic Ocean and 500 miles of the Pacific. The Mississippi, the third largest drainage basin in the world, had grown to full maturity and we glided over water from 31 states.

Like the tree with its branches, the river also has its roots, or distributaries. The Atchafalaya River is the first and largest, exiting just downstream from the Red River. The water that flows into this wide, soggy basin finds its own path to the ocean. This diversion has become the Corps of Engineers most serious challenge; the problem is that the Mississippi wants to move there. Already a quarter of its flow splits off into the Atchafalaya, the steeper and shorter path. The intention of the Corps is to prevent this restless Mississippi from going off in a different direction. If the river were allowed its way, New Orleans, which lies three feet below sea level, would become a slack-water, brackish swamp that would quickly silt in.

Car license plates claim Louisiana the "Sportsman's Paradise." It certainly is a state of diverse beauty and beyond the west bank of the river the flat alluvial plain gives way to the expansive bayous. Bayou comes from "bayuk," the Choctaw word for stream. They are not swamps, but slowly moving bodies of water that teem with wildlife: alligators, crabs, beaver, snakes, crawfish, shrimp, fish, deer, squirrels and coon. Deep in the bayous are remnants of the once royal cypress forest; some trees are said to be over a millennium old, the most ancient living things in the entire Mississippi valley. This region is also home to the Cajun folk.

In 1755 British Canadians rounded up French loyalists living in Acadia, Nova Scotia, and exiled them. They were sailed around the Florida peninsula and into the Gulf of Mexico and after they passed the mouth of the Mississippi River were dumped in the bayous. The British ships then sailed back to Halifax for more Acadians. The British must have assumed the exiled would perish since the environment appeared inhospitable, but in reality the exiles thrived. The Acadians, or Cajuns, built dugouts from the rot-resistant cypress trees and then explored their new home, finding an abundance of food. Today their cuisine is known worldwide in dishes like jambalaya, gumbo and boiled crawfish. As the rest of America grew into the industrial age, this bayou country remained mostly unnoticed and over a couple centuries they have created a unique French dialect that many still speak. With the discovery of oil their isolated culture began to change, but being survivors, they still hold onto much of it, like their foot-stomping Zydeco music.

On the river's east bank are the Tunica Hills. While the French Acadians were living their new found life in the bayous, the British slowly filled the other hilly side with plantations run on legalized slavery. A prominent landmark in the region is the infamous Angola Penitentiary. Walled in behind stone, steel, razor wire and concrete were trapped men; the contrast between their contained reality and ours, freely floating the river, was stark. If I'm ever imprisoned, may it never be on the banks of this river where I can see freedom float right on by without me. Seems like cruel and unusual punishment.

When Gus purchased the sailboat, some very detailed charts were included which he studied as we approached St. Francisville looking for a place to anchor. Bayou Sara looked like the only possibility so we motored into its calm water and a few moments later the motor suddenly went kaput. We both yanked on the pull cord several times but there was no coaxing it; she was dead. Taking to the oars, we managed to paddle the catamaran to shore and tied it off between four large trees. When it was secure, we canoed across the bayou to explore the town.

At the mouth of the bayou was a ferry landing and next to that a small beer shack where a group of men sat in the shade drinking cold ones. We bought them all a beer and then they bought us one and we bought them another. These guys had been living next to Old Big their entire lives and not a one would dare travel out on it in any small boat, especially a canoe. Due to the broken-down motor, we ended up staying in St. Francisville for a week; during that time Gus and I often returned to that shack to share a beer with the locals.

When Pat landed in St. Francisville the year before, he had befriended a man named Benoit and suggested I look him up. While Gus tore the motor apart and cussed its every piece, I headed to town to see if I could find the other guy, whistling while I walked with hands deep in pocket over the crushed seashell road.

The small southern river town was charming, its hub filled with antebellum homes, shops and plantations, the streets lined with live oaks, azaleas, magnolias and pecan trees, all exotic to me. I filled my pockets with the nuts, cracking and snacking along the way. At a general store I asked about Benoit's whereabouts and learned he lived a mile north.

When I found his tar-papered shack, I gave it a knock and Benoit came to the door looking surprised. When I told him I was a friend of Pat's, the fellow who had canoed down the river the previous year, he smiled, and after I explained that I too was on such a journey, he invited me in. Faithful to southern hospitality, he and his wife Kay insisted I stay for dinner, the gumbo ready. We spent the evening on their porch listening to zydeco, drinking wine and indulging in lively conversation.

In the morning after breakfast I walked through the rolling hills back to the catamaran. The sailboat had been interesting enough, Gus, too, but I was feeling the need to move in my own direction again. I still had my canoe and missed it.

Along the way someone stopped to offer me a lift and before dropping me off, the stranger told me about picking pecans for money. My stash was nearly empty so I figured I'd give it a try. That afternoon, bent over like an old man, I combed the forest floor gathering the fallen gems. When my gunnysack was full, I returned to the sailboat, shelled a big pile and made some tasty flat bread, heavy with the meat of the nuts. Over the next few days I returned, filling up several sacks and then went to cash them in at the buyers co-op. It wasn't much, but it paid for food and beer at the shack.

At first light one morning I woke to a light drizzle; intermittent showers came and went but the drizzle never stopped, raining all day and through the night. By noon the next day our tranquil harbor began moving. As the bayou rose it began to seep into the lowlands, picking up all kinds of debris; each hour the driftwood grew bigger and more abundant, all the while the current picking up speed. When we had first anchored, it was like a flat-water lake and we had chosen our landing spot simply because there were a few big trees for tying off. We had paid no attention to the current because there wasn't any; as it fortunately turned out, we had picked the safest spot, in the middle of an inside bend. The faster current was on the opposite shore and with it floated most of the cruising logs.

By late afternoon it was a full-fledged flash flood, entire uprooted trees sweeping right by us, barely missing the sailboat. If one had hit us, it could have easily punctured the hull and snapped our lines, but there was nothing to do but wait it out. It was a sleepless night; every time I started to doze an errant log would bump up against the hull and with each scrape I thought we'd be sent out into the dark midnight river without a motor. The canoes were still tied behind the sailboat, full of water now and tugging violently on their lines. Halfway through the night there was a violent shudder, and

I went up top with a flashlight and noticed one of the canoe lines had snapped. I tried pulling in the taunt line to see which one remained, but the weight of the submerged canoe was too heavy. I was filled with dread, fearing I had lost my canoe so close to the end.

At dawn's first light we scrambled outside to access the scene—Bayou Sara was so full of drifting logs it seemed possible to walk across it. We discovered Gus's canoe had been stolen by the flood; mine was still there, humming on the wet line. He really didn't mind because his sailboat was still in one piece. The clouds parted, the rain ceased and the bayou calmed back down just as quickly as it had erupted. We had survived the deluge and later learned it was Thanksgiving Day.

From upstream came a john-boat. It landed on the point near us and an ancient bearded man hove to shore, debarked, and stretched his creaky limbs. After looking around a bit, he emptied his boat of all his gear and made camp. I watched him pitch his umbrella tent, start a fire, put on a pot, unfold his lawn chair and finally light his pipe. He sat there for an hour smoking, petting his dog and simply gazing at the river. I couldn't resist going over to meet him.

His name was Pat Paterson but he never liked the name so he called himself Clyde. A genuine river rat, this man had spent most of his 77 years cruising about the Mississippi. He'd had several different boats over the years, many crafts taking him around innumerable bends. Employment had always seemed easy enough. Like Alexander, he had worked the tow-boats, put his hand to logging and pulled nets as a commercial fisherman. Now he just camped wherever he pleased, tending to the north in the summer and the south come fall. Wherever he went, he arranged to have his Social Security checks forwarded. For Clyde this was no adventure; it was his chosen lifestyle and the river was his home. He could sit beside it for hours, for days on end; with a big tent, a sack of grub, his boat, dog and pipe he was complete. He told me he had camped there before, out on the point where the bayou and the river met, and he intended on staying again for a while. When I told him about the floods from the night before, he laughed knowingly at the drama.

The old man and I spent Thanksgiving Day walking the forest, pausing often to rest upon the ground and tell each other our tales. He had fled the West Virginia coal mines as a teenager and never looked back. After he bought his first boat, he rowed down the Tennessee River and entered the Mississippi and there he'd remained for 60 years, always following his heart's desire, which seems a wise choice.

At one point he rolled up his pants leg and showed me a patch of his self-cured skin cancer. His treatment was simple: apply liberal amounts of saltpeter directly onto the tender flesh and then light it with a match to cauterize it. "I don't trust doctors. I'd rather treat myself. Living outside is the secret to a long life, and this is where I want to die. I prefer to keel over right here." Today if your grandfather behaved like that, you'd send him to the old folks home, but not Clyde. He was stubbornly independent.

As we rambled about eating fresh pecans, he talked about living off the land: "All you need is a sack of flour, some sugar, a little salt, a rod and a rifle." Clyde led the way as we crossed pastures and thick woods. Moving along at his pace I kept thinking about Thanksgiving; that particular day the holiday didn't seem to have any special meaning. Clyde agreed, "There's only today and any one could be the last."

Meanwhile Gus continued to tinker with the outboard; he completely disassembled the thing and rebuilt it twice, all to no avail. A local fisherman finally solved the problem. A small ten cent ring had cracked and he gave Gus one of his spares, and once reassembled the engine fired right up. He was one happy bloke then, grinning from ear to ear with pride and relief. Ready to continue his journey, he placed a call to his pal Don, who was now ready to rejoin him and planned on leaving the following day for St. Francisville. At that point I knew I would continue alone.

I walked to Benoit and Kay's to bid them farewell and just as I arrived they were heading out the door for a party at a friend's. Lori had been born and raised on the former plantation and all his kinfolk had either died or moved off, leaving him now to maintain the estate alone. The house was a typical antebellum, white-columned mansion, the driveway lined with 200-year-old weighty oaks. Antique furniture on the inside dated back to the early 1800s. Hand-woven tapestries, hand-blown crystal chandeliers, hand-painted family portraits all made me feel like I had entered a museum. After dinner a powerful thunderstorm unleashed itself upon us and we gathered around the lit fireplace to listen to the torrential rains. When a lightening bolt knocked out the electricity, someone went for candles and placed them around the room. The eerie scenario was perfect for telling ghost stories, branches scratching the windowpanes. One of the storytellers, a teacher from New Orleans named Charlotte, gave me her phone number.

Benoit suggested that I canoe down Bayou Sara before resuming my Mississippi journey, offering to deliver me and my canoe 30 miles upstream. "An easy two-day float," he said. Yes, I thought, that would be an appropriate way to reenter the river after a week of landlubbing. He drove me back to the catamaran, and after gathering my belongings, I extended my sincerest thanks to Gus. Benoit dropped me off beside a bridge over the small stream and I was alone again.

STONED
Paimusk to Swamp Lake

To Hudson Bay

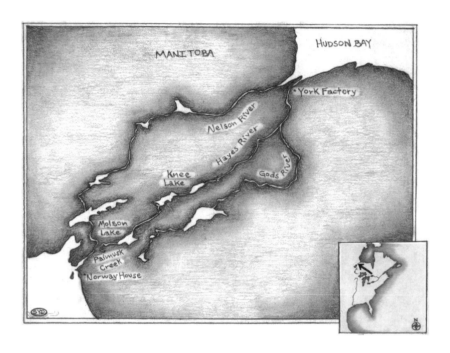

MANITOBA

HUDSON BAY

•York Factory

Nelson River

Hayes River

Gods River

Knee
Lake

Molson
Lake

Paimusk
Creek
•Norway House

N

Jerry, true to his word, was outside the hotel in the morning waiting to transport us to a tributary of the Hayes River. Herb and I were ready, having the night before repacked all our new food stuffs for the last leg of the trip. Our packs were heavier than when we'd first started. We hoisted them into his truck and left Norway House, bumping along a rough road, and then he deposited us at the source of little Paimusk Creek. It was a welcome change to be off the big windy waters and on a stream. We meandered through its crystalline peace all day, passing through large grassy swamps and steep pink granite cliffs. Colonies of black and green lichens painted the rock beside tufts of bonsai jack pine. You could feel the slightest interruption in all that silence; the beating wings of a startled bird felt like the pulse of my own heart, a slight breeze passing through pine boughs like my own sigh.

Towards the end of the Paimusk we stopped to photograph a series of unusual pictographs. At one end of the cliff was a collection of old, faded symbols, very similar to the ones we had seen in the Boundary Waters. On the far end, however, were some very fresh additions: someone had spray-painted a bright red warrior canoe surrounded by mythic symbols onto the wall. A debate on art and culture ensued. Herb questioned why the contemporary natives shouldn't continue the tradition and paint their own work. Who are we to say that the old symbols are magnificent, even sacred, but the new ones are just graffiti?

It felt incongruous to me. The original artist's work seemed cabalistic and surrounded in some mysterious language, a genuine attempt to touch the divine. The contemporary works were like cheap forgeries without much creative juice, and not at all original. At the very least, the modern artists should find their own cliff on which to express their personal existential anguish and leave the integrity of the original ochre tones that have withstood time.

A little further down the river was a large treeless outcrop covered in various shades of lichen where the locals came to leave a different mark; scraping away the very slow-growing lichens, exposing the naked granite underneath, they scratched their names and proclamations of love. It's clear we ephemeral beings feel a need to leave some reminder behind, a lasting footprint, a defining signature that states, "We were here." For me the truth is that more glaciers will come along one day to assure us, "We're just passing through."

The Paimusk empties into beautiful Molson Lake, its waters clean as any I'd seen, cold and sweet to drink, the underwater visibility exceptional. Along the way we came across a fly-in fishing resort, where the clients had just returned with the local guides and were now drinking cold beers. Not at all shy, I asked the owner if we could buy two. "No," he said. "It's illegal to sell alcohol here, but I'd be happy to give you some." He informed us there was a Cree guide working at the camp who had once paddled the Hayes River and we were invited to dinner to meet him. Later when we pulled out our maps, the guide pointed out two valuable shortcuts, as well as some warnings about a couple of particular rapids. It took him three weeks to make York factory, and he did it with a party of 14 teenagers!

Placid water, another ripple-free mirror with a descending moon, everything silent except the sound of rhythmic paddles leaving whirlpools of our force. Halfway to the Hayes came dawn with its awakening birds, a riot of sound and color. We left the moon and Molson behind, entering the first reaches of the river as the sun peeked out, a nice slow current leading us through more high rock bluffs and grassy bends. We portaged around a six-foot waterfall and enjoyed a few small rapids, just enough to get the adrenalin flowing, and then purchased the night on Robinson Lake.

With the sea not that far off, we discussed the completion of our journey, prompting a variety of feelings. This was such an amazing lifestyle: canoeing along from one liquid gem to another all summer long, free and outside. Often I felt as if I could simply go on forever, but it was a lot of work with many discomforts, and so the thought of finishing was not unwelcome. During our fire-ring chat a strong gusty wind appeared from the west, turning the tranquil lake into a blanket of whitecaps. Nature, like us, was stirred.

Dreams of joining the circus. It's good practice to "talk your dreams" after awakening and Herb was always a good ear. We both chortled to the far side of Robinson, the waning moon over our shoulders, as I related the thrill of running away from home with the Fat Lady. More glassy waters made it an easy paddle; cattails arched perfectly, bending down to the lake surface and gracefully touching their own tips.

Our humor diminished at the end of the lake where the river dropped into a series of unnavigable cascades. A nearly two-mile portage awaited. The trail was well marked, leading around a waterfall that we never got to see. All along the path were scattered remnants of an old narrow gauge railway: heavy iron rails, steel wheels, cables, nuts and bolts. During the height of fur trading in this area the merchants used York boats instead of canoes; compared to paddling, these barks were rowed or sailed and could carry more cargo. The Hudson Bay Company constructed railways to portage them for they were bulky and too heavy to carry. Unfortunately, none of this technology was going to help us and we trudged through the muddy path tormented by mosquitoes. Three trips and four and a half miles later we splashed into Logan Lake to refresh. Out in the middle of the water four otters swam with us, diving under the canoe, appearing on one side and then the other.

Beyond Opeminegoka Lake, the Hayes ran through a series of swift rapids with twisted names like Hahasew, Seesep, and Wipanipanis. We didn't feel confident to run any of them. There were no visible portages to be found, and the river banks were a tangle of brush, so lining the canoe was impossible. Instead we stripped down to our skivvies, put on our boots, got right into the water and slowly walked through along the edge of the river, hanging onto the gunwales. Carefully, we went from one tenuous foothold to the next, clutching onto branches when we could, always nervous as thousands of gallons of water spilled around us. Thankfully it was a hot day; the water was cool but the sun quickly dried us off and warmed us between our wades. There was a portage at Wipanipanis Falls, the only one we found that day. Presumably other parties did indeed shoot the rapids, but we chose caution, for if we had run them and spilled it would have been a disaster.

Our reward for the tension-filled day was a deluxe campsite on big Oxford Lake: a soft bed in the grass, a view of 50-foot sheer cliffs painted by the sunset, a small crackling fire, floating islands on the horizon. The far side of the lake was 30 miles away, the distance a canoe can travel in a day. We could see tomorrow's shore.

At the end of Oxford Lake is the village of Oxford House. As we skirted along the shore and passed the first homes, I heard a loud splash near our boat, which I thought was a fish jumping until I saw the trajectory of a thrown rock coming straight for the canoe, and then came another and another. Hiding in the bushes was a group of kids attempting to stone us. They never did connect, but came close enough several times. We tried to outdistance them, paddling fast, but they scrambled along the shore behind us and continued tossing more ammunition. They eventually gave up when we neared the village proper and the episode left me wary about even entering the town. Feeling unwelcome, we walked the dusty road to the Hudson Bay store where an older gang was hanging out on the front steps. They seemed bored with nothing better to do than stare at us. At least they cast no stones. I could overhear many of the older folks speaking Cree and wanted to talk to them and hear their stories, but none from that generation would make eye contact. We bought a few items, dropped our mail and left.

The mists were slowly lifting and ever so carefully we entered more rapids, wading through the first few. Another section seemed easy enough so we tried our skill, aiming for the deep water troughs. We practiced our draw strokes and brace techniques in the slower pools. What was certain: the barge of a plastic boat was not meant for whitewater, being cumbersome and slow to turn. The fast river carried us into more playful waters. We couldn't see how far the rapids ran, but we figured if it got too dangerous we could back-paddle to shore. The river carved through the hills and curved around a cliff and suddenly before us was a big ledge drop followed by a three-foot standing wave. There was no reversing—we plunged over the edge and straight into the wave, the mighty river washing over our spray skirts. We were feeling more competent, but the fear and anxiety never left.

After a long gentle section we approached what our maps referred to as Knife Rapids, the very name frightening us, and without discussion we prepared for our walk in the water. I got out of the canoe and stumbled onto an old overgrown portage. By then we were smart enough to know we should take it. It was a mile of muddy Hell: slippery, swarming with mosquitoes, impossibly tangled in brush and mined with sphagnum moss islands where we post-holed up to our knees. We suffered the discomforts, for it was better to sweat and bleed on the trail than have our canoe sliced by knives.

From far off we could hear the roar of Trout Falls, a thunderous affair with the Hayes now a large river. We decided to make camp beside it. Before even pitching the tent I went for my fishing rod, put on a floating lure, placed it in the pool below the falls and pulled it through the clear water just to see what kind of action it had. Boom, a bite, the whine of line releasing, a shout to Herb, "Grab the net," and within a few minutes there was a walleye flopping on the rocks, the biggest fish I'd ever caught. Herb ran for his own rod then and immediately caught a huge northern that he tossed back. The walleye would feed us both.

That night the constant din of white noise kept me from sleep. When we'd arrived at Trout Falls, I was taken with the idea of sleeping beside its tremendous force, but after a few hours of tossing in my bag I realized it had been a mistake, impossible to cancel out the loud rumbling. Mozart's "C Major #848" mixing with the Rolling Stones "Ruby Tuesday" agitated me all night. It's a romantic thought, sleeping beside a waterfall, but I realized I prefer silence.

In the morning Herb cast for breakfast and instantly caught another northern. We fried it up and savored every morsel. Next to the waterfall someone had constructed a long stick ladder connecting the lower pool to the upper side of the falls. We figured its purpose was to help skid boats up around the falls. While we were eating breakfast, a motorboat appeared from downstream and five Cree men jumped out and began dragging their launch over the ladder. I suggested we help so we pushed from behind with the others. All the while I talked away, bragging about the fish we'd caught, and everyone in the party nodded their heads quite impressed. As soon as we got the boat to the upside of the falls, the one young Cree in the group turned to me and said with a smile that none of the others spoke English. They shoved the boat into the river, fired up the outboard and plowed expertly up through the rapids, laughing all the way. The situation impressed me in two ways: one, we had now paddled far enough into the wilderness to be among non-English speakers; two, they could negotiate those same rapids with a motorboat.

Beyond Trout Falls the Hayes fed into one of our last lakes, Knee. As we ate our lunch on a rock, two speedboats went zooming by. According to our maps this lake was devoid of humans so we were a little surprised. Granted, we had met the party earlier that morning, but we thought that was simply a rare encounter of people going between places. We got back in the canoe, paddled around a point and then saw two float planes tied to a long dock. The closer we got the clearer it became that something was going on. The place was full of workers.

An older gentleman greeted us at the dock. He owned a dozen fishing resorts scattered across high Canada and this was his latest project. They had just recently broken ground and people were hustling everywhere: some were busy clearing land for the future airstrip, others were grooming the lodge grounds, another group was already stirring cement for the footings, while motorboats hauled sand from a nearby beach for the mortar mixes. A separate team was there just to cook for everybody else and we were invited to dine with the crew.

Tommy was the foreman, the person really in charge. He had lived in the Canadian bush all of his life, from the British Columbia Rocky Mountains to high Yukon tundra, from extreme northern Ontario to the Arctic. He was the resourceful jack-of-all-trades who could do anything from fix a bulldozer to build a log cabin, dig a well to fly a plane. Certainly he could build a lodge out of the wilderness. He was one of the most intense men I've ever met, a non-stop enthusiast and gifted talker.

After dinner he took Herb and me on a tour. While strolling along he pulled from his pocket a special smoke, lit it up, and passed it around.

Holy tree tops! I felt good, stoned, wandering around the woods and listening to bush tales.

When we returned to our tent, we found a black bear trying to rip open one of our food packs. We chased it away with our fiercest growls and a loud drumming of pots and pans. That was close: every calorie in that pack was needed if we were to reach the ocean, for there were no more stores. Throughout our journey the only time we ever saw bears was near established campsites or villages. Smart creatures, they know where the bacon is. In the few short months since the project's inception, the bears had already established themselves as residents.

We were served fish and fried potatoes for breakfast. Afterwards Tommy pulled us aside for one more of his rolled strolls, one more fascinating monolog and away we flew with the warm breeze. It was a fine send-off. He had told us about some pictographs further up Knee Lake that were in excellent condition: deer, a few men, a moose and what appeared to be a ladder. The lake was full of splendid paradisiacal islands, one named Magnetite, and passing it our compass went wild. Near the end we found our own island for the night. Herb decided to wet his line and one cast later we had another walleye.

Our island had a pair of nesting bald eagles. We watched them take turns flying away and returning with twigs in their beaks which were woven methodically into a large basket on the top of an old spruce. With their six-foot wingspans the eagles were magnificent, soaring over us and casting shadows, their cries piercing the silence and reminding us who was really in possession of the island. Just before sunset one of them leapt from the perch, hesitated a moment in midair and dove into the lake to pluck out a quivering fish.

For the past couple of months Herb and I had paddled through close to a hundred lakes. The next day, after so many, we finally traversed the last, Swampy Lake; beyond it was all uninterrupted river to the sea. Halfway down its shore I spotted a timber wolf running along a small beach. When it noticed us it froze, then sniffed the air; sensing we were harmless, it resumed its trot and dashed into the bush. It seemed an auspicious omen, so I tossed a pinch of tobacco into the water.

OUTAOUAIS
Mattawa to Montréal

To the St. Lawrence Seaway

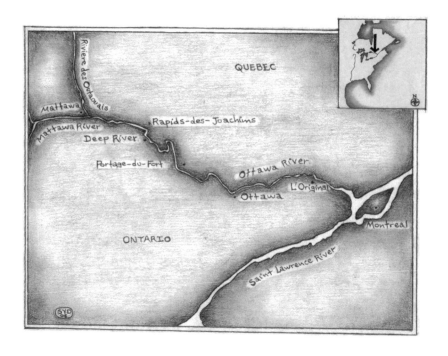

When Paula and I left the Mattawa River and entered the Ottawa River, we were carried into a pair of splendid days. Paddling was easy as warm breezes pushed our kayaks down a fast and sunny river with dramatic scenery and no portages. Québec was now on our left, its Laurentian Mountains topped with lush pines. Ontario was still on our right to the south, and its gentler hills showed maples giving way to fall. We never saw any other humans but the wildlife was abundant— herons and beavers, deer and chickadees, eagle, fish and fox. The music was sweet, too; winds whistled in our ears and sang in the trees, birds volleyed notes from the banks and Paula's voice filled the empty spaces. Food was delicious and plentiful and wild fruit went into everything we ate. That first day ended with an empty beach at the mouth of Ruisseau Creek, where we climbed up into a waterfall and showered under the pummeling force.

On the second day there was no wind, just a quiet peace balancing over the river on the fragile surface between deep sky and deep water. We paddled an easy 30 miles, wending our way through summer's climax. During a break I dove into the river and tried swimming against its current, all I could do to keep apace with the mighty flow. Late in the afternoon we zigged over to Chute Hanna on the Québec side, hoping for a sandbar big enough for our tent, but all we found was a low stream surrounded by steep banks. We zagged a mile over to the Ontario side looking for some flat clearing in the wall of brush. Nothing. Then my keen eyes noticed an opening, a hole in the forest on the opposite shore, so we zigged another mile back over to Québec and found treasure, a flat ledge covered in old growth pine. The floor was padded with a woven needle carpet and the tall trees shaded our tanned bodies. The aromatic resins coming from our twig fire smelled sweet, that first sip of tea after another swim tasted sensual. While pitching in the pine, we felt an absolute unity between ourselves and everything surrounding us. We were the circle. Life itself was sufficient—healthy, free, outside and in wild country.

At Rapids des Joachims are two dams, the first a control structure that backs up the river and the other an electrical generating station. Between them is an island which contains a small hamlet. Our plan was to portage at the control dam because it seemed shorter and less obstructed. As we neared the hopeful path, we instead found a huge billboard: NO PORTAGING ALLOWED. The fine print advised us that the only portage was four miles downstream near the generators. An hour later we spotted another billboard: CANOE PORTAGE LANDING. The designated path, in reality, was a two-mile hike through town, for us, six dusty miles.

We decided to first go into town and solicit help, maybe find a friendly vehicle, and as we entered the quiet village a truck passed and the driver waved. When we waved back, he slowed down and pulled beside us. Since we were on the Québec side, Paula greeted the young man, "Bon jour." Between them it was understood we wished for help in portaging around the dam, preferably early the next morning, and we'd be happy to pay. With no hesitation he agreed to meet us at the landing at 8:00 a.m.

With the easy good news we had the afternoon free, time enough for a stroll through historic Rapids des Joachims. This place was another important outpost during the fur-trading era, strategically located on a portage around a once mighty waterfall which the new dams have since buried. There are several interesting buildings: a mission church, the Hudson Bay warehouse, and an old hotel, The Rapid Inn. Our throats were dry and we ended up spending the rest of the afternoon with the locals; by the time we stumbled out it was turning dark. We found ourselves zigzagging again, this time looking for our camp along some night road. When we finally arrived, we managed to raise the tent and tip in.

As it turned out, our shuttle's chauffeur was the local game warden. If he hadn't told us, we wouldn't have known since he wore no uniform, had no badge and carried no weapon. I remembered a different game warden we met back in Neyes Provincial Park in Ontario, who was outfitted with an impeccably pressed uniform, shiny boots, a polished pistol, a brand new 4x4 truck pulling a new trailer loaded with a slick all-terrain vehicle. When I told this fellow he chuckled, explaining that in Québec the coffers were pretty slim. This amicable French Canadian struck me as a true civil servant; obviously he liked to help people, including the odd kayaker. He drove us to the downstream side of the island and the dam and when I offered him some cash for gas, he just shook his head no. In simple English he said, "You enjoy your trip. Buy yourselves please a hot lunch in Deep River."

The water next to shore was slack, but around the corner by the hydro-electric station was a boiling froth streaming out of the discharge chutes. We launched with trepidation and approached the visible eddy line that separated the calm from the turbulent. We both hesitated a moment before nosing into the swift waters, Paula going first. One moment she was beside me and the next she was two blocks away, the current propelling her into the middle of the river like a shooting star. Gingerly I followed, the mighty sweep of current making me feel powerless as it tossed me around a bend. There was no use fighting it; I stayed low and paddled with it, bobbing about in the flush. In moments I was beside Paula again, the two of us laughing nervously.

Just beyond the hydro-electric dam we passed a nuclear power station, its corrugated tin buildings looking abandoned. I couldn't help but compare these two different approaches to power. Rushing with the whitewater chase below the hydro-electric dam had been very scary and could have easily done us in, but the power was something we could personally battle in our trusty boats. These nuclear plants silently deceive us.

Trying to keep our distance, we hugged the opposite shore and just beyond the hot-pot we stumbled onto something new: a log boom. This mile-long floating chain stretched across the entire river, too big to simply ram over. Instead, we each got out of our kayaks and onto one of the slimy trunks. Keeping our balance against the boat, we were able to nudge them over to the other side one at a time. Fifteen minutes later we were halted by a second boom which held back a forest full of logs waiting for the mill. Seeing no way through that tangle, we were forced back upstream towards the nuclear plant and back over the first boom. Reluctantly, we followed it to shore and finally found a maintained boat passage. None of this was marked on our maps.

The town of Deep River on the Ontario side was quite different from Québec's Rapids des Joachims. The French town felt historically old and funky; in contrast, Deep River was brand new and meticulously clean. More than 2000 government employees resided there servicing the nuclear power plant upstream and, even more importantly, the Chalk River Nuclear Research Center a few miles further downstream. Fusion research, spent nuclear rod disposal and exportation of juice to the U.S. were all integral to its economy.

By the time we finished our rounds about town it was getting late, so we headed across the river to a long sunlit beach and made camp. Upstream the texture of the smooth water started turning white; a big thunderhead loomed above and its advance winds whipped down onto the water. The waves grew fast and we watched them sweeping towards us. The first gust that hit lifted our tent off the beach, and as it hovered on the verge of flying away I dove for it, Paula right behind me. She quickly unzipped the door and we both dashed inside.

The storm unleashed its tremendous power; heavy rain and cracking flashes filled the sky. Anchored safely to the beach, we held down. The best power—natural electricity—better than hydro, better than nuclear. And then the wind stopped blowing, the rain ceased, the lightening fizzled out. I looked out the window and saw a flock of Canadian geese following the storm, pointing to the half moon.

Much too slowly, we passed the White Chalk Nuclear Research Center. A large billboard sign fastened to the high wire fence read NO PICTURE TAKING. Behind it several buildings surrounded a small reactor, and appropriately downstream and adjacent to the facility was a Canadian Forces base. We escaped the meltdown only to enter a military training camp—rifles popped off from the nearby woods and helicopters drummed the silence.

Past Ouiseau Rock the river turned south away from the Laurentian Mountains and into an area filled with cabins. We disembarked at the site of old Fort William and sat on the shady porch of an inn, sipping cold soda and conversing with the locals. I asked them about some upcoming rapids and whether we could run them or not. According to those local shade lovers, the river was easy enough and each knew someone who had gone through. The information still seemed suspect.

It was a hot day and leaving that porch was not easy. We finally headed downstream and encountered another web of old, rotten log booms that extended as far as we could see. Gently pulling ourselves out of the cockpits again, we straddled one slippery wild bronco and slid the kayaks over the link. A few hundred yards later there was another one. Then another. Somewhere in the labyrinth was a boat passage but damned if we could find it.

When we encountered open water again, we moved fast. Near the head of Chute de Culbute we found a fine rock camp and resting after an exhausting day studied the maps. There were no more nuclear power plants for a while, nor any battle fields. All that awaited now was tumbling rapids.

Chute de Culbute was indeed whitewater vicious, the first section beyond our abilities. We anxiously searched the shore for a portage, but found nothing. It was lined with thick brush and portaging was horrible. We forced our way through the thicket, dragging the boats over boulders and under deadfalls, slashed constantly, back and forth three times until we had everything moved to the bottom. We entered the fast river again but our ride didn't last long. Another stretch of water rapidly tumbling over sharp rocks was just around the bend and to get around that jag we portaged through the remains of an old logging sluice.

Here in the late 1800s, men dynamited out a channel to bypass the violent river. Once they cleared the rock channel, they lined it with timber to create a smooth chute to help float all those virgin pines through. Now, all that remains of the sluice are old rotted wood planks and big steel spikes that stick out like dull knives. Halfway through this sluice we encountered a 10-foot-high logjam sealing off the canyon. Up and over we crawled; we were fortunate because the water was relatively low and, since it hadn't rained in a while, the logs were dry. If they had been wet, the moss covering them would turn greasy and leg-breaking slippery. One could easily become impaled on one of the rusty nails. Avoiding them was like an exercise in Tai Chi.

After those two stressful walks we were regaled with Chapeau, a cute French village. The silvery steeple of the Catholic church rose above the wood-framed homes, all roofed in the same tin. On the outskirts of town we noticed a few surviving homestead log cabins. Many fur traders had retired here in the eighteenth century, exchanging the paddle for the plow. We couldn't resist a stroll through its quiet streets; it felt like a place this voyageur could retire.

Past Chapeau the shore became even more populated and we understood the wilds were now gone. The first European settlements in Canada were all downstream from there and along our route. Ottawa City was very close; Montréal follows that and then the city of Québec. Finding a camp site was a challenge. There were still scattered woods of oak, maple and pine, but most were privately owned. On a small island in the shadow of someone's grove, we hid a September night away.

Île du Grand Calumet is a large island that splits the Ottawa River in two. On one side is a long reservoir created by another hydro-dam and on the other is the main free-flowing channel which cascades through world-renowned rapids. Paula and I considered the obvious options: we could take the calm lake paddle and hope for an easy portage around the dam, or we could paddle the river and portage the rapids. A local man in the village of La Passe suggested a third option.

At the bottom of the 15-mile rapid section, near the end of Île du Grand Calumet, was a whitewater rafting company. He told us that every morning they delivered a bus load of tourists off at the head, just downstream from where we were, and then they all rode in rubber rafts through the rapids with guides. They always had an empty bus going back to their resort. We might be able to buy two tickets for the thrilling ride and at the same time have them shuttle our kayaks through.

We rang them up and after a little convincing made an agreement with the manager: for $80 each we could raft down and they would transport our gear. All we had to do was meet them at the designated spot in the morning. And what luck; it just so happened to be their last run of the season.

The bus arrived promptly at 8:00 a.m. and after loading our kayaks and forking out the dough, we were assigned seats in one of the five patched rubber tubs. As we shoved off, our personal guide explained the basics of river rafting. The trick was to move faster than the current in order to have some control over your direction. The rafts were awkward things, but he assured us that just a little forward motion made all the difference. He also coached us briefly on the rescue procedure; if you happen to go overboard, just raise your feet up and point them downstream. We were all told to just relax, go with the current, and someone would come pluck us out.

The swift current carried the flotilla down to the first rapids at McCoy Chute and all but one of the rafts paddled over to a beach to wait their turn. We got out and walked down the shore a little way to watch as the leaders went through. At the chute, the river choked into a bottleneck and then dropped suddenly into the base of a 10-foot standing wave. I couldn't imagine how anyone could navigate that without getting thoroughly drenched. The raft slowly approached the lip and then, as they teetered on the edge, the shout to paddle like hell was heard. I found myself tensing just to watch. The crew did paddle frantically and they easily rode up and over the wave without a hitch.

A second raft shoved off and approached the hole a little closer to shore. It dipped down and as it began to ascend the wave the front end was jerked up, catapulting three paddlers directly into the drink. I noticed that my assigned seat was in the same location in the bow as those who were now swimming. The boat seemed to lose momentum and stalled halfway up the wave, stuck between the awesome current and gravity. I assumed it was going to tip over backwards, but, slowly, paddling hard, they gained the crest. Once they were over, the guide steered to the ejected party and picked them out, one by one, like a crane. In the background I could hear our guide snickering.

Our turn came next. As we neared the plunging moment, I could smell nervous sweat in the air. We dug in, shot down the tongue and then smacked into the huge wave, which was much more frightening seen at eye-level. We all got a good shower from the spray but managed to surf the raft over. The remaining parties took their turns and then we all continued down together, splashing our way through a series of milder rapids, stopping often to swim. It was a slick way to get through the most dangerous stretch of the Ottawa River.

On Labor Day morning, we headed out over a large reservoir and the acrid smell of a pulp mill coated our nostrils all morning. By the time we finally outdistanced the stench, we came upon the old Québec town of Portage du Fort beside another big dam. In the days of yore canoeists had a long portage here, eight miles around intense rapids that dropped 70 feet in elevation. All that whitewater is now pacified and our walk was an easy hop around the wall.

Downstream we had a joyride, weaving through narrow channels that traced a series of small islands. The current was snappy but the thrill was short as we dumped into Lac du Chat. Halfway to its containing dam we came upon another boom, thousands upon thousands of logs trapped behind it. Along the shoreline scattered trunks lay half-submerged, wasted and slowly rotting away, and cabins occupied every lot.

We camped on the one vacant spot we could find, a narrow beach surrounded by swamp. Fortunately there were no longer any mosquitoes, and crawling into the thicket we disappeared from public view. A nearby highway hummed with the traffic of families returning home after holiday. Summer was over.

An older couple sitting on their deck saw us coming down Lac du Chat and waved us in, offering cold drinks. John and Joan were water people. They lived across the river in Arnprior, but since retiring they preferred hanging out in their cabin that had no phone, no electricity, an outhouse and plenty of solitude. Tied to their dock was a handsome sailboat John had built. Strong headwinds began brewing when they offered us hot lunch; that led to dinner and a campsite on their fairway lawn.

In the morning we headed to the Fitroy Dam, four miles of rapids drowned behind its concrete. Once we reached the rocky revetment above it, we tossed our gear out and prepared for the hop-shuttle. Just as soon as we shouldered our first heavy loads, a retired couple from Fitroy drove up in a truck and I asked them if they knew where the quickest path back to the river was. They knew all right, placing all our gear in the bed of the vehicle and delivering us personally. We were liking these retired folks.

Paula had a cousin who lived in Alymer, just outside the city of Ottawa; when we arrived at the marina, we called her and an hour later she arrived by car. As soon as I met her, I liked her: funny, exuberant and thoughtful. She insisted we spend a couple of days and had the menu all planned. There was no argument. Her husband Jim was waiting for us beside the pool with a full cooler.

Bonnie and Paula are both passionate chefs. They worked together in the kitchen and prepared glazed duck with wild rice and an almond spinach salad with maple Dijon dressing, all the ingredients local. During seconds I noticed how happy Paula was. She wore that most comfortable glow as she chatted away with Bonnie, sharing cooking secrets and family recipes.

Jim and I had our own conversation, about parenting mostly. He insisted that our folks did the best job they could given their own upbringing, in their own unique times with their own resources; armed with both personal gifts and baggage, they reared us the way they believed was correct. Whether right or wrong was not important. It was wiser to put it all in perspective and listen to your own voice, let go of the resentments and be tolerant, become your own person, forgive and flow forward. It all seemed pretty sensible to me by sunrise. In just one evening we had figured most everything out.

Jim offered to portage our boats by car from Alymer to Hull, bypassing Chaderie Falls, some serious rapids and most of Ottawa City. With a couple of two-by-fours and a coil of rope we fashioned a rack for the kayaks, which were longer than the car. Once everything was lashed down, it made a curious upside-down catamaran on wheels.

Paula and I crossed over the river to downtown Ottawa and then walked through the capital of Canada. It was a quick visit because the longer one wanders as a nomad the less attractive cities become. The water in Rideau Canal was dirty; Parliament stones were blackened by years of auto exhaust and the shores were littered with trash.

We camped on a small beach in the Petrie Islands. Autumn was extending her fingers: sumacs were on fire, flowers were turning to seed, dry north winds cooled down the night. Sipping my evening tea beside the river, I felt content. We were nearing the end of the Ottawa River and would soon be on the St. Lawrence Seaway, our last stretch to the sea. There were more cities awaiting us, more crowded shores, more unpredictable waters and weather, but it never matters at the end of the day; the only preoccupation was where to find another log.

The wind was at our backs and fog drifted across the water. The fast and wide river felt familiar; it could have been somewhere along the Mississippi. The privately-owned shores were equally populated. Industry mixed with farmlands, cow manure and oil refineries perfuming the air, and swamps fringed the lowlands. Scattered in the reeds were many duck blinds, a reminder that hunting season was coming soon. It was never quiet; a highway's drone mixed with the chirp of crickets, long trains rumbled distantly. And like the Mississippi, the towns felt old, the streets cobbled and the homes made of stone, brick and beam.

The marshy shore thickened, making everything soggy muck and camping nonexistent. We passed an island midstream that had a park-like forest thinned by a herd of grazing cows, the best place seen all day. We landed and while pulling out our equipment, an ATV approached and two young farmer's daughters dismounted and informed us in French that we were on private property. We did our best to explain our journey and asked if we could camp just one night. They drove back to their house to ask father for permission. Paula and I were stuck; neither of us wanted to move, so we waited. A half-hour later the vehicle returned, but this time with dad. Kindly, in his broken English, he gave us formal permission to camp on his island, but he warned us his herd wandered the pasture at night and so we best beware. Taking our chances, we pitched the tent far from the their well-worn paths. Between all their stomping and dung dropping, though, I didn't sleep well.

Halfway through the next day we left the swamps. To our left was Montebello and a ridge of green hills, the banks lined with million-dollar homes that sprawled around old farmsteads. The day had started windy but soon it died and the water calmed, one of only four perfectly glassy days all summer. The skies were clear and the tranquil river moved quickly, carrying us 30 miles downstream.

Just past the town of L'Original we came upon a private campground packed with RVs. We were both ready to quit so we struck shore. These folks didn't travel in their campers; no, they parked them permanently on tiny waterfront slips—the new working-class cabin. Each postage stamp lot was meticulously groomed. It seemed there was a tacit agreement among them: they all had to decorate their yards with flamingoes, twirling daisies, statues of little fishermen, and since it was cool, not let their dogs go without a hand-knit sweater. I was impressed because everyone obeyed the covenant. There were a few empty sites for stragglers so we happily moved in. Once set, a neighbor brought us a pot of coffee and invited us to the evening bonfire. Even though we were still in Ontario, everyone spoke French. Paula's Québécois was improving with every encounter, and we had a wonderful evening with the circle, telling our story as best we could.

In the morning we went strolling through L'Original. Everything felt French: the signs, the mansard roofs, the people's faces and their melodic language. I regretted not having studied the language more. At the local café I did at least understand "crêpes avec sirop d'érable," pancakes with maple syrup.

As we decamped, two of our neighbors presented us with a bon voyage gift, a bag of fresh garden vegetables, and right behind them came another couple with some warm brownies. We were touched by their thoughtfulness and as we were thanking them another couple showed up with yet another gift, four acrylic hand-crocheted, neon-colored butterflies. We couldn't help but hug and kiss them all. Several more campers, curious about all the hugging, came over and by the time we launched the boats, our largest send-off party ever had assembled. The sky was clear and blue, sun glittering off the water and a few tears. Our friends all took turns shouting "Take care" in English and waving us on.

We sailed with the wind. By noon it was blowing so hard that we reached our top speed of six miles an hour and covered over 30 miles while surging ahead in following seas. Entering Parc Carillon, we crossed the provincial border and left Ontario for Québec. We landed at the park to register for a campsite but found the office locked up. In fact, there was nobody anywhere. Assuming it was closed for the season, we chose the deluxe site at the far end, right next to the river, our view out over another large reservoir. Four miles away we could make out the last dam on the Ottawa River. According to the map there was a lock there. Even though it was now off-season, the water was still warm enough for a good swim; sitting naked on the shore we massaged each other's sore muscles.

The map had been correct; there was a lock at the dam. We were glad because for once we didn't have to portage. Right after we pulled the service cord to alert the lockmaster, six uniformed Canadian Park Service personnel appeared to make sure we had a smooth and pleasant experience. The senior park employee gave us a lecture on lock procedure and safety. When he finally took a breath, the other employees all fell into position. We returned to our boats and when the gates opened a man with a headset directed us inside the chamber. Along the wall was a floating catwalk and our designated guide stood there waiting, her job to help us descend. We lashed our boats to the catwalk, the signal was given, and the chamber began to empty. All six employees watched us dutifully to make sure we were safe. On the way down, our chaperon exchanged a few phrases in French with Paula; eventually I dared a response in Spanish. She smiled, apparently understanding that language: an Albertan, a Québécoise and a Minnesotan bounced French, English and Spanish off the slimy cement walls until the gates reopened.

On the Mississippi I had locked through 27 dams, none of which compared to that experience. On the Big Mighty, after the gates were opened and you were allowed to enter, one employee threw you a safety line and then usually you never saw him again. There was little instruction; it was generally assumed that you knew what to do or you wouldn't be there. The gates closed, the chamber emptied, the gates opened and you left. Simple. I found the Canadian experience amusing—it certainly provided more employment and had the added benefit of free language camp.

When the ride was over, we took a jaunt through quaint Carrillon, another remnant colonial French town. Once back on the river, we crossed over to Pointe de la Fortune, having spied a pub inside a marina where we were certain a burger and fries awaited.

With full bellies we left the protective channel, rounded the point and entered Lac des Deux Montagnes, directly into 20-knot headwinds. We fought hard all afternoon to gain forward motion and spent those burgers quickly. I was running on reserves by the time we approached tiny Rita Isle. Our map showed there was a cabin on it; as we neared Montréal the mainland filled with houses and the island seemed our only option. After we tied off at the dock, I lurched around like a thief, checking to see if anyone was home; the lawn was freshly cut but no one was there. Although both uncomfortable with the arrangement, we were exhausted and decided to hide out; if anyone came, we would plead desperation. We only pulled the bare essentials from our kayaks, dinner and a book, and then claimed the far corner of the yard, waiting for dark. The fear of the owner and a nasty dog haunted us all afternoon, but we remained alone. At dawn's first light we disappeared without a trace.

After a quick lunch in a swamp we headed for the town of Oka, hearing the noise from pounding helicopters long before we arrived. Like huge dragonflies, they circled through the sky. A couple of weeks before our arrival, a handful of warriors from First Nation Mohawk had occupied the town's detox center; it seemed they did not want a golf course built on their tribal lands and were willing to defend their treaty rights. The Canadian government considered it trespassing and was equally determined to stand its ground. The two sides had reached an impasse; a Québec provincial policeman and a Mohawk were both dead, and all held their breaths waiting for a solution.

As we neared Oka, I saw a copter parked along the shoreline, next to it two heavily armed soldiers discussing strategy with a couple of worried civilians. A little further down the shore were two manned army tanks on the beach, their turrets aiming toward the detox center; soldiers were crawling through the woods and the town's streets were deserted. Suddenly a green helicopter shot straight toward us; hovering above our heads for a minute, it then buzzed away, evidently unimpressed. We kept our distance just the same. A sailboat passed by; when it appeared to make a deliberate tack towards the village wharf, another helicopter, yellow with Québec Police blazoned on its bottom, zipped right over to intercept it, hovering a few feet above its mast and forcing the boat away with powerful downdrafts.

Outdistancing the standoff, we rounded a bend and entered a different onslaught, 30-knot winds in our face. If there had been any available campsite, we would have taken it, but between the battleground and the populated shore we could find no sanctuary, no place to hide. A marina two miles away offered hope, so we trudged through chalky contaminated waters. Things didn't seem so fun anymore. Two hours later, traveling at a breakneck speed of one mile per hour, we arrived. It was impossible to go further.

Paula had done her undergraduate work in environmental engineering at Magill University in downtown Montréal, and so approaching the city was for her a kind of homecoming. Paula called one of her best friends from then to see if she could save us and Kathleen agreed to come whisk us away to her apartment for the weekend. The only missing detail was where to store the boats.

Arm in arm we walked into the marina office at the Club Nautique. Paula greeted in French the young receptionist and explained how strong winds had stopped us on our long voyage. Would it be possible to leave our kayaks at the marina for the weekend? We'd be happy to pay.

"Non, c'est un club privé. Non," she responded. She continued to present her various arguments for not helping us. I didn't understand much, save "non."

The tide of emotions dashed our spirits again; we felt terribly frustrated as we shuffled outside the office, unsure what to do. Paula cried and I paced. There was no way we were getting back on that tempestuous water; we were unwelcome at the marina, and Kathleen was on her way.

I decided to go back into the office and plead our case again. Alone, I stood before the stubborn woman and begged in English, "I don't think you realize just how desperate we are. The wind is howling, we can't paddle and can't remain here. We're stuck and really need your help. Please, won't you reconsider?" She conceded to at least call her boss and ask permission.

After explaining the situation to him, she handed me the phone. Thankfully he spoke English and I shared our predicament with him. He generously offered us free boat storage for as long as we needed. I thanked him heartily. I went back outside, embraced Paula and shared the good news.

A half hour later Kathleen arrived. Sitting in a car speeding into the city was strange; shopping malls, gray cement apartment complexes, industry, traffic jams and smog all mixed into an absurd smoky image. I remarked aloud how everything can change in a moment. When we arrived at the apartment, Kathleen's boyfriend spun his collection of Stan Rogers records while she offered us wine.

Later Montréal invited us to play. We looked, tasted, listened, inhaled and felt the life in that great city, for two days savoring ethnic cuisine and long strolls with the weekend hordes. Street musicians played, old folks walked poodles, lipsticked hookers solicited and youthful students mixed with Afro-Americans, Pakistanis, Taiwanese, American Indians and all the other gathered children. I kept wondering where all those people came from. Where had they been that summer while we were paddling?

We ambled up to the bluff of Mount Royal and looked out over the St. Lawrence Seaway. After that we descended to the seaway itself and, I admit, the Lachine Rapids frightened me. While having café au lait at some sidewalk bistro, I asked Kathleen if she would car portage us around the city, which would save us a very difficult day of travel. We could be on the downstream side moving easily towards the sea, and she was more than willing.

Back at Club Nautique I dug inside one of our packs, pulled out a couple of the hand-crocheted, neon-colored butterflies and walked into the marina office. The receptionist was there and I presented them to her as a gift, hoping it might soften the edge. She smiled.

We then drove clear across Montréal, in one short car ride skipping over 20 miles of rapids and sprawling city, a compromise we were both happy to make. Near Pointe aux Trembles we found a marina with easy access and I pulled my boat down from the car roof, slipping it halfway into the water. I turned to go for Paula's kayak when an errant wave picked mine up and began to carry it mainstream. Wading into the river to retrieve it, I wasn't sure whether to laugh or be scared. After spending just one weekend in the city, I realized how much I missed my craft; we quickly got reacquainted on a brand new watercourse, the St. Lawrence Seaway.

QUEENS
Baton Rouge to New Orleans

Down the Mississippi

It was a quiet time alone on Bayou Sara. The weather was cool and I was thankful for that—the alligators and snakes would be lethargic. One time I got hung up on a sandbar so I got out to push the canoe; I'm not sure if quicksand is real, but as I stepped into the river, my legs were sucked knee deep. It didn't take long to yank myself back in and I sure never did that again. At night I slept under a bridge during a steady drizzle, staying dry while worrying about flashfloods. When I reached the Mississippi River, Gus had departed. Clyde was still there, and that night I shared his tent, wanting one more moment of his simple visions while sleeping beside his dog Charlie.

After those easy days on the bayou the mighty Mississippi felt overwhelming. I paddled on, staying closer to shore and not taking any risks with New Orleans close at hand. For the past few months my main concern had been survival on the water. I had paddled countless strokes and started many fires, had slept beside the river; I ate, drank, sang, laughed and wept there. Soon it would all end and something else would begin. This river had seeped into my veins and I found it difficult to imagine letting go.

The bottom of the Mississippi drops near Baton Rouge, allowing for the introduction of oceanic ships that come from all over the world to trade in petrochemicals. One of the largest oil refineries in our nation is located just upstream and sprawls out over 2000 acres of prime river frontage, processing crude into gasoline day and night. I kept my distance from the thirsty tankers, hoping none were leaving soon. Instead of a tour of

Louisiana's capital, I opted to move beyond the city and find a safe hole somewhere.

In the hundred river miles between Baton Rouge and New Orleans are endless industrial plants scattered along the shore. Fields of cotton become tank farms and chemical plants, the air fouled with multicolored streaks. In Cancer Alley the camping was unattractive.

The morning breeze stirred early and quickly built into headwinds that made me nervous. Ahead there was one big river loop, and to shave off a few miles I gathered my courage and began crossing the river, cutting inside the bend. When I was out in the middle, I noticed a yacht coming downstream and a ship coming up. My canoe was essentially invisible in the wide river, so I paddled hard to get out of the way of both. The ship was easy to avoid, but as the yacht neared, I noticed it kept shifting direction towards me. I paddled harder but it kept getting closer. Eventually I realized they were trying to track me down so I stopped paddling and waited. The *Chicago Queen* from Lake City, Minnesota, came to an idle beside me.

From the pilot house came a shout, "Where you going?"

It seemed more than obvious: "The Big Easy!"

Another voice chimed in, "Want a lift?"

It was inviting.

"Well, do you want a ride?"

"Sure, yes!"

A rope ladder was unfurled and a line tossed to me. The crew took my gear onboard and I scaled the rope ladder as they hoisted the empty canoe. They were five bikers, and up in the bow were five Harley's strapped down, upright and in position. Pumped for scenes of Easy Rider, the group was also going to Mardi Gras. It had taken them a month to cruise down from Lake Pepin and now they were anxious to make the Crescent City, just a day away. After we introduced ourselves, the captain gunned the engine and away we went. Just like that.

Captain Hank inherited the 50-foot wooden boat from his father, who had used it to give tours on Pepin. Hank wasn't interested in staying in the family business; what he really wanted was to pilot that ship right down to

New Orleans with his buddies and their bikes to party. They amazed me: Stork, Tim, Terry, Glen and, of course, the Captain. All the tattoos, chains, leather and crude talk couldn't disguise their "Minnesota Nice." Everyone on board was flat broke; the last of their change had been spent on fuel, enough to hopefully reach the city. The pantry was down to a couple cups of rice, so I shared what food I had, which didn't last long. The old boat leaked like a sieve and the bilge pump required constant attention, and despite it all no one was worried. To the man they were certain everything would improve once they landed in New Orleans—I could see the river had reached them.

It was enjoyable to sit atop the pilot house. In my canoe I had been so low, but up there the view was grand. Beyond the levee I watched the shore passing: old plantation homes, contemporary tar paper shacks, refineries, swamps and orange trees. We passed ships from Monrovia, Russia, Brazil, and Japan, barges from Pittsburgh, Kansas City and St. Paul. The upstream wind increased and the water became choppy. Captain Hank had the radio on and after listening to the weather report-snowing all over the north we let out a cheer. I took off my shirt to soak up the sun, pleased with the good sense God gave geese. All afternoon and through the night the *Chicago Queen* plowed along.

I was sitting up top when we rounded that last of so many river bends and the skyline of New Orleans appeared. A summer afloat tracing a small stream down, and this my destination at hand. Our plan was to bypass the city center along with the French Quarter and head into the Industrial Canal that connects the Mississippi River with Lake Pontchartrain. Captain Hank figured we could just toss the anchor in some backwater for starters.

We entered the Industrial Canal and slowly approached the locks leading us to Pontchartrain. Not 10 feet away from a cluster of wood pilings, directly in front of the lock gates, the propeller struck a deadhead and was knocked off. Meeting no resistance, the engine whined loudly. Hank realized the prop had sheared off and so cut the engine. That was when I learned the second prop had also recently been lost. With no means to power the huge tub we drifted, waiting for whatever came next.

The lock gates opened and inside was a departing barge; we were directly in its path and the boat's captain began to blow the horn, warning us to move. He kept blowing it while revving the powerful diesel engines, slowly and impatiently advancing, fully capable of crushing us.

Stork lassoed a line around the cluster of piers and when he got a bite we all pulled together, slowly inching the heavy *Chicago Queen* away from harm. The barge passed a few precious feet away and then gave us one more vindictive blast, just for spite. So there we were—barely having survived sinking, powerless, tied off in an illegal spot, and essentially penniless. Welcome to New Orleans.

The city was founded in 1699 by Pierre Lemoyne Sieur d'Iberville. He called his new settlement by the name of the day on which they'd landed there, Mardi Gras, French for "Fat Tuesday," the day before Ash Wednesday, after which for the next 40 days until Easter Catholics repent for their sins. When the first Europeans arrived at this spot, there was nothing but a foot path the natives used as a portage through the surroundings wetlands between Lake Pontchartrain and the Mississippi. The settlers built levees, drained swamps and created their city. With its strategic location at the end of the great river, New Orleans has been fought over since its founding: the Spanish fought the French, the English fought the Americans and the Union fought the Confederacy.

This area quickly became a commercial center, with the first steamboat arriving in 1812. Ten years later it ranked second to New York City as an American seaport and has since then been a lifeline for the United States. Here the exchange between the earth's richest river valley and the rest of the world has taken place for hundreds of years.

I spent the night with the bikers exploring the decadence of the French Quarter: a place American, European, African and Caribbean all at once, where strippers and beggars, street musicians and magicians, artists and tourists were all doing their hustle. In the morning I walked downtown to the office of the *Delta Queen* and filled out a job application, figuring I had enough experience on this river to qualify as a deck hand, and they hired me on the spot. The ship was due back in three days and I was to meet her at the wharf.

I phoned Charlotte, the teacher I'd met in St. Francisville, and she invited me to stay at her house, which sounded much nicer than the *Chicago Queen.* Sitting on her front porch swing, I learned she was a sixth-grade teacher in the inner city. She asked me to be a special guest in her classroom and share my river story, and I gladly accepted. Already I tired of the questions most people asked: how long had it taken, where had I started, what did I want to do next. These youngsters asked the honest questions—didn't you get lonely? weren't you scared? who cooked for you? where did you sleep?

After class Charlotte and I hopped on the trolley and rolled down St. Charles to indulge in the Quarter again; sweet harps, sharp dulcimers, a guitar and fiddle inspired a dance in Jackson Square. We went to her favorite restaurant and indulged in dozens of raw oysters and Jax Beer. I saw how beautiful this new friend was.

I stayed with her for a few more pleasant days, and in that time I managed to retrieve my canoe. Benoit was willing to drive down and store it in case I ever needed it again. Then the *Delta Queen* arrived and for two weeks I worked on the opulent steamer, filling myself with good food and company. We cruised to Natchez and back twice—what a treat to still be a part of the river, only now as a paid traveler.

After tying off in New Orleans I disembarked with a desire to walk the pavement again. When funds became low, I sought another job and got hired as a deck hand on a towboat, the *Spanish Fort*. All we did was shuttle barges of corn up to a grain elevator which then transferred the goods onto ships. Whenever a new ship came in I would wander up to its pilot house and chat with the captain and crew, sailors from around the world. When we returned to the harbor for a shift change after a month, I bailed. Sitting beside the river one more time, I drank a bottle of wine while reflecting on everything I'd experienced since Minnesota. Lake Itasca seemed far away, already belonging to another time. As I sprinkled tobacco over the water, along with a few drops of wine, I felt satisfied. But the journey was far from over.

THE RENT CANOE
Lower Hayes River to York Factory

To Hudson Bay

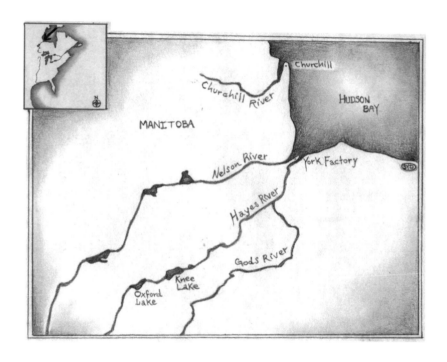

Herb and I entered the lower Hayes River, undoubtedly the most dangerous section of our trip, and camped at the head of the first serious rapids, agreeing a fresh start in the morning was best. After dinner I hopped from one boulder to the next, working my way out to a flat ledge in the middle of the river. I sat down and listened to the churning waters, trying to perceive some message in all the rage. Just below me was an eddy. I felt just like it: clear in my purpose, connected to this place for the moment, but knowing I would soon be released into the surrounding fury, dancing around some very sharp rocks. Hopefully our keen eyes would pick them out, at least most of them.

For the next 20 miles it was essentially all whitewater. Our maps up to that point had been excellent. Their scale provided us with a clear picture of what lay ahead. For some reason no one ever bothered to make such detailed maps for this next leg of our journey, the most rapid-filled section. The best we could find were five times less in scale, a radical difference. On a river cartographers denote rapids with straight bar lines, and our maps for the next few days were littered with them. On these new maps one couldn't really decipher where the rapids truly began nor where they terminated. The best we could do was pause at every bend, survey ahead with binoculars and sensitive ears, and make educated guesses.

Our first day in that frothy place was long and stressful. We were in and out of the canoe all day, sometimes walking the boat through along the shallow shore, other times skillfully paddling our way down. At one point we came to a severe curve in the river created by a flat rocky finger. We got out to line the boat around and halfway through the maneuver I slipped, falling into the river and bashing my leg against a rock. Fortunately Herb held fast to the canoe, because I was swept away. I kept to the surface, raising my legs to avoid any more submerged rocks, and swam safely to shore quite shaken. Herb was a little relieved, too, not particularly happy with the thought of paddling alone. Since our spill at Wheelbarrow Falls, we had dutifully lashed our gear in the boat whenever we entered rapids. The only items we left loose were the spare paddles in case there was a need to grab one in a hurry. When I slipped, my spare fell out. We both watched as the river carried it away, up and over some large standing waves to disappear. The lesson was clear: we had no second chances. That paddle could have just as easily been our canoe.

With tired and frayed nerves we fully appreciated our campsite that night. It was always a relief after all that negotiating, all that guessing, all those surprises, all that hard work to simply pause and watch the river flow by, to look back upstream, up canyon, and know we'd successfully traversed more dangerous waters and arrived safely to be warmed by a fire, a meal and a ceremonial calumet. The camping was superb: whitewater riverside real estate. In such reflective moments I truly felt like I belonged to that place.

Downstream we could see the Brazzy Hills looming, catching the last golden glow of the day. We knew the river passed right through them, cutting its rough path through their foundations. But that would be for tomorrow, for another nervous day.

We came upon three waterfalls that were actually marked on the map, and with a little searching found the portages around each, little used and quite overgrown. The indigenous people were the first to hack them out of the forest and later the voyagers shared them, but only the rare party like us came through now.

The country was spectacular, incredibly wild, uncontrolled, primordial. I had never been so deep into wilderness before. To get to these places you have to work hard, and in spite of all the apprehension we were both feeling a previously unknown excitement. Life had been pared down to the essentials: fast unpredictable water, sleek transportation, adequate clothing, sturdy shelter, nourishing food, friendly fire and uncharted islands for camp. We realized that if we tipped over out there, if our boat was destroyed or went downstream without us, we would have a hellish time getting out. That knowledge lent new drama to the daily prospect of living. Understanding that our survival depended on our skills, on our own actions, was exhilarating: to see the end of day we had to earn it.

The Hayes grew up fast, tranquil in its infancy. Throttling into adolescence it became feisty, riotous and wholly unpredictable, but that too passed quickly. Once we were beyond the Brazzy Hills the river matured to a fast calm with direction and singular purpose: to reach the sea. It traveled between high chalky bluffs and the rocks disappeared, the rapids vanished. What remained of the forest grew thinner the closer we got to the bay. There were bonsai clumps here and there, but mostly the terrain was composed of muskeg swamp. It was lonely, forlorn, desolate land. And there were creatures; we saw tracks in the sandy beaches—deer, bobcat, wolf and moose. I'd been told the polar bears of Hudson Bay have been known to travel as far as 50 miles inland, which would put them just about where we camped.

We, too, felt aged beside the waterway, advancing towards a certain end and already stirred by nostalgia.

In spite of steady headwinds we rode the fast river and covered 40 miles, our best day on record. We camped on the point where the Gods and the Hayes Rivers converged, pitching the tent on the flat dry clay and hoping it wouldn't rain. Where these two rivers join, the Hayes broadens and its volume doubles. Beside the fire with maps in hand, we calculated we had 40 more miles to reach our destination, our salty waters.

Steady ocean breezes blew up the river the next day and I could smell minerals. Despite a valiant effort, we did not gain much. Between Herb's suffering hand and my aching right shoulder we moved slowly. We had hoped it would be our last day, but that is how expectations go, and we rested beside the junction with the Pennycutaway River. The closer we got, the more nervous we became about polar bears, which summer nearby on the bay between York Factory and Churchill. I couldn't forget what I'd read: the only animal on earth that smelling, seeing or hearing a person will pursue it. You.

We could have reached York Factory in one more long day, but decided to delay our arrival, thinking that because of the "bear scare" it would be wisest to camp one more night, and then in the morning, when we were fresh and strong, blast to the end. So our penultimate day was an easy and reflective one; we paused often, swam at every bend, ate the last of our chocolate and camped early.

The river flowed between 50-foot clay bluffs and after dinner we scrambled up to see what was on the other side. All the way to the horizon was endless flat muskeg, a place where you could literally sink out of sight. There were scattered clumps of small trees upon the rim of the bluff. Changing its muddy course, the river constantly eroded away at the banks and eventually these tree islands would become undermined and slide down the steep bank en masse. They lie scattered all along the shore. Our camp was on a gravel peninsula well away from any of them.

Later in the evening, I walked alone along the beach and came upon a sight that chilled me: half-buried was the stern of an aluminum canoe, the boat rent in half by some awesome force. I imagined another party had met some terrible fate further upstream in the violent rapids and the river had carried the wreck here. Who was in that ravaged canoe? What exactly had happened? Did they survive? Later back at camp I told Herb about my discovery. We returned to the sight together and offered up the last of our pipe, for we had been fortunate and were thankful.

After 82 days, 1600 miles, thousands of portage rods, a hundred lakes and untold strokes, we saw it—the ocean. Our pained backs, stiff hands and weary bones felt ecstatic.

The river was slowly moving backwards as the tide flowed in, the wind in our face, which at least meant the polar bears hadn't caught smell of us. Those last miles were strenuous, but by noon we arrived to the old trading post of York Factory, first established in 1684. We pulled up to the dock, tied off and got out of that canoe for the last time.

We ascended the stairway to the top of the bluff and headed for a small white house. Betty opened the door as if she were expecting us. On her table was a batch of cookies fresh from the oven. Her husband Jim appeared through the back door, toting some huge firearm. Neither of them ever left the house without their rifles—the bears were indeed passing through. They joined us at the table and then the questions started. What a pleasant couple, a Cree family who trapped all winter and worked here in the summer for the Canadian Park Service. They were the interpreters for the historical site and informed us we were the only party to paddle the Hayes that summer. They usually saw one or two a year; few people ever came to visit this inaccessible place, and whenever someone did Betty and Jim were glad.

They gave us a tour of Canada's oldest building still standing upon permafrost, the old Hudson Bay Depot constructed in 1831. The reason it has survived so long is because it was built by shipwrights, not carpenters, and so was made to flex with the expanding earth. The floors moved up and down, the walls in and out, like some ship floating over the permanently frozen ground. The ingenious structure had weathered many a storm. Both carpenters, Herb and I were fascinated. Up in the lookout tower was a wall filled with carved signatures, and it was customary to leave your initials when visiting. Ours are there. Jim and Betty then took us to the old cemetery while explaining that in its heyday this place was a bustling town, one of the major trade centers for the fur empire. All of the original structures are gone now, just the depot and the graveyard remain.

The only other buildings in York Factory belong to the Silver Goose Inn, a family-run hunting lodge. Because of bears we weren't too keen on camping anywhere, and so we walked over to see if we could get a place for the night. They gave us a cabin and said dinner was at six. We returned to Jim and Betty's to borrow their radio phone and arrange for a float plane the next day. Jim then led us to a work shed next to their cabin and pulled out an old branding iron he had found with the insignia of the Hudson Bay Company. He fired up a torch, heated the iron and branded both of our paddles. It was another custom he explained: we had been officially recognized now as bona fide voyageurs.

That evening after dinner Herb and I walked along the bluffs out towards Marsh Point, gazing out to sea, looking back up the river we had descended. I thought of all the people who had come this way before. Some never left, their bones frozen below the fragile soil. We had arrived to this place our way, from our own backyard streams. I felt proud. And then Herb shouted, "A bear!" Sure enough, lumbering along sniffing, its head raised, was an enormous polar bear. He paused midwhiff, caught our scent, and started to walk right towards us. Two men have seldom made such haste and we arrived more than a little excited back to the safety of the Silver Goose. The family laughed at what was a common occurrence for them.

Our bush pilot touched down in the river the next morning. Jim, Betty and the Silver Goose family all went out to meet the plane, hoping for mail or a package. We tied our canoe onto one of the pontoons and loaded our gear inside the small cockpit. As we wedged ourselves between the packs, two more polar bears ambled up the shore. Everyone on the dock went for their rifles and our pilot gunned the engines. The float plane was a little slow to lift because of the heavy canoe, but we eventually took to the air, flying up and over the Hayes, circling back over York Factory. The pilot tipped his wings once to bid our friends on shore goodbye.

From the air the scenery was unforgettable. When we flew over the mouth of the Nelson River, I noticed a cluster of white dots. Belugas, the man at the helm informed us. "And see over there, on the far side of the river, more polar bears." We flew north up the coast and the seemingly barren landscape was teeming with life, at every river mouth another pod of belugas and here and there caribou herds. Because of the permafrost the surface water never percolates into the ground, creating hundreds of lakes, and from the eagle-eye view they looked like jewels. Each had a distinct color—jade, turquoise, garnet, obsidian—and every lake seemed its own unique ecosystem. Long esker ridges separated most of the lakes from each other and a few were connected by pristine rivers that fed into the cobalt sea.

We touched down on a lake just outside of Churchill. Herb had a friend living in town, Lily, who knew we were coming, and at her home first came hot showers, followed by lobster and red wine. After dinner she drove us out to Cape Merry to watch the belugas play in the river mouth. Sitting there on the bedrock I learned an interesting geological term: isostatic rebound. Lily explained that 11,000 years ago the glaciers covering this area were more than two miles thick and their weight was tremendous. Since the ice receded the earth has been slowly rebounding from all that massive suppression, and the further north one goes the more measurable this uplift. In Churchill, photos taken a century ago show the shoreline a full meter lower. Just think that in a human lifetime one could see the continent rise.

That night Herb and I wandered over to the only bar in town, celebrating our success with a few of the locals. One man, Charlie, invited us to his home, really a 42-foot fishing boat, the *Arctic Enterprise.* It was in dry dock on the beach just past town, near the mouth of the Churchill River. He was refurbishing it with the intent of taking tourists out to explore Hudson Bay; there was much to be done and he offered us work. Herb was more interested in returning home, but for me the bid was enticing.

To protect their portion of the fur trade, the British built a stone fortress at the mouth of the Churchill River in 1731, Prince of Wales Fort. It was attacked once, by the French in 1782, without a single shot being fired. With the decline in pelts, it was later abandoned. After that not much happened in Churchill until the mid 1900s, when the Canadian government punched in a railhead and a humongous grain elevator. It was realized the surplus grain could be shipped to Europe twice as fast from Hudson Bay than from their already established Great Lake ports. For many years this facility was the only game in town.

More recently, Churchill has become world-renowned for its polar bears. These largest of bears spend the winter out on the ice hunting seals, their favorite food. Every spring as the ice breaks up and drifts south, they become marooned on the southern shores of Hudson Bay, between York Factory and Churchill. They pass the summer scattered along the coast hungry for seal, waiting for winter. In the fall when the temperatures start to drop, they begin migrating north looking for ice sheets where the seals are. Normally right around Halloween they pass through the Churchill area and the town is organized with citizen patrols to warn the neighbors when the creatures are approaching. They don't shoot them but just watch out and make room. "Problem" bears are trapped live and then transported far up the coast. It is a rare example of the humans species learning to adapt to a predator as opposed to annihilating it; in fact, these villagers have learned there is big money in bear-watching.

Our new friend Charlie had part-time work as a tundra buggy driver. These specially adapted vehicles have enormous tires that are filled with low air pressure to limit damage to the terrain and are stuffed with tourists to observe the bears. Charlie invited us for a complimentary ride the next day.

A precarious environment the tundra, extreme winters and a very short growing season offer little hope for life, but it is prolific. Tenacious hardy dwarf plants thrived delicately. When we all got out for a walk, we were warned to stay on the trail to avoid stepping on wild flowers and killing them. Scattered about were clumps of taiga, isolated islands of dwarfed trees, birch, spruce and alder, the tallest perhaps four feet high, all cooperating together to hold the soil. We saw no bears but plenty of birds.

In the late evening after the sun went down, we went for a ride in a freighter canoe. Greg, another fellow we'd met at the bar, had promised us a tour of the Churchill River. I anticipated a day trip, but as Herb, Charlie and I chatted away beside the *Arctic Enterprise,* Greg motored up and onto the beach guided by a flashlight. It was time to go. The river was foggy, which made it even darker; we puttered upstream for a half hour and then in the middle of the river he cut the motor. There was a moment of silence as we drifted in the night, and then we understood why he had brought us there, what he had wanted to share. Surrounding the boat were teeming beluga whales surfacing for air, inhaling deep lungfuls, exhaling fine spray, diving for fish, swishing and splashing, singing and snorting and creating a chorus of sounds I'd never heard before. At one point Greg turned on his flashlight and we could see their glistening bodies roiling about in the river, turning the smooth surface into a living undulating texture. We sat there drifting downstream for an hour, no one talking, all of us just listening to the music. When Greg tapped the side of the canoe with a paddle, a few curious whales came right up to us, spraying their breath and giving me the chance to touch their slippery skin.

Lily and her partner Wilfred invited us over for a gourmet farewell dinner. We ate local scallops, fresh bannock, curried caribou and loganberry pie. After the feast, we walked to the train station; Herb had a ticket on the night train, I did not.

After one last bear hug, he turned and boarded the Polar Bear Express, bound for the city of Winnipeg and then Thunder Bay. Herb and I had lived together every day for the past three months and had created a lifetime friendship.

I remained in Churchill for two more weeks working on Charlie's boat. In between were many pleasures: motorcycle rides along the ocean coast, parties with locals, more wondrous whale encounters, waking up to barking seals, solitary walks, a strange subarctic full moon, unforgettable northern light shows and hours watching the tides. The night before my own departure-return I phoned my daughter. When I told her I was on my way home, she asked if I was going to canoe back.

Coming home by train took two days, covering the same distance we had paddled in three months. Once settled back into my cabin, I took a walk over to Herb's. We drove up the gravel road to Sawbill Lake and sat beside the water, still wondering what might wait around that first bend.

TIDAL ZONE
The St. Lawrence River to Québec

To the St. Lawrence Seaway

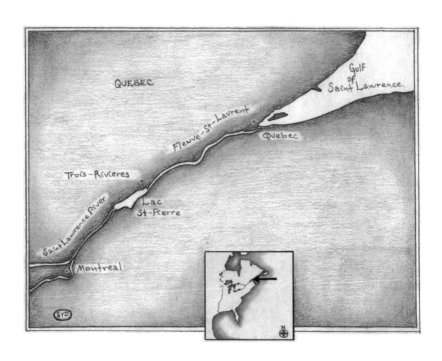

The St. Lawrence River is the artery that connects the Great Lakes with the Atlantic Ocean; all the ships sailing to and from these five lakes eventually pass along it. Because Paula and I had taken the shortcut via the Ottawa River, we hadn't seen any ships since the St. Mary's River, but once we entered the St. Lawrence we saw them frequently. We shoved off as an upstream ship from Liverpool and a downstream one from Monrovia met midriver, their wakes easy, by the time they reached us just smooth swells.

Our first ride on the St. Lawrence's powerful current was easy and fast. Periodic gusts from an offshore Atlantic breeze slowed us down some, but we were happy to be afloat again and shrugged it off. It took us all day to outdistance the Montréal suburbs with their mansions lining the banks. As the light was fading, we landed on Île de Vercheres, a sparsely populated island with a tiny beach on the eastern tip just big enough for our tent.

Lying in our safe house we held onto one another. Frustrations with developed shore, despair in inclement weather and bodily fatigue affected us; we tired of hiding in small woodlots and my right elbow suffered in the headwinds. The combination of departing from a good friend and her familiar city all made Paula melancholic. But there was also an understanding, a guarded joy, that this journey would soon end. Something new and unknown awaited. Sea level was not far away.

The St. Lawrence granted us perfect calm the next day. Fast moving currents textured the surface with swirls and boils, all marked by greasy eddy lines. We slid over the ever-changing hydraulics feeling confident. Fish leapt out of the water, loudly splashing as they came back down. The upper side of their circular wake idled against the current while the lower side expanded with it, growing into enormous elongated ovals. The wind was full of birds, smoky puffs of red-winged blackbirds waving in the sky. At times they rested in the bulrushes and arrowroots chattering madly. Canadian geese grouped up in their aerodynamic angles, honking in concert, while along the shore the herons hunted frogs. Cormorants passed like low linear shadows; hawks circled up high, each doing its part in a sacred concentric dance.

We stopped in the village of Lanoraie along the Chenal du Nord to search for a *pâtisserie*. Walking through the quiet town I realized we were ambling beside some of Canada's oldest homes. The attention to detail in eighteenth-century architecture was evident: leaded windows, gabled eaves on every dormer, built-in bays, cozy porches and colorful tin roofs.

With a swift current and blessed tailwind we sailed past swamps, early autumn hardwoods, grassy sheep farms, scattered industrial sites and a few small towns. The clouds grew dark in the afternoon, storms brewing behind us. There was a big mud flat along the north shore beside a field of corn, and if the river didn't rise overnight, the place would be safe.

All night it stormed and rain began leaking into our weathered tent; a small pool formed near my head, so I mopped it up and fell back asleep. Heavy showers woke me once more and I lay wide awake, worried about the river engulfing us.

We made fast coffee in the mud under the downcast gray morning sky. The rains had ceased and the river was a pane of glass. It felt like I was flying, skimming on that thin delicate line again. Within a few miles the river changed as it spread out into Lac St. Pierre. The current slowed and its silts settled down to the bottom creating a crystal clear St. Lawrence; watery fields of cattail, wild rice and bulrush covered the surface as far as we could see. Scattered throughout fishermen constructed weirs, labyrinths of upright sticks woven with nets. Closer to shore the reeds grew so thick they were impassable and we found ourselves squeezed further out towards the middle of the large shallows. We were lucky because the potentially violent lake remained calm all day; had the winds picked up we would have been in trouble. Instead we wove our way through the fecund marsh, brushing against the reeds and startling snow geese. Halfway down the lake we found a break in the swamp, the only campsite we'd seen in 20 miles.

During the night the level of the reservoir rose and at dawn when I crawled out of the tent, I noticed it was a foot higher from the tide. The morning promised excellent paddling and by noon we reached the end of Lac St. Pierre. Once we were back on the river proper, we rode the receding tide down, traveling fast.

The industrial town of Trois Rivières came upon us quickly, its arch bridge looming in the distance, an engineering marvel with thousands of triangles bolted together to create its lengthy span. Three vessels were anchored at the quay: the first belonged to the Canadian Coast Guard, the middle one to Greenpeace, and the last to the Canadian Navy. *Moby Dick,* the Greenpeace ship, had some serious escort. Its dingy was tied off at the bow and standing up inside were two crew members with paint brushes retouching the image of the great white whale itself. "Keep stirring it up!" I cheered.

A pulp plant and a chemical refinery abutted a playground and we stopped to climb the jungle-jim with a handful of kids before setting off to explore the town. For Saturday afternoon, it was very quiet and eventually we found our way inside the Basilica of Nôtre Dame. As I stood beneath its lofty dome, I noticed an engraving beneath the altar that read, "Où est-il ton Dieu?"

"Outside, on the river," I whispered.

The tide turned and we moved slowly.

When we kayaked over flat water, our average speed was four miles an hour. Past Trois Rivières, on a morning with ideal conditions we set records: the river current, the outgoing tide, the tail wind and our strong arms all worked in favor to double our velocity. The tide reached its low point around noon and the river had by then dropped three feet. As the current shifted back upstream, the tailwinds grew stronger, making difficult choppy water.

A long uninhabited sandy beach appeared at the mouth of a small river, one of the more beautiful sites we'd seen in weeks. Cozy and safe, we watched the passing ships cut into the white-capped river, the waves pounding hard on the sands as the tides surged upstream. We were glad to be off the vast river.

An old man carried a bundle of reeds out to the end of the point beyond the river's mouth. We watched him weave the freshly cut greens into last year's dry brown mat, preparing his duck blind for the opening of the hunting season two days away. Along with us, the fowl were nervous.

A boy appeared on our beach and with curiosity asked us in Québécois if we were camping there. We nodded that yes, this was home for the night. Then he asked where we were from. He'd heard of Lake Superior. Satisfied, he dashed off into a golden aspen grove to reappear in the brown beach grass, turning and waving once more before vanishing beneath a canopy of deep maroon sumacs.

We began this journey a few days before the summer solstice. Now it was the autumnal equinox so, faithfully, Paula and I built another bonfire to celebrate. It had been one full summer on the water, one lively season. Ritualistically we each took a turn leaping over the flames and landing feet-first into autumn. In the nearby village church bells pealed.

Everything about this mode of travel had been new to Paula: the camp life, the self-propelled voyage on big waters, the continental distance, always being outside. And everything about Paula was new to me: watching her navigate her own craft, overcome honest fears, experience a different beauty, discover her innate buoyancy. Of all the expeditions, my shared company with Paula pleased me the most.

Southwest winds blew through the night and into the day, pushing us fast. As we neared the end of this river, we needed tailwinds more than ever; headwinds would make traveling impossible. The waves built to four feet, many breaking from behind and surfing us down into their trough, and we were like two bobbers shoved along through confusing waters. In spite of intermittent showers we persevered for 20 miles. Small limestone bluffs appeared along the shore dressed in beautiful fall foliage, beneath the cliffs immense grassy tidal flats. We knew it was best to exit before the tide dropped or we would have to march through those zones. I spied a small sandy opening beyond one swamp and we plunged into the reeds until the boats became stuck and then I got out and wallowed a few more yards through the muck to check it out. We had found an excellent little hole, high and dry, invisible to the nearby farms and cabins. An immense cormorant flock complimented the sunset. The smell of decomposing leaves scented the air, gusts of wind sending them flying from the trees. A Russian ship headed upstream, perhaps for the last grain run to Duluth.

Gunfire sounded from both sides of the river at exactly 6:00 in the morning. Hunters surrounded us, spraying the air with a constant "pop-pop-pop." All the birds were distraught; the ducks frantically looked for places to hide, the gulls whined and cried in fevered pitch, even the herons seemed scared as they barked to warn their fellow winged ones. It frightened me to think of going out on the water amidst all the falling shot and chaos. It was doubtful the hunters would see us sitting in the middle of that wide waterway. I rolled over in my sleeping bag and looked at Paula: her face was pale and she rolled her eyes.

Not only were ducks falling out of the sky but also, overnight, the river had moved. A hundred feet of muddy boulder-strewn flats now separated our boats from the river. I walked to the edge of the vegetation line where the mud began, testing the ankle-deep, slurping yuck. Portaging through that ooze would be difficult. We decided to wait for the river's return, and hopefully a break in the hunt.

Throughout the morning the shotguns were relentless, but by late morning the tide was licking at our boats so we took our chances and launched into the whitecaps and pellets. We were both extremely wound up and nerved. The wind helped push us along and around a big bend, Cap Santé, and suddenly the swampy shore turned to steep shale cliffs and the rich fowl feeding grounds disappeared. Like two terrified ducks we had outdistanced the hunters unscathed. The gusty winds died out, leaving us a smooth fast current and feeling calmer by the stroke.

We camped that night on a narrow beach at the base of the cliffs, hidden in fiery sumac. There was plenty of driftwood to rekindle our fires, and a soft flat spot for the tent. It was a straight 20-mile fetch down the river to the city of Québec and we could already see its first bridge and smell the ocean.

I had a fitful sleep. All night a steady sea breeze blew up the river, throwing crashing waves onto our tiny beach. At first the surf lulled me to sleep, but a few hours later I awoke and realized how close they really were. I reckoned we'd be safe, having pitched the tent above the high water mark. Just the same, I was unsure; we had our backs to the cliffs and were hemmed in. Perhaps, I worried, was this the night of the highest tide? We would become embayed. By midnight the waves were washing up within three feet of us. The river idled there for another hour before beginning its slow descent. At two in the morning I finally fell back into a relieved sleep.

When we woke at dawn, the river had vanished; between the cliffs and the main river channel was nothing but a flat, jagged rock shelf extending out to the middle of the valley. The exposed river floor was nearly level so it was easy to see that the water didn't have to drop much for the river to recede a long ways out. Paula thought she could see the river about a mile away. There was nothing to do but wait for it to come back. We relaxed, enjoying the respite of the sunny fall day, staring giddily at the portal of our final trek.

By late morning the surge returned. We rode that current down fast and easy, reaching the far side of the very fetch we had been gazing at. Just upstream from the bridge and the city of Québec we camped our last night, sharing one more dinner in our last patch of woods. The conversation was filled with reflections on so many intimate moments that had brought us so far. As it grew dark, we lit a candle.

It was Paula's golden birthday, 27 on the 27th. After a kiss my companion rolled over and fell back asleep. The rains let up and I went outside to gather flowers and prepare breakfast. We sat inside our fabric home eating, watching the world outside: colorful autumn leaves were falling fast, the tide was advancing towards us visibly as the river became higher and higher. Soon my stern was afloat, and then my bow. One last time we loaded up.

We passed under a suspension bridge built of clean and simple straight lines, and then around one more bend we slipped under an old steel truss bridge, the very last one to span the St. Lawrence River. Each of us let out a robust holler as we crossed that symbolic threshold.

The tidal current grew stronger. At one point I stopped paddling to peel off a sweater and I noticed we were actually moving backwards, back towards Minnesota. Paddling hard against it, we searched for a place to rest and wait it out. All we could find was a dirty beach next to a tank farm, which had to suffice. As the sun broke through the waters began to flow seaward, and the city of Québec was at hand. We could hear its heartbeat mixed with bluejay song. We could smell its diesel fumes blending with rotting poplar leaves. We could see its construction beyond the red shale cliffs draped in wild grape vines.

Everything narrowed at Québec. A cement seawall rose straight out of the river and beyond it the old city stood boldly with its citadel and the Château Frontenac. Beside the bottlenecked waters industrial wharfs lined the shore where several ships, sleeping giants, were tied fast; others plied the midstream current and deep channel. Spotting a ferry landing downstream, with great scrutiny we calculated our next move to get beyond all the traffic to the far side of town and the safety of a marina.

Idling into the busy commercial port we approached the car ferry, and the decision whether to back-paddle or go. The boat was only half-full and it seemed we had time. Giving it plenty of berth, we began the dash. Once abreast the dragon, the engines suddenly began to hum; there was one toot, the lines were tossed and with its prop wash churning up the water it slowly drifted downstream towards us. Two other ships were passing midstream, and soon colliding wakes from the ferry and the ships reached our kayaks; the ferry kept getting closer and we were certain it couldn't see us. Fearful, in the midst of our last mile with nowhere to hide, we paddled furiously trying to slip away from the screws.

When it was safe to go, the ferry revved its engines and created the deadliest wake we'd encountered, a four-foot comber that headed straight for us. Then a tug boat appeared chugging along in our direction, making its own nasty wake, and they both arrived at the same time, giving us a frightening series of soaking waves. With enough hip swivels and hard pulls we managed to escape the congested chop. The excitement of finishing our journey was shaken by the all too real necessity of simple survival. One last river moment.

Having finally passed the danger of so many ships, we stopped to catch our breath. Before us the river broadened out into the Gulf of St. Lawrence: sea level. Just below the city was a long sandy beach home to a sailing club. We were hoping to leave our boats there and check into a hotel. Celebrations were planned: a birthday, a dream fulfilled.

A swarm of children played on the beach. They'd each constructed a little boat and had come to the shore to test their unique designs. After paddling over a hundred days, covering over a thousand miles, we slid onto those same sands. One boy carefully placed his dreamboat into the water just as I pulled mine out.

My gratitude to Pat Wilch, Herb Wills and Paula Magdich: better companions would be hard to find. Thanks to Jay Miskowiec who whipped this text into shape, Dave Grinstead for helping with the maps and Salvador Yrízar who knew how to finish them. A few friends guided me with the early manuscript: Bob, Kent, Peter, Tomás, Paul and Obie; their suggestions were invaluable.

Finally, without Blanca, my compass, I'd still be drifting.

AK, San Felipe del Agua, June 2006